FRENCH
VOCABULARY

ENGLISH-
FRENCH

The most useful words
To expand your lexicon and sharpen
your language skills

9000 words

French vocabulary for English speakers - 9000 words
By Andrey Taranov

T&P Books vocabularies are intended for helping you learn, memorize and review foreign words. The dictionary is divided into themes, covering all major spheres of everyday activities, business, science, culture, etc.

The process of learning words using T&P Books' theme-based dictionaries gives you the following advantages:

- Correctly grouped source information predetermines success at subsequent stages of word memorization
- Availability of words derived from the same root allowing memorization of word units (rather than separate words)
- Small units of words facilitate the process of establishing associative links needed for consolidation of vocabulary
- Level of language knowledge can be estimated by the number of learned words

T&P Books Publishing
www.tpbooks.com

ISBN: 978-1-78071-295-6

This book is also available in E-book formats.
Please visit www.tpbooks.com or the major online bookstores.

FRENCH VOCABULARY
for English speakers

T&P Books vocabularies are intended to help you learn, memorize, and review foreign words. The vocabulary contains over 9000 commonly used words arranged thematically.

- Vocabulary contains the most commonly used words
- Recommended as an addition to any language course
- Meets the needs of beginners and advanced learners of foreign languages
- Convenient for daily use, revision sessions, and self-testing activities
- Allows you to assess your vocabulary

Special features of the vocabulary

- Words are organized according to their meaning, not alphabetically
- Words are presented in three columns to facilitate the reviewing and self-testing processes
- Words in groups are divided into small blocks to facilitate the learning process
- The vocabulary offers a convenient and simple transcription of each foreign word

The vocabulary has 256 topics including:

Basic Concepts, Numbers, Colors, Months, Seasons, Units of Measurement, Clothing & Accessories, Food & Nutrition, Restaurant, Family Members, Relatives, Character, Feelings, Emotions, Diseases, City, Town, Sightseeing, Shopping, Money, House, Home, Office, Working in the Office, Import & Export, Marketing, Job Search, Sports, Education, Computer, Internet, Tools, Nature, Countries, Nationalities and more …

T&P BOOKS' THEME-BASED DICTIONARIES

The Correct System for Memorizing Foreign Words

Acquiring vocabulary is one of the most important elements of learning a foreign language, because words allow us to express our thoughts, ask questions, and provide answers. An inadequate vocabulary can impede communication with a foreigner and make it difficult to understand a book or movie well.

The pace of activity in all spheres of modern life, including the learning of modern languages, has increased. Today, we need to memorize large amounts of information (grammar rules, foreign words, etc.) within a short period. However, this does not need to be difficult. All you need to do is to choose the right training materials, learn a few special techniques, and develop your individual training system.

Having a system is critical to the process of language learning. Many people fail to succeed in this regard; they cannot master a foreign language because they fail to follow a system comprised of selecting materials, organizing lessons, arranging new words to be learned, and so on. The lack of a system causes confusion and eventually, lowers self-confidence.

T&P Books' theme-based dictionaries can be included in the list of elements needed for creating an effective system for learning foreign words. These dictionaries were specially developed for learning purposes and are meant to help students effectively memorize words and expand their vocabulary.

Generally speaking, the process of learning words consists of three main elements:

- Reception (creation or acquisition) of a training material, such as a word list
- Work aimed at memorizing new words
- Work aimed at reviewing the learned words, such as self-testing

All three elements are equally important since they determine the quality of work and the final result. All three processes require certain skills and a well-thought-out approach.

New words are often encountered quite randomly when learning a foreign language and it may be difficult to include them all in a unified list. As a result, these words remain written on scraps of paper, in book margins, textbooks, and so on. In order to systematize such words, we have to create and continually update a "book of new words." A paper notebook, a netbook, or a tablet PC can be used for these purposes.

This "book of new words" will be your personal, unique list of words. However, it will only contain the words that you came across during the learning process. For example, you might have written down the words "Sunday," "Tuesday," and "Friday." However, there are additional words for days of the week, for example, "Saturday," that are missing, and your list of words would be incomplete. Using a theme dictionary, in addition to the "book of new words," is a reasonable solution to this problem.

The theme-based dictionary may serve as the basis for expanding your vocabulary.

It will be your big "book of new words" containing the most frequently used words of a foreign language already included. There are quite a few theme-based dictionaries available, and you should ensure that you make the right choice in order to get the maximum benefit from your purchase.

Therefore, we suggest using theme-based dictionaries from T&P Books Publishing as an aid to learning foreign words. Our books are specially developed for effective use in the sphere of vocabulary systematization, expansion and review.

Theme-based dictionaries are not a magical solution to learning new words. However, they can serve as your main database to aid foreign-language acquisition. Apart from theme dictionaries, you can have copybooks for writing down new words, flash cards, glossaries for various texts, as well as other resources; however, a good theme dictionary will always remain your primary collection of words.

T&P Books' theme-based dictionaries are specialty books that contain the most frequently used words in a language.

The main characteristic of such dictionaries is the division of words into themes. For example, the *City* theme contains the words "street," "crossroads," "square," "fountain," and so on. The *Talking* theme might contain words like "to talk," "to ask," "question," and "answer".

All the words in a theme are divided into smaller units, each comprising 3–5 words. Such an arrangement improves the perception of words and makes the learning process less tiresome. Each unit contains a selection of words with similar meanings or identical roots. This allows you to learn words in small groups and establish other associative links that have a positive effect on memorization.

The words on each page are placed in three columns: a word in your native language, its translation, and its transcription. Such positioning allows for the use of techniques for effective memorization. After closing the translation column, you can flip through and review foreign words, and vice versa. "This is an easy and convenient method of review – one that we recommend you do often."

Our theme-based dictionaries contain transcriptions for all the foreign words. Unfortunately, none of the existing transcriptions are able to convey the exact nuances of foreign pronunciation. That is why we recommend using the transcriptions only as a supplementary learning aid. Correct pronunciation can only be acquired with the help of sound. Therefore our collection includes audio theme-based dictionaries.

The process of learning words using T&P Books' theme-based dictionaries gives you the following advantages:

- You have correctly grouped source information, which predetermines your success at subsequent stages of word memorization
- Availability of words derived from the same root (lazy, lazily, lazybones), allowing you to memorize word units instead of separate words
- Small units of words facilitate the process of establishing associative links needed for consolidation of vocabulary
- You can estimate the number of learned words and hence your level of language knowledge
- The dictionary allows for the creation of an effective and high-quality revision process
- You can revise certain themes several times, modifying the revision methods and techniques
- Audio versions of the dictionaries help you to work out the pronunciation of words and develop your skills of auditory word perception

The T&P Books' theme-based dictionaries are offered in several variants differing in the number of words: 1.500, 3.000, 5.000, 7.000, and 9.000 words. There are also dictionaries containing 15,000 words for some language combinations. Your choice of dictionary will depend on your knowledge level and goals.

We sincerely believe that our dictionaries will become your trusty assistant in learning foreign languages and will allow you to easily acquire the necessary vocabulary.

TABLE OF CONTENTS

PRONUNCIATION GUIDE

Letter	French example	T&P phonetic alphabet	English example

Vowels

Letter	French example	T&P phonetic alphabet	English example
A a	cravate	[a]	shorter than in ask
E e	mer	[ɛ]	man, bad
I i [1]	hier	[j]	yes, New York
I i [2]	musique	[i]	shorter than in feet
O o	porte	[o], [ɔ]	drop, baught
U u	rue	[y]	fuel, tuna
Y y [3]	yacht	[j]	yes, New York
Y y [4]	type	[i]	shorter than in feet

Consonants

Letter	French example	T&P phonetic alphabet	English example
B b	robe	[b]	baby, book
C c [5]	place	[s]	city, boss
C c [6]	canard	[k]	clock, kiss
Ç ç	leçon	[s]	city, boss
D d	disque	[d]	day, doctor
F f	femme	[f]	face, food
G g [7]	page	[ʒ]	forge, pleasure
G g [8]	gare	[g]	game, gold
H h	héros	[h]	silent [h]
J j	jour	[ʒ]	forge, pleasure
K k	kilo	[k]	clock, kiss
L l	aller	[l]	lace, people
M m	maison	[m]	magic, milk
N n	nom	[n]	name, normal
P p	papier	[p]	pencil, private
Q q	cinq	[k]	clock, kiss
R r	mars	[r]	rolled [r]
S s [9]	raison	[z]	zebra, please
S s [10]	sac	[s]	city, boss
T t	table	[t]	tourist, trip
V v	verre	[v]	very, river
W w	Taïwan	[w]	vase, winter

Letter	French example	T&P phonetic alphabet	English example
X x [11]	expliquer	[ks]	box, taxi
X x [12]	exact	[gz]	exam, exact
X x [13]	dix	[s]	city, boss
X x [14]	dixième	[z]	zebra, please
Z z	zéro	[z]	zebra, please

Combinations of letters

ai	faire	[ɛ]	man, bad
au	faute	[o], [oː]	floor, doctor
ay	payer	[eɪ]	age, today
ei	treize	[ɛ]	man, bad
eau	eau	[o], [oː]	floor, doctor
eu	beurre	[ø]	eternal, church
œ	œil	[ø]	eternal, church
œu	cœur	[øː]	first, thirsty
ou	nous	[u]	book
oi	noir	[wa]	watt, white
oy	voyage	[wa]	watt, white
qu	quartier	[k]	clock, kiss
ch	chat	[ʃ]	machine, shark
th	thé	[t]	tourist, trip
ph	photo	[f]	face, food
gu [15]	guerre	[g]	game, gold
ge [16]	géographie	[ʒ]	forge, pleasure
gn	ligne	[ɲ]	canyon, new
on, om	maison, nom	[ɔ̃]	strong

Comments

[1] before vowels
[2] elsewhere
[3] before vowels
[4] elsewhere
[5] before e, i, y
[6] elsewhere
[7] before e, i, y
[8] elsewhere
[9] between two vowels
[10] elsewhere
[11] most of cases
[12] rarely
[13] in dix, six, soixante

[14] in dixième, sixième
[15] before e, i, u
[16] before a, o, y

ABBREVIATIONS
used in the vocabulary

ab.	-	about
adj	-	adjective
adv	-	adverb
anim.	-	animate
as adj	-	attributive noun used as adjective
e.g.	-	for example
etc.	-	et cetera
fam.	-	familiar
fem.	-	feminine
form.	-	formal
inanim.	-	inanimate
masc.	-	masculine
math	-	mathematics
mil.	-	military
n	-	noun
pl	-	plural
pron.	-	pronoun
sb	-	somebody
sing.	-	singular
sth	-	something
v aux	-	auxiliary verb
vi	-	intransitive verb
vi, vt	-	intransitive, transitive verb
vt	-	transitive verb
m	-	masculine noun
f	-	feminine noun
m pl	-	masculine plural
f pl	-	feminine plural
m, f	-	masculine, feminine
conj	-	conjunction
prep	-	preposition
v imp	-	impersonnel verb
vp	-	pronominal verb

BASIC CONCEPTS

Basic concepts. Part 1

1. Pronouns

I, me	**je**	[ʒə]
you	**tu**	[ty]
he	**il**	[il]
she	**elle**	[εl]
it	**ça**	[sa]
we	**nous**	[nu]
you (to a group)	**vous**	[vu]
they (masc.)	**ils**	[il]
they (fem.)	**elles**	[εl]

2. Greetings. Salutations. Farewells

Hello! (fam.)	**Bonjour!**	[bɔ̃ʒur]
Hello! (form.)	**Bonjour!**	[bɔ̃ʒur]
Good morning!	**Bonjour!**	[bɔ̃ʒur]
Good afternoon!	**Bonjour!**	[bɔ̃ʒur]
Good evening!	**Bonsoir!**	[bɔ̃swar]
to say hello	**dire bonjour**	[dir bɔ̃ʒur]
Hi! (hello)	**Salut!**	[saly]
greeting (n)	**salut** (m)	[saly]
to greet (vt)	**saluer** (vt)	[salɥe]
How are you? (form.)	**Comment allez-vous?**	[kɔmɑ̃talevu]
How are you? (fam.)	**Comment ça va?**	[kɔmɑ̃ sa va]
What's new?	**Quoi de neuf?**	[kwa də nœf]
Bye-Bye! Goodbye!	**Au revoir!**	[orəvwar]
See you soon!	**À bientôt!**	[a bjɛ̃to]
Farewell!	**Adieu!**	[adjø]
to say goodbye	**dire au revoir**	[dir ərəvwar]
So long!	**Salut!**	[saly]
Thank you!	**Merci!**	[mεrsi]
Thank you very much!	**Merci beaucoup!**	[mεrsi boku]
You're welcome	**Je vous en prie**	[ʒə vuzɑ̃pri]

Don't mention it!	Il n'y a pas de quoi	[il njapɑ də kwa]
It was nothing	Pas de quoi	[pɑ də kwa]
Excuse me! (fam.)	Excuse-moi!	[ɛkskyz mwa]
Excuse me! (form.)	Excusez-moi!	[ɛkskyze mwa]
to excuse (forgive)	excuser (vt)	[ɛkskyze]
to apologize (vi)	s'excuser (vp)	[sɛkskyze]
My apologies	Mes excuses	[me zɛkskyz]
I'm sorry!	Pardonnez-moi!	[pardɔne mwa]
to forgive (vt)	pardonner (vt)	[pardɔne]
It's okay!	C'est pas grave	[sepagrav]
please (adv)	s'il vous plaît	[silvuple]
Don't forget!	N'oubliez pas!	[nublije pɑ]
Certainly!	Bien sûr!	[bjɛ̃ sy:r]
Of course not!	Bien sûr que non!	[bjɛ̃ syr kə nõ]
Okay! (I agree)	D'accord!	[dakɔr]
That's enough!	Ça suffit!	[sa syfi]

3. How to address

mister, sir	monsieur	[məsjø]
ma'am	madame	[madam]
miss	mademoiselle	[madmwazɛl]
young man	jeune homme	[ʒœn ɔm]
young man (little boy)	petit garçon	[pti garsõ]
miss (little girl)	petite fille	[ptit fij]

4. Cardinal numbers. Part 1

0 zero	zéro	[zero]
1 one	un	[œ̃]
2 two	deux	[dø]
3 three	trois	[trwa]
4 four	quatre	[katr]
5 five	cinq	[sɛ̃k]
6 six	six	[sis]
7 seven	sept	[sɛt]
8 eight	huit	[ɥit]
9 nine	neuf	[nœf]
10 ten	dix	[dis]
11 eleven	onze	[õz]
12 twelve	douze	[duz]
13 thirteen	treize	[trɛz]
14 fourteen	quatorze	[katɔrz]

15 fifteen	quinze	[kɛ̃z]
16 sixteen	seize	[sɛz]
17 seventeen	dix-sept	[disɛt]
18 eighteen	dix-huit	[dizɥit]
19 nineteen	dix-neuf	[diznœf]
20 twenty	vingt	[vɛ̃]
21 twenty-one	vingt et un	[vɛ̃teœ̃]
22 twenty-two	vingt-deux	[vɛ̃tdø]
23 twenty-three	vingt-trois	[vɛ̃trwa]
30 thirty	trente	[trɑ̃t]
31 thirty-one	trente et un	[trɑ̃teœ̃]
32 thirty-two	trente-deux	[trɑ̃t dø]
33 thirty-three	trente-trois	[trɑ̃t trwa]
40 forty	quarante	[karɑ̃t]
41 forty-one	quarante et un	[karɑ̃teœ̃]
42 forty-two	quarante-deux	[karɑ̃t dø]
43 forty-three	quarante-trois	[karɑ̃t trwa]
50 fifty	cinquante	[sɛ̃kɑ̃t]
51 fifty-one	cinquante et un	[sɛ̃kɑ̃teœ̃]
52 fifty-two	cinquante-deux	[sɛ̃kɑ̃t dø]
53 fifty-three	cinquante-trois	[sɛ̃kɑ̃t trwa]
60 sixty	soixante	[swasɑ̃t]
61 sixty-one	soixante et un	[swasɑ̃teœ̃]
62 sixty-two	soixante-deux	[swasɑ̃t dø]
63 sixty-three	soixante-trois	[swasɑ̃t trwa]
70 seventy	soixante-dix	[swasɑ̃tdis]
71 seventy-one	soixante et onze	[swasɑ̃te ɔ̃z]
72 seventy-two	soixante-douze	[swasɑ̃t duz]
73 seventy-three	soixante-treize	[swasɑ̃t trɛz]
80 eighty	quatre-vingts	[katrəvɛ̃]
81 eighty-one	quatre-vingt et un	[katrəvɛ̃teœ̃]
82 eighty-two	quatre-vingt deux	[katrəvɛ̃ dø]
83 eighty-three	quatre-vingt trois	[katrəvɛ̃ trwa]
90 ninety	quatre-vingt-dix	[katrəvɛ̃dis]
91 ninety-one	quatre-vingt et onze	[katrəvɛ̃ teɔ̃z]
92 ninety-two	quatre-vingt-douze	[katrəvɛ̃ duz]
93 ninety-three	quatre-vingt-treize	[katrəvɛ̃ trɛz]

5. Cardinal numbers. Part 2

100 one hundred	cent	[sɑ̃]
200 two hundred	deux cents	[dø sɑ̃]

300 three hundred	**trois cents**	[trwa sã]
400 four hundred	**quatre cents**	[katr sã]
500 five hundred	**cinq cents**	[sɛ̃k sã]
600 six hundred	**six cents**	[si sã]
700 seven hundred	**sept cents**	[sɛt sã]
800 eight hundred	**huit cents**	[ɥi sã]
900 nine hundred	**neuf cents**	[nœf sã]
1000 one thousand	**mille**	[mil]
2000 two thousand	**deux mille**	[dø mil]
3000 three thousand	**trois mille**	[trwa mil]
10000 ten thousand	**dix mille**	[di mil]
one hundred thousand	**cent mille**	[sã mil]
million	**million** (m)	[miljɔ̃]
billion	**milliard** (m)	[miljar]

6. Ordinal numbers

first (adj)	**premier** (adj)	[prəmje]
second (adj)	**deuxième** (adj)	[døzjɛm]
third (adj)	**troisième** (adj)	[trwazjɛm]
fourth (adj)	**quatrième** (adj)	[katrijɛm]
fifth (adj)	**cinquième** (adj)	[sɛ̃kjɛm]
sixth (adj)	**sixième** (adj)	[sizjɛm]
seventh (adj)	**septième** (adj)	[sɛtjɛm]
eighth (adj)	**huitième** (adj)	[ɥitjɛm]
ninth (adj)	**neuvième** (adj)	[nœvjɛm]
tenth (adj)	**dixième** (adj)	[dizjɛm]

7. Numbers. Fractions

fraction	**fraction** (f)	[fraksjɔ̃]
one half	**un demi**	[œ̃ dəmi]
one third	**un tiers**	[œ̃ tjɛr]
one quarter	**un quart**	[œ̃ kar]
one eighth	**un huitième**	[œn ɥitjɛm]
one tenth	**un dixième**	[œ̃ dizjɛm]
two thirds	**deux tiers**	[dø tjɛr]
three quarters	**trois quarts**	[trwa kar]

8. Numbers. Basic operations

subtraction	**soustraction** (f)	[sustraksjɔ̃]
to subtract (vi, vt)	**soustraire** (vt)	[sustrɛr]

| division | division (f) | [divizjɔ̃] |
| to divide (vt) | diviser (vt) | [divize] |

addition	addition (f)	[adisjɔ̃]
to add up (vt)	additionner (vt)	[adisjɔne]
to add (vi, vt)	ajouter (vt)	[aʒute]
multiplication	multiplication (f)	[myltiplikasjɔ̃]
to multiply (vt)	multiplier (vt)	[myltiplije]

9. Numbers. Miscellaneous

digit, figure	chiffre (m)	[ʃifr]
number	nombre (m)	[nɔ̃br]
numeral	adjectif (m) numéral	[adʒɛktif nymeral]
minus sign	moins (m)	[mwɛ̃]
plus sign	plus (m)	[ply]
formula	formule (f)	[fɔrmyl]

calculation	calcul (m)	[kalkyl]
to count (vt)	compter (vt)	[kɔ̃te]
to count up	calculer (vt)	[kalkyle]
to compare (vt)	comparer (vt)	[kɔ̃pare]

How much?	Combien?	[kɔ̃bjɛ̃]
sum, total	somme (f)	[sɔm]
result	résultat (m)	[rezylta]
remainder	reste (m)	[rɛst]

a few ...	quelques`...	[kɛlkə]
few, little (adv)	peu de ...	[pø də]
the rest	reste (m)	[rɛst]
one and a half	un et demi	[œne dəmi]
dozen	douzaine (f)	[duzɛn]

in half (adv)	en deux	[ɑ̃ dø]
equally (evenly)	en parties égales	[ɑ̃ parti egal]
half	moitié (f)	[mwatje]
time (three ~s)	fois (f)	[fwa]

10. The most important verbs. Part 1

to advise (vt)	conseiller (vt)	[kɔ̃seje]
to agree (say yes)	être d'accord	[ɛtr dakɔr]
to answer (vi, vt)	répondre (vi, vt)	[repɔ̃dr]
to apologize (vi)	s'excuser (vp)	[sɛkskyze]
to arrive (vi)	venir (vi)	[vənir]
to ask (~ oneself)	demander (vt)	[dəmɑ̃de]
to ask (~ sb to do sth)	demander (vt)	[dəmɑ̃de]

to be (vi)	être (vi)	[ɛtr]
to be afraid	avoir peur	[avwar pœr]
to be hungry	avoir faim	[avwar fɛ̃]
to be interested in ...	s'intéresser (vp)	[sɛ̃terese]
to be needed	être nécessaire	[ɛtr nesesɛr]
to be surprised	s'étonner (vp)	[setɔne]
to be thirsty	avoir soif	[avwar swaf]
to begin (vt)	commencer (vt)	[kɔmɑ̃se]
to belong to ...	appartenir à ...	[apartənir a]
to boast (vi)	se vanter (vp)	[sə vɑ̃te]
to break (split into pieces)	casser (vt)	[kase]
to call (for help)	appeler (vt)	[aple]
can (v aux)	pouvoir (v aux)	[puvwar]
to catch (vt)	attraper (vt)	[atrape]
to change (vt)	changer (vt)	[ʃɑ̃ʒe]
to choose (select)	choisir (vt)	[ʃwazir]
to come down	descendre (vi)	[desɑ̃dr]
to come in (enter)	entrer (vi)	[ɑ̃tre]
to compare (vt)	comparer (vt)	[kɔ̃pare]
to complain (vi, vt)	se plaindre (vp)	[sə plɛ̃dr]
to confuse (mix up)	confondre (vt)	[kɔ̃fɔ̃dr]
to continue (vt)	continuer (vt)	[kɔ̃tinɥe]
to control (vt)	contrôler (vt)	[kɔ̃trole]
to cook (dinner)	préparer (vt)	[prepare]
to cost (vt)	coûter (vt)	[kute]
to count (add up)	compter (vi, vt)	[kɔ̃te]
to count on ...	compter sur ...	[kɔ̃te syr]
to create (vt)	créer (vt)	[kree]
to cry (weep)	pleurer (vi)	[plœre]

11. The most important verbs. Part 2

to deceive (vi, vt)	tromper (vt)	[trɔ̃pe]
to decorate (tree, street)	décorer (vt)	[dekɔre]
to defend (a country, etc.)	défendre (vt)	[defɑ̃dr]
to demand (request firmly)	exiger (vt)	[ɛgziʒe]
to dig (vt)	creuser (vt)	[krøze]
to discuss (vt)	discuter (vt)	[diskyte]
to do (vt)	faire (vt)	[fɛr]
to doubt (have doubts)	douter (vt)	[dute]
to drop (let fall)	faire tomber	[fɛr tɔ̃be]
to excuse (forgive)	excuser (vt)	[ɛkskyze]
to exist (vi)	exister (vi)	[ɛgziste]

to expect (foresee)	**prévoir** (vt)	[prevwar]
to explain (vt)	**expliquer** (vt)	[ɛksplike]
to fall (vi)	**tomber** (vi)	[tɔ̃be]
to find (vt)	**trouver** (vt)	[truve]
to finish (vt)	**finir** (vt)	[finir]
to fly (vi)	**voler** (vi)	[vɔle]
to follow ... (come after)	**suivre** (vt)	[sɥivr]
to forget (vi, vt)	**oublier** (vt)	[ublije]
to forgive (vt)	**pardonner** (vt)	[pardɔne]
to give (vt)	**donner** (vt)	[dɔne]
to give a hint	**donner un indice**	[dɔne ynɛ̃dis]
to go (on foot)	**aller** (vi)	[ale]
to go for a swim	**se baigner** (vp)	[sə beɲe]
to go out (from ...)	**sortir** (vi)	[sɔrtir]
to guess right	**deviner** (vt)	[dəvine]
to have (vt)	**avoir** (vt)	[avwar]
to have breakfast	**prendre le petit déjeuner**	[prɑ̃dr ləpti deʒœne]
to have dinner	**dîner** (vi)	[dine]
to have lunch	**déjeuner** (vi)	[deʒœne]
to hear (vt)	**entendre** (vt)	[ɑ̃tɑ̃dr]
to help (vt)	**aider** (vt)	[ede]
to hide (vt)	**cacher** (vt)	[kaʃe]
to hope (vi, vt)	**espérer** (vi)	[ɛspere]
to hunt (vi, vt)	**chasser** (vi, vt)	[ʃase]
to hurry (vi)	**être pressé**	[ɛtr prese]

12. The most important verbs. Part 3

to inform (vt)	**informer** (vt)	[ɛ̃fɔrme]
to insist (vi, vt)	**insister** (vi)	[ɛ̃siste]
to insult (vt)	**insulter** (vt)	[ɛ̃sylte]
to invite (vt)	**inviter** (vt)	[ɛ̃vite]
to joke (vi)	**plaisanter** (vi)	[plɛzɑ̃te]
to keep (vt)	**garder** (vt)	[garde]
to keep silent	**rester silencieux**	[rɛste silɑ̃sjø]
to kill (vt)	**tuer** (vt)	[tɥe]
to know (sb)	**connaître** (vt)	[kɔnɛtr]
to know (sth)	**savoir** (vt)	[savwar]
to laugh (vi)	**rire** (vi)	[rir]
to liberate (city, etc.)	**libérer** (vt)	[libere]
to like (I like ...)	**plaire** (vt)	[plɛr]
to look for ... (search)	**chercher** (vt)	[ʃɛrʃe]
to love (sb)	**aimer** (vt)	[eme]

to make a mistake	**se tromper** (vp)	[sə trõpe]
to manage, to run	**diriger** (vt)	[diriʒe]
to mean (signify)	**signifier** (vt)	[siɲifje]
to mention (talk about)	**mentionner** (vt)	[mãsjɔne]
to miss (school, etc.)	**manquer** (vt)	[mãke]
to notice (see)	**apercevoir** (vt)	[apɛrsəvwar]
to object (vi, vt)	**objecter** (vt)	[ɔbʒɛkte]
to observe (see)	**observer** (vt)	[ɔpsɛrve]
to open (vt)	**ouvrir** (vt)	[uvrir]
to order (meal, etc.)	**commander** (vt)	[kɔmãde]
to order (mil.)	**ordonner** (vt)	[ɔrdɔne]
to own (possess)	**posséder** (vt)	[pɔsede]
to participate (vi)	**participer à …**	[partisipe a]
to pay (vi, vt)	**payer** (vi, vt)	[peje]
to permit (vt)	**permettre** (vt)	[pɛrmɛtr]
to plan (vt)	**planifier** (vt)	[planifje]
to play (children)	**jouer** (vt)	[ʒwe]
to pray (vi, vt)	**prier** (vt)	[prije]
to prefer (vt)	**préférer** (vt)	[prefere]
to promise (vt)	**promettre** (vt)	[prɔmɛtr]
to pronounce (vt)	**prononcer** (vt)	[prɔnõse]
to propose (vt)	**proposer** (vt)	[prɔpoze]
to punish (vt)	**punir** (vt)	[pynir]
to read (vi, vt)	**lire** (vi, vt)	[lir]
to recommend (vt)	**recommander** (vt)	[rəkɔmãde]
to refuse (vi, vt)	**se refuser** (vp)	[sə rəfyze]
to regret (be sorry)	**regretter** (vt)	[rəgrɛte]
to rent (sth from sb)	**louer** (vt)	[lwe]
to repeat (say again)	**répéter** (vt)	[repete]
to reserve, to book	**réserver** (vt)	[rezɛrve]
to run (vi)	**courir** (vt)	[kurir]

13. The most important verbs. Part 4

to save (rescue)	**sauver** (vt)	[sove]
to say (~ thank you)	**dire** (vt)	[dir]
to scold (vt)	**gronder** (vt)	[grõde]
to see (vt)	**voir** (vt)	[vwar]
to sell (vt)	**vendre** (vt)	[vãdr]
to send (vt)	**envoyer** (vt)	[ãvwaje]
to shoot (vi)	**tirer** (vi)	[tire]
to shout (vi)	**crier** (vi)	[krije]
to show (vt)	**montrer** (vt)	[mõtre]
to sign (document)	**signer** (vt)	[siɲe]

to sit down (vi)	s'asseoir (vp)	[saswar]
to smile (vi)	sourire (vi)	[surir]
to speak (vi, vt)	parler (vi, vt)	[parle]
to steal (money, etc.)	voler (vt)	[vɔle]
to stop (please ~ calling me)	cesser (vt)	[sese]
to stop (for pause, etc.)	s'arrêter (vp)	[sarete]
to study (vt)	étudier (vt)	[etydje]
to swim (vi)	nager (vi)	[naʒe]
to take (vt)	prendre (vt)	[prɑ̃dr]
to think (vi, vt)	penser (vi, vt)	[pɑ̃se]
to threaten (vt)	menacer (vt)	[mənase]
to touch (with hands)	toucher (vt)	[tuʃe]
to translate (vt)	traduire (vt)	[tradɥir]
to trust (vt)	avoir confiance	[avwar kɔ̃fjɑ̃s]
to try (attempt)	essayer (vt)	[eseje]
to turn (~ to the left)	tourner (vi)	[turne]
to underestimate (vt)	sous-estimer (vt)	[suzɛstime]
to understand (vt)	comprendre (vt)	[kɔ̃prɑ̃dr]
to unite (vt)	réunir (vt)	[reynir]
to wait (vt)	attendre (vt)	[atɑ̃dr]
to want (wish, desire)	vouloir (vt)	[vulwar]
to warn (vt)	avertir (vt)	[avɛrtir]
to work (vi)	travailler (vi)	[travaje]
to write (vt)	écrire (vt)	[ekrir]
to write down	prendre en note	[prɑ̃dr ɑ̃ nɔt]

14. Colors

color	couleur (f)	[kulœr]
shade (tint)	teinte (f)	[tɛ̃t]
hue	ton (m)	[tɔ̃]
rainbow	arc-en-ciel (m)	[arkɑ̃sjɛl]
white (adj)	blanc (adj)	[blɑ̃]
black (adj)	noir (adj)	[nwar]
gray (adj)	gris (adj)	[gri]
green (adj)	vert (adj)	[vɛr]
yellow (adj)	jaune (adj)	[ʒon]
red (adj)	rouge (adj)	[ruʒ]
blue (adj)	bleu (adj)	[blø]
light blue (adj)	bleu clair (adj)	[blø klɛr]
pink (adj)	rose (adj)	[roz]
orange (adj)	orange (adj)	[ɔrɑ̃ʒ]

violet (adj)	**violet** (adj)	[vjɔlɛ]
brown (adj)	**brun** (adj)	[brœ̃]
golden (adj)	**d'or** (adj)	[dɔr]
silvery (adj)	**argenté** (adj)	[arʒɑ̃te]
beige (adj)	**beige** (adj)	[bɛʒ]
cream (adj)	**crème** (adj)	[krɛm]
turquoise (adj)	**turquoise** (adj)	[tyrkwaz]
cherry red (adj)	**rouge cerise** (adj)	[ruʒ səriz]
lilac (adj)	**lilas** (adj)	[lila]
crimson (adj)	**framboise** (adj)	[frɑ̃bwaz]
light (adj)	**clair** (adj)	[klɛr]
dark (adj)	**foncé** (adj)	[fɔ̃se]
bright, vivid (adj)	**vif** (adj)	[vif]
colored (pencils)	**de couleur** (adj)	[də kulœr]
color (e.g., ~ film)	**en couleurs** (adj)	[ɑ̃ kulœr]
black-and-white (adj)	**noir et blanc** (adj)	[nwar e blɑ̃]
plain (one-colored)	**monochrome** (adj)	[mɔnɔkrom]
multicolored (adj)	**multicolore** (adj)	[myltikɔlɔr]

15. Questions

Who?	**Qui?**	[ki]
What?	**Quoi?**	[kwa]
Where? (at, in)	**Où?**	[u]
Where (to)?	**Où?**	[u]
From where?	**D'où?**	[du]
When?	**Quand?**	[kɑ̃]
Why? (What for?)	**Pourquoi?**	[purkwa]
Why? (reason)	**Pourquoi?**	[purkwa]
What for?	**À quoi bon?**	[ɑ kwa bɔ̃]
How? (in what way)	**Comment?**	[kɔmɑ̃]
What? (What kind of ...?)	**Quel?**	[kɛl]
Which?	**Lequel?**	[ləkɛl]
To whom?	**À qui?**	[ɑ ki]
About whom?	**De qui?**	[də ki]
About what?	**De quoi?**	[də kwa]
With whom?	**Avec qui?**	[avɛk ki]
How many? How much?	**Combien?**	[kɔ̃bjɛ̃]
Whose?	**À qui?**	[ɑ ki]

16. Prepositions

with (accompanied by)	**avec ...** (prep)	[avɛk]
without	**sans ...** (prep)	[sɑ̃]
to (indicating direction)	**à ...** (prep)	[ɑ]
about (talking ~ ...)	**de ...** (prep)	[də]
before (in time)	**avant** (prep)	[avɑ̃]
in front of ...	**devant** (prep)	[dəvɑ̃]
under (beneath, below)	**sous ...** (prep)	[su]
above (over)	**au-dessus de ...** (prep)	[odsy də]
on (atop)	**sur ...** (prep)	[syr]
from (off, out of)	**de ...** (prep)	[də]
of (made from)	**en ...** (prep)	[ɑ̃]
in (e.g., ~ ten minutes)	**dans ...** (prep)	[dɑ̃]
over (across the top of)	**par dessus ...** (prep)	[par dəsy]

17. Function words. Adverbs. Part 1

Where? (at, in)	**Où?**	[u]
here (adv)	**ici** (adv)	[isi]
there (adv)	**là-bas** (adv)	[laba]
somewhere (to be)	**quelque part** (adv)	[kɛlkə par]
nowhere (not anywhere)	**nulle part** (adv)	[nyl par]
by (near, beside)	**près de ...** (prep)	[prɛ də]
by the window	**près de la fenêtre**	[prɛdə la fənɛtr]
Where (to)?	**Où?**	[u]
here (e.g., come ~!)	**ici** (adv)	[isi]
there (e.g., to go ~)	**là-bas** (adv)	[laba]
from here (adv)	**d'ici** (adv)	[disi]
from there (adv)	**de là-bas** (adv)	[də laba]
close (adv)	**près** (adv)	[prɛ]
far (adv)	**loin** (adv)	[lwɛ̃]
near (e.g., ~ Paris)	**près de ...**	[prɛ də]
nearby (adv)	**tout près** (adv)	[tu prɛ]
not far (adv)	**pas loin** (adv)	[pɑ lwɛ̃]
left (adj)	**gauche** (adj)	[goʃ]
on the left	**à gauche** (adv)	[agoʃ]
to the left	**à gauche** (adv)	[agoʃ]
right (adj)	**droit** (adj)	[drwa]
on the right	**à droite** (adv)	[adrwat]

to the right	**à droite** (adv)	[adrwat]
in front (adv)	**devant** (adv)	[dəvã]
front (as adj)	**de devant** (adj)	[də dəvã]
ahead (look ~)	**en avant** (adv)	[ɑn avã]
behind (adv)	**derrière** (adv)	[dɛrjɛr]
from behind	**par derrière** (adv)	[par dɛrjɛr]
back (towards the rear)	**en arrière** (adv)	[ɑn arjɛr]
middle	**milieu** (m)	[miljø]
in the middle	**au milieu** (adv)	[omiljø]
at the side	**de côté** (adv)	[də kote]
everywhere (adv)	**partout** (adv)	[partu]
around (in all directions)	**autour** (adv)	[otur]
from inside	**de l'intérieur**	[də lɛ̃terjœr]
somewhere (to go)	**quelque part** (adv)	[kɛlkə par]
straight (directly)	**tout droit** (adv)	[tu drwa]
back (e.g., come ~)	**en arrière** (adv)	[ɑn arjɛr]
from anywhere	**de quelque part**	[də kɛlkə par]
from somewhere	**de quelque part**	[də kɛlkə par]
firstly (adv)	**premièrement** (adv)	[prəmjɛrmã]
secondly (adv)	**deuxièmement** (adv)	[døzjɛmmã]
thirdly (adv)	**troisièmement** (adv)	[trwazjɛmmã]
suddenly (adv)	**soudain** (adv)	[sudɛ̃]
at first (adv)	**au début** (adv)	[odeby]
for the first time	**pour la première fois**	[pur la prəmjɛr fwa]
long before …	**bien avant …**	[bjɛn avã]
anew (over again)	**de nouveau** (adv)	[də nuvo]
for good (adv)	**pour toujours** (adv)	[pur tuʒur]
never (adv)	**jamais** (adv)	[ʒamɛ]
again (adv)	**encore** (adv)	[ãkɔr]
now (adv)	**maintenant** (adv)	[mɛ̃tnã]
often (adv)	**souvent** (adv)	[suvã]
then (adv)	**alors** (adv)	[alɔr]
urgently (quickly)	**d'urgence** (adv)	[dyrʒãs]
usually (adv)	**d'habitude** (adv)	[dabityd]
by the way, …	**à propos, …**	[apropo]
possible (that is ~)	**c'est possible**	[sepɔsibl]
probably (adv)	**probablement** (adv)	[prɔbabləmã]
maybe (adv)	**peut-être** (adv)	[pøtɛtr]
besides …	**en plus, …**	[ãplys]
that's why …	**c'est pourquoi …**	[se purkwa]
in spite of …	**malgré …**	[malgre]
thanks to …	**grâce à …**	[gras a]
what (pron.)	**quoi** (pron.)	[kwa]

that (conj.)	que (conj)	[kə]
something	quelque chose (pron.)	[kɛlkə ʃoz]
anything (something)	quelque chose (pron.)	[kɛlkə ʃoz]
nothing	rien	[rjɛ̃]

who (pron.)	qui (pron.)	[ki]
someone	quelqu'un (pron.)	[kɛlkœ̃]
somebody	quelqu'un (pron.)	[kɛlkœ̃]

nobody	personne (pron.)	[pɛrsɔn]
nowhere (a voyage to ~)	nulle part (adv)	[nyl par]
nobody's	de personne	[də pɛrsɔn]
somebody's	de n'importe qui	[də nɛ̃pɔrt ki]

so (I'm ~ glad)	comme ça (adv)	[kɔmsa]
also (as well)	également (adv)	[egalmɑ̃]
too (as well)	aussi (adv)	[osi]

18. Function words. Adverbs. Part 2

Why?	Pourquoi?	[purkwa]
for some reason	on ne sait pourquoi	[ɔ̃nə sɛ purkwa]
because ...	parce que ...	[parskə]
for some purpose	pour une raison quelconque	[pur yn rɛzɔ̃ kɛlkɔ̃k]

and	et (conj)	[e]
or	ou (conj)	[u]
but	mais (conj)	[mɛ]
for (e.g., ~ me)	pour ... (prep)	[pur]

too (~ many people)	trop (adv)	[tro]
only (exclusively)	seulement (adv)	[sœlmɑ̃]
exactly (adv)	précisément (adv)	[presizemɑ̃]
about (more or less)	autour de ... (prep)	[otur də]

approximately (adv)	approximativement	[aprɔksimativmɑ̃]
approximate (adj)	approximatif (adj)	[aprɔksimatif]
almost (adv)	presque (adv)	[prɛsk]
the rest	reste (m)	[rɛst]

the other (second)	l'autre (adj)	[lotr]
other (different)	autre (adj)	[otr]
each (adj)	chaque (adj)	[ʃak]
any (no matter which)	n'importe quel (adj)	[nɛ̃pɔrt kɛl]
many, much (a lot of)	beaucoup (adv)	[boku]
many people	plusieurs (pron.)	[plyzjœr]
all (everyone)	touts les ... , toutes les ...	[tut le], [tut le]

in return for ...	en échange de ...	[ɑn eʃɑ̃ʒ də ...]

in exchange (adv)	**en échange** (adv)	[ɑn eʃɑ̃ʒ]
by hand (made)	**à la main** (adv)	[ɑlamɛ̃]
hardly (negative opinion)	**peu probable** (adj)	[pø prɔbabl]
probably (adv)	**probablement** (adv)	[prɔbabləmɑ̃]
on purpose (adv)	**exprès** (adv)	[ɛksprɛ]
by accident (adv)	**par hasard** (adv)	[par azar]
very (adv)	**très** (adv)	[trɛ]
for example (adv)	**par exemple** (adv)	[par ɛgzɑ̃p]
between	**entre …** (prep)	[ɑ̃tr]
among	**parmi …** (prep)	[parmi]
so much (such a lot)	**autant** (adv)	[otɑ̃]
especially (adv)	**surtout** (adv)	[syrtu]

Basic concepts. Part 2

19. Weekdays

Monday	**lundi** (m)	[lœ̃di]
Tuesday	**mardi** (m)	[mardi]
Wednesday	**mercredi** (m)	[mɛrkrədi]
Thursday	**jeudi** (m)	[ʒødi]
Friday	**vendredi** (m)	[vɑ̃drədi]
Saturday	**samedi** (m)	[samdi]
Sunday	**dimanche** (m)	[dimɑ̃ʃ]

today (adv)	**aujourd'hui** (adv)	[oʒurdɥi]
tomorrow (adv)	**demain** (adv)	[dəmɛ̃]
the day after tomorrow	**après-demain** (adv)	[aprɛdmɛ̃]
yesterday (adv)	**hier** (adv)	[ijɛr]
the day before yesterday	**avant-hier** (adv)	[avɑ̃tjɛr]

day	**jour** (m)	[ʒur]
working day	**jour** (m) **ouvrable**	[ʒur uvrabl]
public holiday	**jour** (m) **férié**	[ʒur ferje]
day off	**jour** (m) **de repos**	[ʒur də rəpo]
weekend	**week-end** (m)	[wikɛnd]

all day long	**toute la journée**	[tut la ʒurne]
next day (adv)	**le lendemain**	[lɑ̃dmɛ̃]
two days ago	**il y a 2 jours**	[ilja də ʒur]
the day before	**la veille**	[la vɛj]
daily (adj)	**quotidien** (adj)	[kɔtidjɛ̃]
every day (adv)	**tous les jours**	[tu le ʒur]

week	**semaine** (f)	[səmɛn]
last week (adv)	**la semaine dernière**	[la səmɛn dɛrnjɛr]
next week (adv)	**la semaine prochaine**	[la səmɛn prɔʃɛn]
weekly (adj)	**hebdomadaire** (adj)	[ɛbdɔmadɛr]
every week (adv)	**chaque semaine**	[ʃak səmɛn]
twice a week	**2 fois par semaine**	[dø fwa par səmɛn]
every Tuesday	**tous les mardis**	[tu le mardi]

20. Hours. Day and night

morning	**matin** (m)	[matɛ̃]
in the morning	**le matin**	[lə matɛ̃]
noon, midday	**midi** (m)	[midi]

in the afternoon	dans l'après-midi	[dɑ̃ laprɛmidi]
evening	soir (m)	[swar]
in the evening	le soir	[lə swar]
night	nuit (f)	[nɥi]
at night	la nuit	[la nɥi]
midnight	minuit (f)	[minɥi]
second	seconde (f)	[səgɔ̃d]
minute	minute (f)	[minyt]
hour	heure (f)	[œr]
half an hour	demi-heure (f)	[dəmijœr]
quarter of an hour	un quart d'heure	[œ̃ kar dœr]
fifteen minutes	quinze minutes	[kɛ̃z minyt]
24 hours	vingt-quatre heures	[vɛ̃tkatr œr]
sunrise	lever (m) du soleil	[ləve dy sɔlɛj]
dawn	aube (f)	[ob]
early morning	pointe (f) du jour	[pwɛ̃t dy ʒur]
sunset	coucher (m) du soleil	[kuʃe dy sɔlɛj]
early in the morning	tôt le matin	[to lə matɛ̃]
this morning	ce matin	[sə matɛ̃]
tomorrow morning	demain matin	[dəmɛ̃ matɛ̃]
this afternoon	cet après-midi	[sɛt aprɛmidi]
in the afternoon	dans l'après-midi	[dɑ̃ laprɛmidi]
tomorrow afternoon	demain après-midi	[dəmɛn aprɛmidi]
tonight (this evening)	ce soir	[sə swar]
tomorrow night	demain soir	[dəmɛ̃ swar]
at 3 o'clock sharp	à 3 heures précises	[ɑ trwa zœr presiz]
about 4 o'clock	autour de 4 heures	[otur də katr œr]
by 12 o'clock	vers midi	[vɛr midi]
in 20 minutes	dans 20 minutes	[dɑ̃ vɛ̃ minyt]
in an hour	dans une heure	[dɑ̃zyn œr]
on time (adv)	à temps	[ɑ tɑ̃]
a quarter of ...	moins le quart	[mwɛ̃ lə kar]
within an hour	en une heure	[ɑnyn œr]
every 15 minutes	tous les quarts d'heure	[tu le kar dœr]
round the clock	24 heures sur 24	[vɛ̃tkatr œr syr vɛ̃tkatr]

21. Months. Seasons

January	janvier (m)	[ʒɑ̃vje]
February	février (m)	[fevrije]
March	mars (m)	[mars]
April	avril (m)	[avril]

| May | mai (m) | [mɛ] |
| June | juin (m) | [ʒɥɛ̃] |

July	juillet (m)	[ʒɥijɛ]
August	août (m)	[ut]
September	septembre (m)	[separemã]
October	octobre (m)	[ɔktɔbr]
November	novembre (m)	[nɔvãbr]
December	décembre (m)	[desãbr]

spring	printemps (m)	[prɛ̃tã]
in spring	au printemps	[oprɛ̃tã]
spring (as adj)	de printemps (adj)	[də prɛ̃tã]

summer	été (m)	[ete]
in summer	en été	[ɑn ete]
summer (as adj)	d'été (adj)	[dete]

fall	automne (m)	[otɔn]
in fall	en automne	[ɑn otɔn]
fall (as adj)	d'automne (adj)	[dotɔn]

winter	hiver (m)	[ivɛr]
in winter	en hiver	[ɑn ivɛr]
winter (as adj)	d'hiver (adj)	[divɛr]

month	mois (m)	[mwa]
this month	ce mois	[sə mwa]
next month	le mois prochain	[lə mwa prɔʃɛ̃]
last month	le mois dernier	[lə mwa dɛrnje]

a month ago	il y a un mois	[ilja œ̃ mwa]
in a month	dans un mois	[dãzœn mwa]
in two months	dans 2 mois	[dã də mwa]
the whole month	tout le mois	[tu lə mwa]
all month long	tout un mois	[tutœ̃ mwa]

monthly (~ magazine)	mensuel (adj)	[mãsɥɛl]
monthly (adv)	tous les mois	[tu le mwa]
every month	chaque mois	[ʃak mwa]
twice a month	2 fois par mois	[də fwa par mwa]

year	année (f)	[ane]
this year	cette année	[sɛt ane]
next year	l'année prochaine	[lane prɔʃɛn]
last year	l'année dernière	[lane dɛrnjɛr]

a year ago	il y a un an	[ilja œnã]
in a year	dans un an	[dãzœn ã]
in two years	dans 2 ans	[dã də zã]
the whole year	toute l'année	[tut lane]
all year long	toute une année	[tutyn ane]

every year	**chaque année**	[ʃak ane]
annual (adj)	**annuel** (adj)	[anyɛl]
annually (adv)	**tous les ans**	[tu lezɑ̃]
4 times a year	**4 fois par an**	[katr fwa parɑ̃]

date (e.g., today's ~)	**date** (f)	[dat]
date (e.g., ~ of birth)	**date** (f)	[dat]
calendar	**calendrier** (m)	[kalɑ̃drije]

half a year	**six mois**	[si mwa]
six months	**semestre** (m)	[səmɛstr]
season (summer, etc.)	**saison** (f)	[sɛzɔ̃]
century	**siècle** (m)	[sjɛkl]

22. Time. Miscellaneous

time	**temps** (m)	[tɑ̃]
instant (n)	**instant** (m)	[ɛ̃stɑ̃]
moment	**moment** (m)	[mɔmɑ̃]
instant (adj)	**instantané** (adj)	[ɛ̃stɑ̃tane]
lapse (of time)	**laps** (m) **de temps**	[laps də tɑ̃]
life	**vie** (f)	[vi]
eternity	**éternité** (f)	[etɛrnite]

epoch	**époque** (f)	[epɔk]
era	**ère** (f)	[ɛr]
cycle	**cycle** (m)	[sikl]
period	**période** (f)	[perjɔd]
term (short-~)	**délai** (m)	[delɛ]

the future	**avenir** (m)	[avnir]
future (as adj)	**prochain** (adj)	[prɔʃɛ̃]
next time	**la fois prochaine**	[la fwa prɔʃɛn]
the past	**passé** (m)	[pɑse]
past (recent)	**passé** (adj)	[pɑse]
last time	**la fois passée**	[la fwa pɑse]

later (adv)	**plus tard** (adv)	[ply tar]
after (prep.)	**après ...** (prep)	[aprɛ]
nowadays (adv)	**à présent** (adv)	[aprezɑ̃]
now (adv)	**maintenant** (adv)	[mɛ̃tnɑ̃]
immediately (adv)	**immédiatement** (adv)	[imedjatmɑ̃]
soon (adv)	**bientôt** (adv)	[bjɛ̃to]
in advance (beforehand)	**d'avance** (adv)	[davɑ̃s]

a long time ago	**il y a longtemps**	[ilja lɔ̃tɑ̃]
recently (adv)	**récemment** (adv)	[resamɑ̃]
destiny	**destin** (m)	[dɛstɛ̃]
memories (childhood ~)	**souvenirs** (m pl)	[suvnir]
archives	**archives** (f pl)	[arʃiv]

during …   pendant … (prep)   [pãdã]
long, a long time (adv)   longtemps (adv)   [lɔ̃tã]
not long (adv)   pas longtemps (adv)   [pɑ lɔ̃tã]
early (in the morning)   tôt (adv)   [to]
late (not early)   tard (adv)   [tar]

forever (for good)   pour toujours (adv)   [pur tuʒur]
to start (begin)   commencer (vt)   [kɔmãse]
to postpone (vt)   reporter (vt)   [rəpɔrte]

at the same time   en même temps (adv)   [ã mɛm tã]
permanently (adv)   tout le temps (adv)   [tu lə tã]
constant (noise, pain)   constant (adj)   [kɔ̃stã]
temporary (adj)   temporaire (adj)   [tãpɔrɛr]

sometimes (adv)   parfois (adv)   [parfwa]
rarely (adv)   rarement (adv)   [rarmã]
often (adv)   souvent (adv)   [suvã]

23. Opposites

rich (adj)   riche (adj)   [riʃ]
poor (adj)   pauvre (adj)   [povr]

ill, sick (adj)   malade (adj)   [malad]
healthy (adj)   en bonne santé   [ã bɔn sãte]

big (adj)   grand (adj)   [grã]
small (adj)   petit (adj)   [pti]

quickly (adv)   vite (adv)   [vit]
slowly (adv)   lentement (adv)   [lãtmã]

fast (adj)   rapide (adj)   [rapid]
slow (adj)   lent (adj)   [lã]

cheerful (adj)   joyeux (adj)   [ʒwajø]
sad (adj)   triste (adj)   [trist]

together (adv)   ensemble (adv)   [ãsãbl]
separately (adv)   séparément (adv)   [separemã]

aloud (to read)   à haute voix (adv)   [ɑ ot vwa]
silently (to oneself)   à part soi   [ɑ par swa]

tall (adj)   haut (adj)   [o]
low (adj)   bas (adj)   [ba]

deep (adj)   profond (adj)   [prɔfɔ̃]
shallow (adj)   peu profond (adj)   [pø prɔfɔ̃]

yes	**oui** (adv)	[wi]
no	**non** (adv)	[nɔ̃]
distant (in space)	**lointain** (adj)	[lwɛ̃tɛ̃]
nearby (adj)	**proche** (adj)	[prɔʃ]
far (adv)	**loin** (adv)	[lwɛ̃]
nearby (adv)	**près** (adv)	[prɛ]
long (adj)	**long** (adj)	[lɔ̃]
short (adj)	**court** (adj)	[kur]
good (kindhearted)	**bon** (adj)	[bɔ̃]
evil (adj)	**méchant** (adj)	[meʃɑ̃]
married (adj)	**marié** (adj)	[marje]
single (adj)	**célibataire** (adj)	[selibatɛr]
to forbid (vt)	**interdire** (vt)	[ɛ̃tɛrdir]
to permit (vt)	**permettre** (vt)	[pɛrmɛtr]
end	**fin** (f)	[fɛ̃]
beginning	**début** (m)	[debu]
left (adj)	**gauche** (adj)	[goʃ]
right (adj)	**droit** (adj)	[drwa]
first (adj)	**premier** (adj)	[prəmje]
last (adj)	**dernier** (adj)	[dɛrnje]
crime	**crime** (m)	[krim]
punishment	**punition** (f)	[pynisjɔ̃]
to order (vt)	**ordonner** (vt)	[ɔrdɔne]
to obey (vi, vt)	**obéir** (vt)	[ɔbeir]
straight (adj)	**droit** (adj)	[drwa]
curved (adj)	**courbé** (adj)	[kurbe]
paradise	**paradis** (m)	[paradi]
hell	**enfer** (m)	[ɑ̃fɛr]
to be born	**naître** (vi)	[nɛtr]
to die (vi)	**mourir** (vi)	[murir]
strong (adj)	**fort** (adj)	[fɔr]
weak (adj)	**faible** (adj)	[fɛbl]
old (adj)	**vieux** (adj)	[vjø]
young (adj)	**jeune** (adj)	[ʒœn]
old (adj)	**vieux** (adj)	[vjø]
new (adj)	**neuf** (adj)	[nœf]

| hard (adj) | dur (adj) | [dyr] |
| soft (adj) | mou (adj) | [mu] |

| warm (adj) | chaud (adj) | [ʃo] |
| cold (adj) | froid (adj) | [frwa] |

| fat (adj) | gros (adj) | [gro] |
| thin (adj) | maigre (adj) | [mɛgr] |

| narrow (adj) | étroit (adj) | [etrwa] |
| wide (adj) | large (adj) | [larʒ] |

| good (adj) | bon (adj) | [bɔ̃] |
| bad (adj) | mauvais (adj) | [movɛ] |

| brave (adj) | vaillant (adj) | [vajɑ̃] |
| cowardly (adj) | peureux (adj) | [pœrø] |

24. Lines and shapes

square	carré (m)	[kare]
square (as adj)	carré (adj)	[kare]
circle	cercle (m)	[sɛrkl]
round (adj)	rond (adj)	[rɔ̃]
triangle	triangle (m)	[trijɑ̃gl]
triangular (adj)	triangulaire (adj)	[trijɑ̃gylɛr]

oval	ovale (m)	[ɔval]
oval (as adj)	ovale (adj)	[ɔval]
rectangle	rectangle (m)	[rɛktɑ̃gl]
rectangular (adj)	rectangulaire (adj)	[rɛktɑ̃gylɛr]

pyramid	pyramide (f)	[piramid]
rhombus	losange (m)	[lɔzɑ̃ʒ]
trapezoid	trapèze (m)	[trapɛz]
cube	cube (m)	[kyb]
prism	prisme (m)	[prism]

circumference	circonférence (f)	[sirkɔ̃ferɑ̃s]
sphere	sphère (f)	[sfɛr]
ball (solid sphere)	globe (m)	[glɔb]
diameter	diamètre (m)	[djamɛtr]
radius	rayon (m)	[rɛjɔ̃]
perimeter (circle's ~)	périmètre (m)	[perimɛtr]
center	centre (m)	[sɑ̃tr]

horizontal (adj)	horizontal (adj)	[ɔrizɔ̃tal]
vertical (adj)	vertical (adj)	[vɛrtikal]
parallel (n)	parallèle (f)	[paralɛl]
parallel (as adj)	parallèle (adj)	[paralɛl]

line	**ligne** (f)	[liɲ]
stroke	**trait** (m)	[trɛ]
straight line	**ligne** (f) **droite**	[liɲ drwat]
curve (curved line)	**courbe** (f)	[kurb]
thin (line, etc.)	**fin** (adj)	[fɛ̃]
contour (outline)	**contour** (m)	[kɔ̃tur]
intersection	**croisement** (m)	[krwazmɑ̃]
right angle	**angle** (m) **droit**	[ɑ̃gl drwa]
segment	**segment** (m)	[sɛgmɑ̃]
sector	**secteur** (m)	[sɛktœr]
side (of triangle)	**côté** (m)	[kote]
angle	**angle** (m)	[ɑ̃gl]

25. Units of measurement

weight	**poids** (m)	[pwa]
length	**longueur** (f)	[lɔ̃gœr]
width	**largeur** (f)	[larʒœr]
height	**hauteur** (f)	[otœr]
depth	**profondeur** (f)	[prɔfɔ̃dœr]
volume	**volume** (m)	[vɔlym]
area	**surface** (f)	[syrfas]
gram	**gramme** (m)	[gram]
milligram	**milligramme** (m)	[miligram]
kilogram	**kilogramme** (m)	[kilɔgram]
ton	**tonne** (f)	[tɔn]
pound	**livre** (f)	[livr]
ounce	**once** (f)	[ɔ̃s]
meter	**mètre** (m)	[mɛtr]
millimeter	**millimètre** (m)	[milimɛtr]
centimeter	**centimètre** (m)	[sɑ̃timɛtr]
kilometer	**kilomètre** (m)	[kilɔmɛtr]
mile	**mille** (m)	[mil]
inch	**pouce** (m)	[pus]
foot	**pied** (m)	[pje]
yard	**yard** (m)	[jard]
square meter	**mètre** (m) **carré**	[mɛtr kare]
hectare	**hectare** (m)	[ɛktar]
liter	**litre** (m)	[litr]
degree	**degré** (m)	[degre]
volt	**volt** (m)	[vɔlt]
ampere	**ampère** (m)	[ɑ̃pɛr]
horsepower	**cheval-vapeur** (m)	[ʃevalvapœr]
quantity	**quantité** (f)	[kɑ̃tite]

a little bit of ...	**un peu de ...**	[œ̃ pø də]
half	**moitié** (f)	[mwatje]
dozen	**douzaine** (f)	[duzɛn]
piece (item)	**pièce** (f)	[pjɛs]
size	**dimension** (f)	[dimɑ̃sjõ]
scale (map ~)	**échelle** (f)	[eʃɛl]
minimal (adj)	**minimal** (adj)	[minimal]
the smallest (adj)	**le plus petit** (adj)	[lə ply pəti]
medium (adj)	**moyen** (adj)	[mwajɛ̃]
maximal (adj)	**maximal** (adj)	[maksimal]
the largest (adj)	**le plus grand** (adj)	[lə ply grɑ̃]

26. Containers

jar (glass)	**bocal** (m)	[bɔkal]
can	**boîte** (f) **en fer-blanc**	[bwat ɑ̃ fɛrblɑ̃]
bucket	**seau** (m)	[so]
barrel	**tonneau** (m)	[tɔno]
basin (for washing)	**bassine** (f)	[basin]
tank (for liquid, gas)	**réservoir** (m)	[rezɛrvwar]
hip flask	**flasque** (f)	[flask]
jerrycan	**jerrycan** (m)	[ʒerikan]
cistern (tank)	**citerne** (f)	[sitɛrn]
mug	**grande tasse** (f)	[grɑ̃d tɑs]
cup (of coffee, etc.)	**tasse** (f)	[tɑs]
saucer	**soucoupe** (f)	[sukup]
glass (tumbler)	**verre** (m)	[vɛr]
wineglass	**verre** (m) **à pied**	[vɛr ɑ pje]
saucepan	**casserole** (f)	[kasrɔl]
bottle (~ of wine)	**bouteille** (f)	[butɛj]
neck (of the bottle)	**goulot** (m)	[gulo]
carafe	**carafe** (f)	[karaf]
pitcher (earthenware)	**cruche** (f)	[kryʃ]
vessel (container)	**récipient** (m)	[resipjɑ̃]
pot (crock)	**pot** (m)	[po]
vase	**vase** (m)	[vɑz]
bottle (~ of perfume)	**flacon** (m)	[flakõ]
vial, small bottle	**fiole** (f)	[fjɔl]
tube (of toothpaste)	**tube** (m)	[tyb]
sack (bag)	**sac** (m)	[sak]
bag (paper ~, plastic ~)	**sac** (m)	[sak]
pack (of cigarettes, etc.)	**paquet** (m)	[pakɛ]

box (e.g., shoebox)	boîte (f)	[bwat]
crate	caisse (f)	[kɛs]
basket	panier (m)	[panje]

27. Materials

material	matériau (m)	[materjo]
wood	bois (m)	[bwa]
wooden (adj)	en bois (adj)	[ɑ̃ bwa]

| glass (n) | verre (m) | [vɛr] |
| glass (as adj) | en verre (adj) | [ɑ̃ vɛr] |

| stone (n) | pierre (f) | [pjɛr] |
| stone (as adj) | en pierre (adj) | [ɑ̃ pjɛr] |

| plastic (n) | plastique (m) | [plastik] |
| plastic (as adj) | en plastique (adj) | [ɑ̃ plastik] |

| rubber (n) | caoutchouc (m) | [kautʃu] |
| rubber (as adj) | en caoutchouc (adj) | [ɑ̃ kautʃu] |

| cloth, fabric (n) | tissu (m) | [tisy] |
| fabric (as adj) | en tissu (adj) | [ɑ̃ tisy] |

| paper (n) | papier (m) | [papje] |
| paper (as adj) | de papier (adj) | [də papje] |

| cardboard (n) | carton (m) | [kartɔ̃] |
| cardboard (as adj) | en carton (adj) | [ɑ̃ kartɔ̃] |

polyethylene	polyéthylène (m)	[pɔlietilɛn]
cellophane	cellophane (f)	[selɔfan]
linoleum	linoléum (m)	[linɔleɔm]
plywood	contreplaqué (m)	[kɔ̃trəplake]

porcelain (n)	porcelaine (f)	[pɔpylasjɔ̃]
porcelain (as adj)	de porcelaine (adj)	[də pɔrselɛn]
clay (n)	argile (f)	[arʒil]
clay (as adj)	en argile (adj)	[ɑn arʒil]
ceramics (n)	céramique (f)	[seramik]
ceramic (as adj)	en céramique (adj)	[ɑ̃ seramik]

28. Metals

metal (n)	métal (m)	[metal]
metal (as adj)	métallique (adj)	[metalik]
alloy (n)	alliage (m)	[aljaʒ]

gold (n)	or (m)	[ɔr]
gold, golden (adj)	en or (adj)	[ɑn ɔr]
silver (n)	argent (m)	[arʒɑ̃]
silver (as adj)	en argent (adj)	[ɑn asje]
iron (n)	fer (m)	[fɛr]
iron (adj), made of iron	en fer (adj)	[ɑ̃ fɛr]
steel (n)	acier (m)	[asje]
steel (as adj)	en acier	[ɑn asje]
copper (n)	cuivre (m)	[kɥivr]
copper (as adj)	en cuivre (adj)	[ɑ̃ kɥivr]
aluminum (n)	aluminium (m)	[alyminjɔm]
aluminum (as adj)	en aluminium (adj)	[ɑn alyminjɔm]
bronze (n)	bronze (m)	[brɔ̃z]
bronze (as adj)	en bronze (adj)	[ɑ̃ brɔ̃z]
brass	laiton (m)	[lɛtɔ̃]
nickel	nickel (m)	[nikɛl]
platinum	platine (f)	[platin]
mercury	mercure (m)	[mɛrkyr]
tin	étain (m)	[etɛ̃]
lead	plomb (m)	[plɔ̃]
zinc	zinc (m)	[zɛ̃g]

HUMAN BEING

Human being. The body

29. Humans. Basic concepts

human being	**être** (m) **humain**	[ɛtr ymɛ̃]
man (adult male)	**homme** (m)	[ɔm]
woman	**femme** (f)	[fam]
child	**enfant** (m, f)	[ɑ̃fɑ̃]
girl	**fille** (f)	[fij]
boy	**garçon** (m)	[garsɔ̃]
teenager	**adolescent** (m)	[adɔlesɑ̃]
old man	**vieillard** (m)	[vjɛjar]
old woman	**vieille femme** (f)	[vjɛj fam]

30. Human anatomy

organism	**organisme** (m)	[ɔrganism]
heart	**cœur** (m)	[kœr]
blood	**sang** (m)	[sɑ̃]
artery	**artère** (f)	[artɛr]
vein	**veine** (f)	[vɛn]
brain	**cerveau** (m)	[sɛrvo]
nerve	**nerf** (m)	[nɛr]
nerves	**nerfs** (m pl)	[nɛr]
vertebra	**vertèbre** (f)	[vɛrtɛbr]
spine	**colonne** (f) **vertébrale**	[kɔlɔn vɛrtebral]
stomach (organ)	**estomac** (m)	[ɛstɔma]
intestines, bowel	**intestin** (m)	[ɛ̃tɛstɛ̃]
intestine (e.g., large ~)	**boyau** (m)	[bwajo]
liver	**foie** (m)	[fwa]
kidney	**rein** (m)	[rɛ̃]
bone	**os** (m)	[ɔs]
skeleton	**squelette** (f)	[skəlɛt]
rib	**côte** (f)	[kot]
skull	**crâne** (m)	[kran]
muscle	**muscle** (m)	[myskl]
biceps	**biceps** (m)	[bisɛps]

triceps	triceps (m)	[trisɛps]
tendon	tendon (m)	[tɑ̃dɔ̃]
joint	articulation (f)	[artikylasjɔ̃]
lungs	poumons (m pl)	[pumɔ̃]
genitals	organes (m pl) génitaux	[ɔrgan ʒenito]
skin	peau (f)	[po]

31. Head

head	tête (f)	[tɛt]
face	visage (m)	[vizaʒ]
nose	nez (m)	[ne]
mouth	bouche (f)	[buʃ]

eye	œil (m)	[œj]
eyes	les yeux	[lezjø]
pupil	pupille (f)	[pypij]
eyebrow	sourcil (m)	[sursi]
eyelash	cil (m)	[sil]
eyelid	paupière (f)	[popjɛr]

tongue	langue (f)	[lɑ̃g]
tooth	dent (f)	[dɑ̃]
lips	lèvres (f pl)	[lɛvr]
cheekbones	pommettes (f pl)	[pɔmɛt]
gum	gencive (f)	[ʒɑ̃siv]
palate	palais (m)	[palɛ]

nostrils	narines (f pl)	[narin]
chin	menton (m)	[mɑ̃tɔ̃]
jaw	mâchoire (f)	[mɑʃwar]
cheek	joue (f)	[ʒu]

forehead	front (m)	[frɔ̃]
temple	tempe (f)	[tɑ̃p]
ear	oreille (f)	[ɔrɛj]
back of the head	nuque (f)	[nyk]
neck	cou (m)	[ku]
throat	gorge (f)	[gɔrʒ]

hair	cheveux (m pl)	[ʃəvø]
hairstyle	coiffure (f)	[kwɑfyr]
haircut	coupe (f)	[kup]
wig	perruque (f)	[peryk]

mustache	moustache (f)	[mustaʃ]
beard	barbe (f)	[barb]
to have (a beard, etc.)	porter (vt)	[pɔrte]
braid	tresse (f)	[trɛs]
sideburns	favoris (m pl)	[favɔri]

red-haired (adj)	roux (adj)	[ru]
gray (hair)	gris (adj)	[gri]
bald (adj)	chauve (adj)	[ʃov]
bald patch	calvitie (f)	[kalvisi]
ponytail	queue (f) de cheval	[kø də ʃəval]
bangs	frange (f)	[frɑ̃ʒ]

32. Human body

hand	main (f)	[mɛ̃]
arm	bras (m)	[bra]
finger	doigt (m)	[dwa]
toe	orteil (m)	[ɔrtɛj]
thumb	pouce (m)	[pus]
little finger	petit doigt (m)	[pəti dwa]
nail	ongle (m)	[ɔ̃gl]
fist	poing (m)	[pwɛ̃]
palm	paume (f)	[pom]
wrist	poignet (m)	[pwaɲɛ]
forearm	avant-bras (m)	[avɑ̃bra]
elbow	coude (m)	[kud]
shoulder	épaule (f)	[epol]
leg	jambe (f)	[ʒɑ̃b]
foot	pied (m)	[pje]
knee	genou (m)	[ʒənu]
calf (part of leg)	mollet (m)	[mɔlɛ]
hip	hanche (f)	[ɑ̃ʃ]
heel	talon (m)	[talɔ̃]
body	corps (m)	[kɔr]
stomach	ventre (m)	[vɑ̃tr]
chest	poitrine (f)	[pwatrin]
breast	sein (m)	[sɛ̃]
flank	côté (m)	[kote]
back	dos (m)	[do]
lower back	reins (m pl)	[rɛ̃]
waist	taille (f)	[taj]
navel	nombril (m)	[nɔ̃bril]
buttocks	fesses (f pl)	[fɛs]
bottom	derrière (m)	[dɛrjɛr]
beauty mark	grain (m) de beauté	[grɛ̃ də bote]
birthmark	tache (f) de vin	[taʃ də vɛ̃]
tattoo	tatouage (m)	[tatwaʒ]
scar	cicatrice (f)	[sikatris]

Clothing & Accessories

33. Outerwear. Coats

clothes	**vêtement** (m)	[vɛtmɑ̃]
outer clothes	**survêtement** (m)	[syrvɛtmɑ̃]
winter clothes	**vêtement** (m) **d'hiver**	[vɛtmɑ̃ divɛr]
overcoat	**manteau** (m)	[mɑ̃to]
fur coat	**manteau** (m) **de fourrure**	[mɑ̃to də furyr]
fur jacket	**veste** (f) **en fourrure**	[vɛst ɑ̃ furyr]
down coat	**manteau** (m) **de duvet**	[manto də dyvɛ]
jacket (e.g., leather ~)	**veste** (f)	[vɛst]
raincoat	**imperméable** (m)	[ɛ̃pɛrmeabl]
waterproof (adj)	**imperméable** (adj)	[ɛ̃pɛrmeabl]

34. Men's & women's clothing

shirt	**chemise** (f)	[ʃəmiz]
pants	**pantalon** (m)	[pɑ̃talɔ̃]
jeans	**jean** (m)	[dʒin]
jacket (of man's suit)	**veston** (m)	[vɛstɔ̃]
suit	**complet** (m)	[kɔ̃plɛ]
dress (frock)	**robe** (f)	[rɔb]
skirt	**jupe** (f)	[ʒyp]
blouse	**chemisette** (f)	[ʃəmizɛt]
knitted jacket	**gilet** (m) **en laine**	[ʒilɛ ɑ̃ lɛn]
jacket (of woman's suit)	**jaquette** (f)	[ʒakɛt]
T-shirt	**tee-shirt** (m)	[tiʃœrt]
shorts (short trousers)	**short** (m)	[ʃɔrt]
tracksuit	**costume** (m) **de sport**	[kɔstym də spɔr]
bathrobe	**peignoir** (m) **de bain**	[pɛɲwar də bɛ̃]
pajamas	**pyjama** (m)	[piʒama]
sweater	**chandail** (m)	[ʃɑ̃daj]
pullover	**pull-over** (m)	[pylɔvɛr]
vest	**gilet** (m)	[ʒilɛ]
tailcoat	**queue-de-pie** (f)	[kødpi]
tuxedo	**smoking** (m)	[smɔkiŋ]
uniform	**uniforme** (m)	[ynifɔrm]

workwear	tenue (f) de travail	[təny də travaj]
overalls	salopette (f)	[salɔpɛt]
coat (e.g., doctor's smock)	blouse (f)	[bluz]

35. Clothing. Underwear

underwear	sous-vêtements (m pl)	[suvɛtmɑ̃]
boxers	boxer (m)	[bɔksɛr]
panties	slip (m) de femme	[slip də fam]
undershirt (A-shirt)	maillot (m) de corps	[majo də kɔr]
socks	chaussettes (f pl)	[ʃosɛt]

nightgown	chemise (f) de nuit	[ʃəmiz də nɥi]
bra	soutien-gorge (m)	[sutjɛ̃gɔrʒ]
knee highs	chaussettes (f pl) hautes	[ʃosɛt ot]
tights	collants (m pl)	[kɔlɑ̃]
stockings (thigh highs)	bas (m pl)	[ba]
bathing suit	maillot (m) de bain	[majo də bɛ̃]

36. Headwear

hat	bonnet (m)	[bɔnɛ]
fedora	chapeau (m) feutre	[ʃapo føtr]
baseball cap	casquette (f) de base-ball	[kaskɛt də bɛzbol]
flatcap	casquette (f)	[kaskɛt]

beret	béret (m)	[berɛ]
hood	capuche (f)	[kapyʃ]
panama hat	panama (m)	[panama]
knitted hat	bonnet (m) de laine	[bɔnɛ də lɛn]

| headscarf | foulard (m) | [fular] |
| women's hat | chapeau (m) de femme | [ʃapo də fam] |

hard hat	casque (m)	[kask]
garrison cap	calot (m)	[kalo]
helmet	casque (m)	[kask]

| derby | melon (m) | [məlɔ̃] |
| top hat | haut-de-forme (m) | [o də fɔrm] |

37. Footwear

footwear	chaussures (f pl)	[ʃosyr]
ankle boots	bottines (f pl)	[bɔtin]
shoes (low-heeled ~)	souliers (m pl)	[sulje]

| boots (cowboy ~) | **bottes** (f pl) | [bɔt] |
| slippers | **chaussons** (m pl) | [ʃosɔ̃] |

tennis shoes	**tennis** (m pl)	[tenis]
sneakers	**baskets** (f pl)	[baskɛt]
sandals	**sandales** (f pl)	[sɑ̃dal]

cobbler	**cordonnier** (m)	[kɔrdɔnje]
heel	**talon** (m)	[talɔ̃]
pair (of shoes)	**paire** (f)	[pɛr]

shoestring	**lacet** (m)	[lase]
to lace (vt)	**lacer** (vt)	[lase]
shoehorn	**chausse-pied** (m)	[ʃospje]
shoe polish	**cirage** (m)	[siraʒ]

38. Textile. Fabrics

cotton (n)	**coton** (m)	[kɔtɔ̃]
cotton (as adj)	**de coton** (adj)	[də kɔtɔ̃]
flax (n)	**lin** (m)	[lɛ̃]
flax (as adj)	**de lin** (adj)	[də lɛ̃]

silk (n)	**soie** (f)	[swa]
silk (as adj)	**de soie** (adj)	[də swa]
wool (n)	**laine** (f)	[lɛn]
woolen (adj)	**en laine** (adj)	[ɑ̃ lɛn]

velvet	**velours** (m)	[vəlur]
suede	**chamois** (m)	[ʃamwa]
corduroy	**velours** (m) **côtelé**	[vəlur kotle]

nylon (n)	**nylon** (m)	[nilɔ̃]
nylon (as adj)	**en nylon** (adj)	[ɑ̃ nilɔ̃]
polyester (n)	**polyester** (m)	[pɔliɛstɛr]
polyester (as adj)	**en polyester** (adj)	[ɑ̃ pɔliɛstɛr]

leather (n)	**cuir** (m)	[kɥir]
leather (as adj)	**en cuir** (adj)	[ɑ̃ kɥir]
fur (n)	**fourrure** (f)	[furyr]
fur (e.g., ~ coat)	**en fourrure** (adj)	[ɑ̃ furyr]

39. Personal accessories

gloves	**gants** (m pl)	[gɑ̃]
mittens	**moufles** (f pl)	[mufl]
scarf (muffler)	**écharpe** (f)	[eʃarp]
glasses	**lunettes** (f pl)	[lynɛt]

frame (eyeglass ~)	monture (f)	[mɔ̃tyr]
umbrella	parapluie (m)	[paraplyi]
walking stick	canne (f)	[kan]
hairbrush	brosse (f) à cheveux	[brɔs a ʃəvø]
fan	éventail (m)	[evɑ̃taj]
necktie	cravate (f)	[kravat]
bow tie	nœud papillon (m)	[nø papijɔ̃]
suspenders	bretelles (f pl)	[brətɛl]
handkerchief	mouchoir (m)	[muʃwar]
comb	peigne (m)	[pɛɲ]
barrette	barrette (f)	[barɛt]
hairpin	épingle (f) à cheveux	[epɛ̃gl a ʃəvø]
buckle	boucle (f)	[bukl]
belt	ceinture (f)	[sɛ̃tyr]
shoulder strap	bandoulière (f)	[bɑ̃duljɛr]
bag (handbag)	sac (m)	[sak]
purse	sac (m) à main	[sak a mɛ̃]
backpack	sac (m) à dos	[sak a do]

40. Clothing. Miscellaneous

fashion	mode (f)	[mɔd]
in vogue (adj)	à la mode (adj)	[alamɔd]
fashion designer	couturier (m)	[kutyrje]
collar	col (m)	[kɔl]
pocket	poche (f)	[pɔʃ]
pocket (as adj)	de poche (adj)	[də pɔʃ]
sleeve	manche (f)	[mɑ̃ʃ]
hanging loop	bride (f)	[brid]
fly (on trousers)	braguette (f)	[bragɛt]
zipper (fastener)	fermeture (f) à glissière	[fɛrmətyr a glisjɛr]
fastener	agrafe (f)	[agraf]
button	bouton (m)	[butɔ̃]
buttonhole	boutonnière (f)	[butɔnjɛr]
to come off (ab. button)	s'arracher (vp)	[saraʃe]
to sew (vi, vt)	coudre (vi, vt)	[kudr]
to embroider (vi, vt)	broder (vt)	[brɔde]
embroidery	broderie (f)	[brɔdri]
sewing needle	aiguille (f)	[egɥij]
thread	fil (m)	[fil]
seam	couture (f)	[kutyr]
to get dirty (vi)	se salir (vp)	[sə salir]
stain (mark, spot)	tache (f)	[taʃ]

to crease, crumple (vi)	se froisser (vp)	[sə frwase]
to tear (vt)	déchirer (vt)	[defire]
clothes moth	mite (f)	[mit]

41. Personal care. Cosmetics

toothpaste	dentifrice (m)	[dãtifris]
toothbrush	brosse (f) à dents	[brɔs a dã]
to brush one's teeth	se brosser les dents	[sə brɔse le dã]

razor	rasoir (m)	[razwar]
shaving cream	crème (f) à raser	[krɛm a raze]
to shave (vi)	se raser (vp)	[sə raze]

| soap | savon (m) | [savõ] |
| shampoo | shampooing (m) | [fãpwɛ̃] |

scissors	ciseaux (m pl)	[sizo]
nail file	lime (f) à ongles	[lim a õgl]
nail clippers	pinces (f pl) à ongles	[pɛ̃s a õgl]
tweezers	pince (f)	[pɛ̃s]

cosmetics	produits (m pl) de beauté	[prɔdyi də bote]
face mask	masque (m) de beauté	[mask də bote]
manicure	manucure (f)	[manykyr]
to have a manicure	se faire les ongles	[sə fɛr le zõgl]
pedicure	pédicurie (f)	[pedikyri]

make-up bag	trousse (f) de toilette	[trus də twalɛt]
face powder	poudre (f)	[pudr]
powder compact	poudrier (m)	[pudrije]
blusher	fard (m) à joues	[far a ʒu]

perfume (bottled)	parfum (m)	[parfœ̃]
toilet water (perfume)	eau (f) de toilette	[o də twalɛt]
lotion	lotion (f)	[losjõ]
cologne	eau de Cologne (f)	[o də kɔlɔɲ]

eyeshadow	fard (m) à paupières	[far a popjɛr]
eyeliner	crayon (m) à paupières	[krɛjõ a popjɛr]
mascara	mascara (m)	[maskara]

lipstick	rouge (m) à lèvres	[ruʒ a lɛvr]
nail polish, enamel	vernis (m) à ongles	[vɛrni a õgl]
hair spray	laque (f) pour les cheveux	[lak pur le ʃəvø]
deodorant	déodorant (m)	[deodorã]

| cream | crème (f) | [krɛm] |
| face cream | crème (f) pour le visage | [krɛm pur lə vizaʒ] |

hand cream	crème (f) pour les mains	[krɛm pur le mɛ̃]
anti-wrinkle cream	crème (f) anti-rides	[krɛm ɑ̃tirid]
day cream	crème (f) de jour	[krɛm də ʒur]
night cream	crème (f) de nuit	[krɛm də nɥi]
day (as adj)	de jour (adj)	[də ʒur]
night (as adj)	de nuit (adj)	[də nɥi]

tampon	tampon (m)	[tɑ̃põ]
toilet paper	papier (m) de toilette	[papje də twalɛt]
hair dryer	sèche-cheveux (m)	[sɛʃəvø]

42. Jewelry

jewelry	bijoux (m pl)	[biʒu]
precious (e.g., ~ stone)	précieux (adj)	[presjø]
hallmark	poinçon (m)	[pwɛ̃sõ]

ring	bague (f)	[bag]
wedding ring	alliance (f)	[aljɑ̃s]
bracelet	bracelet (m)	[braslɛ]

earrings	boucles (f pl) d'oreille	[bukl dɔrɛj]
necklace (~ of pearls)	collier (m)	[kɔlje]
crown	couronne (f)	[kurɔn]
bead necklace	collier (m)	[kɔlje]

diamond	diamant (m)	[djamɑ̃]
emerald	émeraude (f)	[emrod]
ruby	rubis (m)	[rybi]
sapphire	saphir (m)	[safir]
pearl	perle (f)	[pɛrl]
amber	ambre (m)	[ɑ̃br]

43. Watches. Clocks

watch (wristwatch)	montre (f)	[mõtr]
dial	cadran (m)	[kadrɑ̃]
hand (of clock, watch)	aiguille (f)	[egɥij]
metal watch band	bracelet (m)	[braslɛ]
watch strap	bracelet (m)	[braslɛ]

battery	pile (f)	[pil]
to be dead (battery)	être déchargé	[ɛtr deʃarʒe]
to change a battery	changer de pile	[ʃɑ̃ʒe də pil]
to run fast	avancer (vi)	[avɑ̃se]
to run slow	retarder (vi)	[rətarde]
wall clock	pendule (f)	[pɑ̃dyl]
hourglass	sablier (m)	[sablije]

sundial	**cadran** (m) **solaire**	[kadrã sɔlɛr]
alarm clock	**réveil** (m)	[revɛj]
watchmaker	**horloger** (m)	[ɔrlɔʒe]
to repair (vt)	**réparer** (vt)	[repare]

Food. Nutricion

44. Food

meat	viande (f)	[vjɑ̃d]
chicken	poulet (m)	[pulɛ]
young chicken	poulet (m)	[pulɛ]
duck	canard (m)	[kanar]
goose	oie (f)	[wa]
game	gibier (m)	[ʒibje]
turkey	dinde (f)	[dɛ̃d]
pork	du porc	[dy pɔr]
veal	du veau	[dy vo]
lamb	du mouton	[dy mutɔ̃]
beef	du bœuf	[dy bœf]
rabbit	lapin (m)	[lapɛ̃]
sausage (salami, etc.)	saucisson (m)	[sosisɔ̃]
vienna sausage	saucisse (f)	[sosis]
bacon	bacon (m)	[bekɔn]
ham	jambon (m)	[ʒɑ̃bɔ̃]
gammon (ham)	cuisse (f)	[kɥis]
pâté	pâté (m)	[pɑte]
liver	foie (m)	[fwa]
lard	lard (m)	[lar]
ground beef	farce (f)	[fars]
tongue	langue (f)	[lɑ̃g]
egg	œuf (m)	[œf]
eggs	les œufs	[lezø]
egg white	blanc (m) d'œuf	[blɑ̃ dœf]
egg yolk	jaune (m) d'œuf	[ʒon dœf]
fish	poisson (m)	[pwasɔ̃]
seafood	fruits (m pl) de mer	[frɥi də mɛr]
crustaceans	crustacés (m pl)	[krystase]
caviar	caviar (m)	[kavjar]
crab	crabe (m)	[krab]
shrimp	crevette (f)	[krəvɛt]
oyster	huître (f)	[ɥitr]
spiny lobster	langoustine (f)	[lɑ̃gustin]
octopus	poulpe (m)	[pulp]

squid	calamar (m)	[kalamar]
sturgeon	esturgeon (m)	[ɛstyrʒɔ̃]
salmon	saumon (m)	[somɔ̃]
halibut	flétan (m)	[fletɑ̃]

cod	morue (f)	[mɔry]
mackerel	maquereau (m)	[makro]
tuna	thon (m)	[tɔ̃]
eel	anguille (f)	[ɑ̃gij]

| trout | truite (f) | [trɥit] |
| sardine | sardine (f) | [sardin] |

| pike | brochet (m) | [brɔʃɛ] |
| herring | hareng (m) | [arɑ̃] |

| bread | pain (m) | [pɛ̃] |
| cheese | fromage (m) | [frɔmaʒ] |

| sugar | sucre (m) | [sykr] |
| salt | sel (m) | [sɛl] |

rice	riz (m)	[ri]
pasta	pâtes (m pl)	[pɑt]
noodles	nouilles (f pl)	[nuj]

butter	beurre (m)	[bœr]
vegetable oil	huile (f) végétale	[ɥil veʒetal]
sunflower oil	huile (f) de tournesol	[ɥil də turnəsɔl]
margarine	margarine (f)	[margarin]

| olives | olives (f pl) | [ɔliv] |
| olive oil | huile (f) d'olive | [ɥil dɔliv] |

milk	lait (m)	[lɛ]
condensed milk	lait (m) condensé	[lɛ kɔ̃dɑ̃se]
yogurt	yogourt (m)	[jaurt]

| sour cream | crème (f) aigre | [krɛm ɛgr] |
| cream (of milk) | crème (f) | [krɛm] |

| mayonnaise | sauce (f) mayonnaise | [sos majɔnɛz] |
| buttercream | crème (f) au beurre | [krɛm o bœr] |

cereal grain (wheat, etc.)	gruau (m)	[gryo]
flour	farine (f)	[farin]
canned food	conserves (f pl)	[kɔ̃sɛrv]

cornflakes	pétales (m pl) de maïs	[petal də mais]
honey	miel (m)	[mjɛl]
jam	confiture (f)	[kɔ̃fityr]
chewing gum	gomme (f) à mâcher	[gɔm a maʃe]

45. Drinks

water	eau (f)	[o]
drinking water	eau (f) potable	[o pɔtabl]
mineral water	eau (f) minérale	[o mineral]

still (adj)	plate (adj)	[plat]
carbonated (adj)	gazeuse (adj)	[gazøz]
sparkling (adj)	pétillante (adj)	[petijãt]
ice	glace (f)	[glas]
with ice	avec de la glace	[avɛk dəla glas]

non-alcoholic (adj)	sans alcool	[sã zalkɔl]
soft drink	boisson (f)	[bwasɔ̃
	non alcoolisée	nonalkɔlize]
cool soft drink	rafraîchissement (m)	[rafrɛʃismã]
lemonade	limonade (f)	[limɔnad]

liquor	boissons (f pl)	[bwasɔ̃
	alcoolisées	alkɔlize]
wine	vin (m)	[vɛ̃]
white wine	vin (m) blanc	[vɛ̃ blã]
red wine	vin (m) rouge	[vɛ̃ ruʒ]

liqueur	liqueur (f)	[likœr]
champagne	champagne (m)	[ʃãpaɲ]
vermouth	vermouth (m)	[vɛrmut]

whisky	whisky (m)	[wiski]
vodka	vodka (f)	[vɔdka]
gin	gin (m)	[dʒin]
cognac	cognac (m)	[kɔɲak]
rum	rhum (m)	[rɔm]

coffee	café (m)	[kafe]
black coffee	café (m) noir	[kafe nwar]
coffee with milk	café (m) au lait	[kafe o lɛ]
cappuccino	cappuccino (m)	[kaputʃino]
instant coffee	café (m) soluble	[kafe sɔlybl]

milk	lait (m)	[lɛ]
cocktail	cocktail (m)	[kɔktɛl]
milk shake	cocktail (m) au lait	[kɔktɛl o lɛ]

juice	jus (m)	[ʒy]
tomato juice	jus (m) de tomate	[ʒy də tɔmat]
orange juice	jus (m) d'orange	[ʒy dɔrãʒ]
freshly squeezed juice	jus (m) pressé	[ʒy prese]

| beer | bière (f) | [bjɛr] |
| light beer | bière (f) blonde | [bjɛr blɔ̃d] |

dark beer	bière (f) brune	[bjɛr bryn]
tea	thé (m)	[te]
black tea	thé (m) noir	[te nwar]
green tea	thé (m) vert	[te vɛr]

46. Vegetables

| vegetables | légumes (m pl) | [legym] |
| greens | verdure (f) | [vɛrdyr] |

tomato	tomate (f)	[tɔmat]
cucumber	concombre (m)	[kɔ̃kɔ̃br]
carrot	carotte (f)	[karɔt]
potato	pomme (f) de terre	[pɔm də tɛr]
onion	oignon (m)	[ɔɲɔ̃]
garlic	ail (m)	[aj]

cabbage	chou (m)	[ʃu]
cauliflower	chou-fleur (m)	[ʃuflœr]
Brussels sprouts	chou (m) de Bruxelles	[ʃu də brysɛl]
broccoli	brocoli (m)	[brɔkɔli]

beetroot	betterave (f)	[bɛtrav]
eggplant	aubergine (f)	[obɛrʒin]
zucchini	courgette (f)	[kurʒɛt]
pumpkin	potiron (m)	[pɔtirɔ̃]
turnip	navet (m)	[navɛ]

parsley	persil (m)	[pɛrsi]
dill	fenouil (m)	[fənuj]
lettuce	laitue (f), salade (f)	[lety], [salad]
celery	céleri (m)	[selri]
asparagus	asperge (f)	[aspɛrʒ]
spinach	épinard (m)	[epinar]

pea	pois (m)	[pwa]
beans	fèves (f pl)	[fɛv]
corn (maize)	maïs (m)	[mais]
kidney bean	haricot (m)	[ariko]

pepper	poivron (m)	[pwavrɔ̃]
radish	radis (m)	[radi]
artichoke	artichaut (m)	[artiʃo]

47. Fruits. Nuts

| fruit | fruit (m) | [frɥi] |
| apple | pomme (f) | [pɔm] |

pear	poire (f)	[pwar]
lemon	citron (m)	[sitrɔ̃]
orange	orange (f)	[ɔrɑ̃ʒ]
strawberry	fraise (f)	[frɛz]

mandarin	mandarine (f)	[mɑ̃darin]
plum	prune (f)	[pryn]
peach	pêche (f)	[pɛʃ]
apricot	abricot (m)	[abriko]
raspberry	framboise (f)	[frɑ̃bwaz]
pineapple	ananas (m)	[anana]

banana	banane (f)	[banan]
watermelon	pastèque (f)	[pastɛk]
grape	raisin (m)	[rɛzɛ̃]
sour cherry	cerise (f)	[səriz]
sweet cherry	merise (f)	[məriz]
melon	melon (m)	[məlɔ̃]

grapefruit	pamplemousse (m)	[pɑ̃pləmus]
avocado	avocat (m)	[avɔka]
papaya	papaye (f)	[papaj]
mango	mangue (f)	[mɑ̃g]
pomegranate	grenade (f)	[grənad]

redcurrant	groseille (f) rouge	[grozɛj ruʒ]
blackcurrant	cassis (m)	[kasis]
gooseberry	groseille (f) verte	[grozɛj vɛrt]
bilberry	myrtille (f)	[mirtij]
blackberry	mûre (f)	[myr]

raisin	raisin (m) sec	[rɛzɛ̃ sɛk]
fig	figue (f)	[fig]
date	datte (f)	[dat]

peanut	cacahuète (f)	[kakawɛt]
almond	amande (f)	[amɑ̃d]
walnut	noix (f)	[nwa]
hazelnut	noisette (f)	[nwazɛt]
coconut	noix (f) de coco	[nwa də kɔkɔ]
pistachios	pistaches (f pl)	[pistaʃ]

48. Bread. Candy

confectionery (pastry)	confiserie (f)	[kɔ̃fizri]
bread	pain (m)	[pɛ̃]
cookies	biscuit (m)	[biskɥi]

| chocolate (n) | chocolat (m) | [ʃɔkɔla] |
| chocolate (as adj) | en chocolat (adj) | [ɑ̃ ʃɔkɔla] |

candy	**bonbon** (m)	[bɔ̃bɔ̃]
cake (e.g., cupcake)	**gâteau** (m)	[gato]
cake (e.g., birthday ~)	**tarte** (f)	[tart]
pie (e.g., apple ~)	**gâteau** (m)	[gato]
filling (for cake, pie)	**garniture** (f)	[garnityr]
whole fruit jam	**confiture** (f)	[kɔ̃fityr]
marmalade	**marmelade** (f)	[marmǝlad]
waffle	**gaufre** (f)	[gofr]
ice-cream	**glace** (f)	[glas]
pudding	**pudding** (m)	[pudiŋ]

49. Cooked dishes

course, dish	**plat** (m)	[pla]
cuisine	**cuisine** (f)	[kɥizin]
recipe	**recette** (f)	[rǝsɛt]
portion	**portion** (f)	[pɔrsjɔ̃]
salad	**salade** (f)	[salad]
soup	**soupe** (f)	[sup]
clear soup (broth)	**bouillon** (m)	[bujɔ̃]
sandwich (bread)	**sandwich** (m)	[sãdwitʃ]
fried eggs	**les œufs brouillés**	[lezø bruje]
cutlet (croquette)	**boulette** (f)	[bulɛt]
hamburger (beefburger)	**hamburger** (m)	[ãbœrgœr]
beefsteak	**steak** (m)	[stɛk]
stew	**rôti** (m)	[roti]
side dish	**garniture** (f)	[garnityr]
spaghetti	**spaghettis** (m pl)	[spagɛti]
mashed potatoes	**purée** (f)	[pyre]
pizza	**pizza** (f)	[pidza]
porridge (oatmeal, etc.)	**bouillie** (f)	[buji]
omelet	**omelette** (f)	[ɔmlɛt]
boiled (e.g., ~ beef)	**cuit à l'eau** (adj)	[kɥitɑlo]
smoked (adj)	**fumé** (adj)	[fyme]
fried (adj)	**frit** (adi)	[fri]
dried (adj)	**sec** (adj)	[sɛk]
frozen (adj)	**congelé** (adj)	[kɔ̃ʒle]
pickled (adj)	**mariné** (adj)	[marine]
sweet (sugary)	**sucré** (adj)	[sykre]
salty (adj)	**salé** (adj)	[sale]
cold (adj)	**froid** (adj)	[frwa]
hot (adj)	**chaud** (adj)	[ʃo]

bitter (adj)	**amer** (adj)	[amɛr]
tasty (adj)	**bon** (adj)	[bõ]
to cook in boiling water	**cuire à l'eau**	[kɥir ɑ lo]
to cook (dinner)	**préparer** (vt)	[prepare]
to fry (vt)	**faire frire**	[fɛr frir]
to heat up (food)	**réchauffer** (vt)	[reʃofe]
to salt (vt)	**saler** (vt)	[sale]
to pepper (vt)	**poivrer** (vt)	[pwavre]
to grate (vt)	**râper** (vt)	[rɑpe]
peel (n)	**peau** (f)	[po]
to peel (vt)	**éplucher** (vt)	[eplyʃe]

50. Spices

salt	**sel** (m)	[sɛl]
salty (adj)	**salé** (adj)	[sale]
to salt (vt)	**saler** (vt)	[sale]
black pepper	**poivre** (m) **noir**	[pwavr nwar]
red pepper	**poivre** (m) **rouge**	[pwavr ruʒ]
mustard	**moutarde** (f)	[mutard]
horseradish	**raifort** (m)	[rɛfɔr]
condiment	**condiment** (m)	[kõdimã]
spice	**épice** (f)	[epis]
sauce	**sauce** (f)	[sos]
vinegar	**vinaigre** (m)	[vinɛgr]
anise	**anis** (m)	[ani(s)]
basil	**basilic** (m)	[bazilik]
cloves	**clou** (m) **de girofle**	[klu də ʒirɔfl]
ginger	**gingembre** (m)	[ʒɛ̃ʒãbr]
coriander	**coriandre** (m)	[kɔrjãdr]
cinnamon	**cannelle** (f)	[kanɛl]
sesame	**sésame** (m)	[sezam]
bay leaf	**feuille** (f) **de laurier**	[fœj də lɔrje]
paprika	**paprika** (m)	[paprika]
caraway	**cumin** (m)	[kymɛ̃]
saffron	**safran** (m)	[safrã]

51. Meals

food	**nourriture** (f)	[nurityr]
to eat (vi, vt)	**manger** (vi, vt)	[mãʒe]
breakfast	**petit déjeuner** (m)	[pəti deʒœne]

to have breakfast	**prendre le petit déjeuner**	[prãdr ləpti deʒœne]
lunch	**déjeuner** (m)	[deʒœne]
to have lunch	**déjeuner** (vi)	[deʒœne]
dinner	**dîner** (m)	[dine]
to have dinner	**dîner** (vi)	[dine]
appetite	**appétit** (m)	[apeti]
Enjoy your meal!	**Bon appétit!**	[bɔn apeti]
to open (~ a bottle)	**ouvrir** (vt)	[uvrir]
to spill (liquid)	**renverser** (vt)	[rãvɛrse]
to spill out (vi)	**se renverser** (vp)	[sə rãvɛrse]
to boil (vi)	**bouillir** (vi)	[bujir]
to boil (vt)	**faire bouillir**	[fɛr bujir]
boiled (~ water)	**bouilli** (adj)	[buji]
to chill, cool down (vt)	**refroidir** (vt)	[rəfrwadir]
to chill (vi)	**se refroidir** (vp)	[sə rəfrwadir]
taste, flavor	**goût** (m)	[gu]
aftertaste	**arrière-goût** (m)	[arjɛrgu]
to be on a diet	**suivre un régime**	[sɥivr œ̃ reʒim]
diet	**régime** (m)	[reʒim]
vitamin	**vitamine** (f)	[vitamin]
calorie	**calorie** (f)	[kalɔri]
vegetarian (n)	**végétarien** (m)	[veʒetarjɛ̃]
vegetarian (adj)	**végétarien** (adj)	[veʒetarjɛ̃]
fats (nutrient)	**lipides** (m pl)	[lipid]
proteins	**protéines** (f pl)	[prɔtein]
carbohydrates	**glucides** (m pl)	[glysid]
slice (of lemon, ham)	**tranche** (f)	[trãʃ]
piece (of cake, pie)	**morceau** (m)	[mɔrso]
crumb (of bread)	**miette** (f)	[mjɛt]

52. Table setting

spoon	**cuillère** (f)	[kɥijɛr]
knife	**couteau** (m)	[kutʊ]
fork	**fourchette** (f)	[furʃɛt]
cup (of coffee)	**tasse** (f)	[tɑs]
plate (dinner ~)	**assiette** (f)	[asjɛt]
saucer	**soucoupe** (f)	[sukup]
napkin (on table)	**serviette** (f)	[sɛrvjɛt]
toothpick	**cure-dent** (m)	[kyrdã]

53. Restaurant

restaurant	**restaurant** (m)	[rɛstɔrɑ̃]
coffee house	**salon** (m) **de café**	[salɔ̃ də kafe]
pub, bar	**bar** (m)	[bar]
tearoom	**salon** (m) **de thé**	[salɔ̃ də te]
waiter	**serveur** (m)	[sɛrvœr]
waitress	**serveuse** (f)	[sɛrvøz]
bartender	**barman** (m)	[barman]
menu	**carte** (f)	[kart]
wine list	**carte** (f) **des vins**	[kart de vɛ̃]
to book a table	**réserver une table**	[rezɛrve yn tabl]
course, dish	**plat** (m)	[pla]
to order (meal)	**commander** (vt)	[kɔmɑ̃de]
to make an order	**faire la commande**	[fɛr la kɔmɑ̃d]
aperitif	**apéritif** (m)	[aperitif]
appetizer	**hors-d'œuvre** (m)	[ɔrdœvr]
dessert	**dessert** (m)	[desɛr]
check	**addition** (f)	[adisjɔ̃]
to pay the check	**régler l'addition**	[regle ladisjɔ̃]
to give change	**rendre la monnaie**	[rɑ̃dr la mɔnɛ]
tip	**pourboire** (m)	[purbwar]

Family, relatives and friends

54. Personal information. Forms

name, first name	prénom (m)	[prenɔ̃]
family name	nom (m) de famille	[nɔ̃ də famij]
date of birth	date (f) de naissance	[dat də nɛsɑ̃s]
place of birth	lieu (m) de naissance	[ljø də nɛsɑ̃s]
nationality	nationalité (f)	[nasjɔnalite]
place of residence	domicile (m)	[dɔmisil]
country	pays (m)	[pei]
profession (occupation)	profession (f)	[prɔfɛsjɔ̃]
gender, sex	sexe (m)	[sɛks]
height	taille (f)	[taj]
weight	poids (m)	[pwa]

55. Family members. Relatives

mother	mère (f)	[mɛr]
father	père (m)	[pɛr]
son	fils (m)	[fis]
daughter	fille (f)	[fij]
younger daughter	fille (f) cadette	[fij kadɛt]
younger son	fils (m) cadet	[fis kadɛ]
eldest daughter	fille (f) aînée	[fij ene]
eldest son	fils (m) aîné	[fis ene]
brother	frère (m)	[frɛr]
sister	sœur (f)	[sœr]
cousin (masc.)	cousin (m)	[kuzɛ̃]
cousin (fem.)	cousine (f)	[kuzin]
mom	maman (f)	[mamɑ̃]
dad, daddy	papa (m)	[papa]
parents	parents (pl)	[parɑ̃]
child	enfant (m, f)	[ɑ̃fɑ̃]
children	enfants (pl)	[ɑ̃fɑ̃]
grandmother	grand-mère (f)	[grɑ̃mɛr]
grandfather	grand-père (m)	[grɑ̃pɛr]
grandson	petit-fils (m)	[pti fis]

granddaughter	**petite-fille** (f)	[ptit fij]
grandchildren	**petits-enfants** (pl)	[pətizãfã]
uncle	**oncle** (m)	[ɔ̃kl]
aunt	**tante** (f)	[tɑ̃t]
nephew	**neveu** (m)	[nəvø]
niece	**nièce** (f)	[njɛs]
mother-in-law (wife's mother)	**belle-mère** (f)	[bɛlmɛr]
father-in-law (husband's father)	**beau-père** (m)	[bopɛr]
son-in-law (daughter's husband)	**gendre** (m)	[ʒɑ̃dr]
stepmother	**belle-mère, marâtre** (f)	[bɛlmɛr], [marɑtr]
stepfather	**beau-père** (m)	[bopɛr]
infant	**nourrisson** (m)	[nurisɔ̃]
baby (infant)	**bébé** (m)	[bebe]
little boy, kid	**petit** (m)	[pti]
wife	**femme** (f)	[fam]
husband	**mari** (m)	[mari]
spouse (husband)	**époux** (m)	[epu]
spouse (wife)	**épouse** (f)	[epuz]
married (masc.)	**marié** (adj)	[marje]
married (fem.)	**mariée** (adj)	[marje]
single (unmarried)	**célibataire** (adj)	[selibatɛr]
bachelor	**célibataire** (m)	[selibatɛr]
divorced (masc.)	**divorcé** (adj)	[divɔrse]
widow	**veuve** (f)	[vœv]
widower	**veuf** (m)	[vœf]
relative	**parent** (m)	[parã]
close relative	**parent** (m) **proche**	[parã prɔʃ]
distant relative	**parent** (m) **éloigné**	[parã elwaɲe]
relatives	**parents** (m pl)	[parã]
orphan (boy)	**orphelin** (m)	[ɔrfəlɛ̃]
orphan (girl)	**orpheline** (f)	[ɔrfəlin]
guardian (of minor)	**tuteur** (m)	[tytœr]
to adopt (a boy)	**adopter** (vt)	[adɔpte]
to adopt (a girl)	**adopter** (vt)	[adɔpte]

56. Friends. Coworkers

friend (masc.)	**ami** (m)	[ami]
friend (fem.)	**amie** (f)	[ami]
friendship	**amitié** (f)	[amitje]

to be friends	être ami	[ɛtr ami]
buddy (masc.)	copain (m)	[kɔpɛ̃]
buddy (fem.)	copine (f)	[kɔpin]
partner	partenaire (m)	[partənɛr]

chief (boss)	chef (m)	[ʃɛf]
superior	supérieur (m)	[syperjœr]
owner, proprietor	propriétaire (m)	[prɔprijetɛr]
subordinate	subordonné (m)	[sybɔrdɔne]
colleague	collègue (m, f)	[kɔlɛg]

acquaintance (person)	connaissance (f)	[kɔnɛsɑ̃s]
fellow traveler	compagnon (m) de route	[kɔ̃paɲɔ̃ də rut]
classmate	copain (m) de classe	[kɔpɛ̃ də klas]

neighbor (masc.)	voisin (m)	[vwazɛ̃]
neighbor (fem.)	voisine (f)	[vwazin]
neighbors	voisins (m pl)	[vwazɛ̃]

57. Man. Woman

woman	femme (f)	[fam]
girl (young woman)	jeune fille (f)	[ʒœn fij]
bride	fiancée (f)	[fijɑ̃se]

beautiful (adj)	belle (adj)	[bɛl]
tall (adj)	de grande taille	[də grɑ̃d taj]
slender (adj)	svelte (adj)	[svɛlt]
short (adj)	de petite taille	[də ptit taj]

| blonde (n) | blonde (f) | [blɔ̃d] |
| brunette (n) | brune (f) | [brœn] |

ladies' (adj)	de femme (adj)	[də fam]
virgin (girl)	vierge (f)	[vjɛrʒ]
pregnant (adj)	enceinte (adj)	[ɑ̃sɛ̃t]

man (adult male)	homme (m)	[ɔm]
blond (n)	blond (m)	[blɔ̃]
brunet (n)	brun (m)	[brœ̃]
tall (adj)	de grande taille	[də grɑ̃d taj]
short (adj)	de petite taille	[də ptit taj]

rude (rough)	rude (adj)	[ryd]
stocky (adj)	trapu (adj)	[trapy]
robust (adj)	robuste (adj)	[rɔbyst]
strong (adj)	fort (adj)	[fɔr]
strength	force (f)	[fɔrs]
stout, fat (adj)	gros (adj)	[gro]
swarthy (adj)	basané (adj)	[bazane]

| well-built (adj) | svelte (adj) | [svɛlt] |
| elegant (adj) | élégant (adj) | [elegɑ̃] |

58. Age

age	âge (m)	[ɑʒ]
youth (young age)	jeunesse (f)	[ʒœnɛs]
young (adj)	jeune (adj)	[ʒœn]

| younger (adj) | plus jeune (adj) | [ply ʒœn] |
| older (adj) | plus âgé (adj) | [plyzɑʒe] |

young man	jeune homme (m)	[ʒœn ɔm]
teenager	adolescent (m)	[adɔlesɑ̃]
guy, fellow	gars (m)	[ga]

| old man | vieillard (m) | [vjɛjar] |
| old woman | vieille femme (f) | [vjɛj fam] |

adult	adulte (m)	[adylt]
middle-aged (adj)	d'âge moyen (adj)	[dɑʒ mwajɛ̃]
elderly (adj)	âgé (adj)	[ɑʒe]
old (adj)	vieux (adj)	[vjø]

retirement	retraite (f)	[rətrɛt]
to retire (from job)	prendre sa retraite	[prɑ̃dr sa rətrɛt]
retiree	retraité (m)	[rətrɛte]

59. Children

child	enfant (m, f)	[ɑ̃fɑ̃]
children	enfants (pl)	[ɑ̃fɑ̃]
twins	jumeaux (m pl)	[ʒymo]

cradle	berceau (m)	[bɛrso]
rattle	hochet (m)	[ɔʃɛ]
diaper	couche (f)	[kuʃ]

pacifier	tétine (f)	[tetin]
baby carriage	poussette (m)	[pusɛt]
kindergarten	école (f) maternelle	[ekɔl matɛrnɛl]
babysitter	baby-sitter (m, f)	[bebisitœr]

childhood	enfance (f)	[ɑ̃fɑ̃s]
doll	poupée (f)	[pupe]
toy	jouet (m)	[ʒwɛ]
construction set	jeu (m) de construction	[ʒø də kɔ̃stryksjɔ̃]
well-bred (adj)	bien élevé (adj)	[bjɛn elve]

ill-bred (adj)	mal élevé (adj)	[mal elve]
spoiled (adj)	gâté (adj)	[gɑte]
to be naughty	faire le vilain	[fɛr lə vilɛ̃]
mischievous (adj)	vilain (adj)	[vilɛ̃]
mischievousness	espièglerie (f)	[ɛspjɛgləri]
mischievous child	vilain (m)	[vilɛ̃]
obedient (adj)	obéissant (adj)	[ɔbeisɑ̃]
disobedient (adj)	désobéissant (adj)	[dezɔbeisɑ̃]
docile (adj)	sage (adj)	[saʒ]
clever (smart)	intelligent (adj)	[ɛ̃teliʒɑ̃]
child prodigy	l'enfant prodige	[lɑ̃fɑ̃ prɔdiʒ]

60. Married couples. Family life

to kiss (vt)	embrasser (vt)	[ɑ̃brase]
to kiss (vi)	s'embrasser (vp)	[sɑ̃brase]
family (n)	famille (f)	[famij]
family (as adj)	familial (adj)	[familjal]
couple	couple (m)	[kupl]
marriage (state)	mariage (m)	[marjaʒ]
hearth (home)	foyer (m) familial	[fwaje familjal]
dynasty	dynastie (f)	[dinasti]
date	rendez-vous (m)	[rɑ̃devu]
kiss	baiser (m)	[beze]
love (for sb)	amour (m)	[amur]
to love (sb)	aimer (vt)	[eme]
beloved	aimé (adj)	[eme]
tenderness	tendresse (f)	[tɑ̃drɛs]
tender (affectionate)	tendre (adj)	[tɑ̃dr]
faithfulness	fidélité (f)	[fidelite]
faithful (adj)	fidèle (adj)	[fidɛl]
care (attention)	soin (m)	[swk]
caring (~ father)	attentionné (adj)	[atɑ̃sjɔne]
newlyweds	jeunes mariés (pl)	[ʒœ̃ marje]
honeymoon	lune (f) de miel	[lyn də mjɛl]
to get married	se marier (vp)	[sə marje]
(ab. woman)		
to get married (ab. man)	se marier (vp)	[sə marje]
wedding	mariage (m)	[marjaʒ]
golden wedding	les noces d'or	[le nɔs dɔr]
anniversary	anniversaire (m)	[anivɛrsɛr]
lover (masc.)	amant (m)	[amɑ̃]

mistress	**maîtresse** (f)	[mɛtrɛs]
adultery	**adultère** (m)	[adyltɛr]
to cheat on … (commit adultery)	**commettre l'adultère**	[kɔmɛtr ladyltɛr]
jealous (adj)	**jaloux** (adj)	[ʒalu]
to be jealous	**être jaloux**	[ɛtr ʒalu]
divorce	**divorce** (m)	[divɔrs]
to divorce (vi)	**divorcer** (vi)	[divɔrse]
to quarrel (vi)	**se disputer** (vp)	[sə dispyte]
to be reconciled	**se réconcilier** (vp)	[sə rekɔ̃silje]
together (adv)	**ensemble** (adv)	[ɑ̃sɑ̃bl]
sex	**sexe** (m)	[sɛks]
happiness	**bonheur** (m)	[bɔnœr]
happy (adj)	**heureux** (adj)	[œrø]
misfortune (accident)	**malheur** (m)	[malœr]
unhappy (adj)	**malheureux** (adj)	[malœrø]

Character. Feelings. Emotions

61. Feelings. Emotions

feeling (emotion)	sentiment (m)	[sɑ̃timɑ̃]
feelings	sentiments (m pl)	[sɑ̃timɑ̃]
to feel (vt)	sentir (vt)	[sɑ̃tir]
hunger	faim (f)	[fɛ̃]
to be hungry	avoir faim	[avwar fɛ̃]
thirst	soif (f)	[swaf]
to be thirsty	avoir soif	[avwar swaf]
sleepiness	somnolence (f)	[sɔmnifɛr]
to feel sleepy	avoir sommeil	[avwar sɔmɛj]
tiredness	fatigue (f)	[fatig]
tired (adj)	fatigué (adj)	[fatige]
to get tired	être fatigué	[ɛtr fatige]
mood (humor)	humeur (f)	[ymœr]
boredom	ennui (m)	[ɑ̃nɥi]
to be bored	s'ennuyer (vp)	[sɑ̃nɥije]
seclusion	solitude (f)	[sɔlityd]
to seclude oneself	s'isoler (vp)	[sizɔle]
to worry (make anxious)	inquiéter (vt)	[ɛ̃kjete]
to be worried	s'inquiéter (vp)	[sɛ̃kjete]
worrying (n)	inquiétude (f)	[ɛ̃kjetyd]
anxiety	préoccupation (f)	[preɔkypasjɔ̃]
preoccupied (adj)	soucieux (adj)	[susjø]
to be nervous	s'énerver (vp)	[senɛrve]
to panic (vi)	paniquer (vi)	[panike]
hope	espoir (m)	[ɛspwar]
to hope (vi, vt)	espérer (vi)	[ɛspere]
certainty	certitude (f)	[sɛrtityd]
certain, sure (adj)	certain (adj)	[sɛrtɛ̃]
uncertainty	incertitude (f)	[ɛ̃sɛrtityd]
uncertain (adj)	incertain (adj)	[ɛ̃sɛrtɛ̃]
drunk (adj)	ivre (adj)	[ivr]
sober (adj)	sobre (adj)	[sɔbr]
weak (adj)	faible (adj)	[fɛbl]
happy (adj)	heureux (adj)	[œrø]
to scare (vt)	faire peur	[fɛr pœr]

| fury (madness) | **fureur** (f) | [fyrœr] |
| rage (fury) | **rage** (f), **colère** (f) | [raʒ], [kɔlɛr] |

depression	**dépression** (f)	[depresjɔ̃]
discomfort	**inconfort** (m)	[ɛ̃kɔ̃fɔr]
comfort	**confort** (m)	[kɔ̃fɔr]
to regret (be sorry)	**regretter** (vt)	[rəgrɛte]
regret	**regret** (m)	[rəgrɛ]
bad luck	**malchance** (f)	[malʃɑ̃s]
sadness	**tristesse** (f)	[tristɛs]

shame (remorse)	**honte** (f)	[ɔ̃t]
gladness	**joie, allégresse** (f)	[ʒwa], [alegrɛs]
enthusiasm, zeal	**enthousiasme** (m)	[ɑ̃tuzjasm]
enthusiast	**enthousiaste** (m)	[ɑ̃tuzjast]
to show enthusiasm	**avoir de l'enthousiasme**	[avwar də lɑ̃tuzjasm]

62. Character. Personality

character	**caractère** (m)	[karaktɛr]
character flaw	**défaut** (m)	[defo]
mind	**esprit** (m)	[ɛspri]
reason	**raison** (f)	[rɛzɔ̃]

conscience	**conscience** (f)	[kɔ̃sjɑ̃s]
habit (custom)	**habitude** (f)	[abityd]
ability	**capacité** (f)	[kapasite]
can (e.g., ~ swim)	**savoir** (vt)	[savwar]

patient (adj)	**patient** (adj)	[pasjɑ̃]
impatient (adj)	**impatient** (adj)	[ɛ̃pasjɑ̃]
curious (inquisitive)	**curieux** (adj)	[kyrjø]
curiosity	**curiosité** (f)	[kyrjozite]

modesty	**modestie** (f)	[mɔdɛsti]
modest (adj)	**modeste** (adj)	[mɔdɛst]
immodest (adj)	**vaniteux** (adj)	[vanitø]

laziness	**paresse** (f)	[parɛs]
lazy (adj)	**paresseux** (adj)	[parɛsø]
lazy person (masc.)	**paresseux** (m)	[parɛsø]

cunning (n)	**astuce** (f)	[astys]
cunning (as adj)	**rusé** (adj)	[ryze]
distrust	**méfiance** (f)	[mefjɑ̃s]
distrustful (adj)	**méfiant** (adj)	[mefjɑ̃]

generosity	**générosité** (f)	[ʒenerozite]
generous (adj)	**généreux** (adj)	[ʒenerø]
talented (adj)	**doué** (adj)	[dwe]

talent	**talent** (m)	[talɑ̃]
courageous (adj)	**courageux** (adj)	[kuraʒø]
courage	**courage** (m)	[kuraʒ]
honest (adj)	**honnête** (adj)	[ɔnɛt]
honesty	**honnêteté** (f)	[ɔnɛtte]
careful (cautious)	**prudent** (adj)	[prydɑ̃]
brave (courageous)	**courageux** (adj)	[kuraʒø]
serious (adj)	**sérieux** (adj)	[serjø]
strict (severe, stern)	**sévère** (adj)	[sevɛr]
decisive (adj)	**décidé** (adj)	[deside]
indecisive (adj)	**indécis** (adj)	[ɛ̃desi]
shy, timid (adj)	**timide** (adj)	[timid]
shyness, timidity	**timidité** (f)	[timidite]
confidence (trust)	**confiance** (f)	[kɔ̃fjɑ̃s]
to believe (trust)	**croire** (vt)	[krwar]
trusting (naïve)	**confiant** (adj)	[kɔ̃fjɑ̃]
sincerely (adv)	**sincèrement** (adv)	[sɛ̃sɛrmɑ̃]
sincere (adj)	**sincère** (adj)	[sɛ̃sɛr]
sincerity	**sincérité** (f)	[sɛ̃serite]
open (person)	**ouvert** (adj)	[uvɛr]
calm (adj)	**calme** (adj)	[kalm]
frank (sincere)	**franc** (adj)	[frɑ̃]
naïve (adj)	**naïf** (adj)	[naif]
absent-minded (adj)	**distrait** (adj)	[distrɛ]
funny (odd)	**drôle, amusant** (adj)	[drol], [amyzɑ̃]
greed	**avidité** (f)	[avidite]
greedy (adj)	**avare** (adj)	[avar]
stingy (adj)	**radin** (adj)	[radɛ̃]
evil (adj)	**méchant** (adj)	[meʃɑ̃]
stubborn (adj)	**têtu** (adj)	[tety]
unpleasant (adj)	**désagréable** (adj)	[dezagreabl]
selfish person (masc.)	**égoïste** (m)	[egɔist]
selfish (adj)	**égoïste** (adj)	[egɔist]
coward	**peureux** (m)	[pœrø]
cowardly (adj)	**peureux** (adj)	[pœrø]

63. Sleep. Dreams

to sleep (vi)	**dormir** (vi)	[dɔrmir]
sleep, sleeping	**sommeil** (m)	[sɔmɛj]
dream	**rêve** (m)	[rɛv]
to dream (in sleep)	**rêver** (vi)	[rɛve]
sleepy (adj)	**endormi** (adj)	[ɑ̃dɔrmi]

bed	lit (m)	[li]
mattress	matelas (m)	[matla]
blanket (comforter)	couverture (f)	[kuvɛrtyr]
pillow	oreiller (m)	[ɔrɛje]
sheet	drap (m)	[dra]

insomnia	insomnie (f)	[ɛ̃sɔmni]
sleepless (adj)	sans sommeil (adj)	[sɑ̃ sɔmɛj]
sleeping pill	somnifère (m)	[sɔmnifɛr]
to take a sleeping pill	prendre un somnifère	[prɑ̃dr œ̃ sɔmnifɛr]

to feel sleepy	avoir sommeil	[avwar sɔmɛj]
to yawn (vi)	bâiller (vi)	[baje]
to go to bed	aller se coucher	[ale sə kuʃe]
to make up the bed	faire le lit	[fɛr le li]
to fall asleep	s'endormir (vp)	[sɑ̃dɔrmir]

nightmare	cauchemar (m)	[koʃmar]
snoring	ronflement (m)	[rɔ̃fləmɑ̃]
to snore (vi)	ronfler (vi)	[rɔ̃fle]

alarm clock	réveil (m)	[revɛj]
to wake (vt)	réveiller (vt)	[reveje]
to wake up	se réveiller (vp)	[sə reveje]
to get up (vp)	se lever (vp)	[sə ləve]
to wash up (vi)	se laver (vp)	[sə lave]

64. Humour. Laughter. Gladness

humor (wit, fun)	humour (m)	[ymur]
sense of humor	sens (m) de l'humour	[sɑ̃s də lymur]
to have fun	s'amuser (vp)	[samyze]
cheerful (adj)	joyeux (adj)	[ʒwajø]
merriment, fun	joie, allégresse (f)	[ʒwa], [alegrɛs]

smile	sourire (m)	[surir]
to smile (vi)	sourire (vi)	[surir]
to start laughing	se mettre à rire	[sə mɛtr ɑ rir]
to laugh (vi)	rire (vi)	[rir]
laugh, laughter	rire (m)	[rir]

anecdote	anecdote (f)	[anɛkdɔt]
funny (anecdote, etc.)	drôle (adj)	[drol]
funny (odd)	comique, ridicule (adj)	[kɔmik], [ridikyl]

to joke (vi)	plaisanter (vi)	[plɛzɑ̃te]
joke (verbal)	plaisanterie (f)	[plɛzɑ̃tri]
joy (emotion)	joie (f)	[ʒwa]
to rejoice (vi)	se réjouir (vp)	[sə reʒwir]
glad, cheerful (adj)	joyeux (adj)	[ʒwajø]

65. Discussion, conversation. Part 1

| communication | communication (f) | [kɔmynikasjɔ̃] |
| to communicate | communiquer (vi) | [kɔmynike] |

conversation	conversation (f)	[kɔ̃vɛrsasjɔ̃]
dialog	dialogue (m)	[djalɔg]
discussion (discourse)	discussion (f)	[diskysjɔ̃]
debate	débat (m)	[deba]
to debate (vi)	discuter (vi)	[diskyte]

interlocutor	interlocuteur (m)	[ɛ̃tɛrlɔkytœr]
topic (theme)	sujet (m)	[syʒɛ]
point of view	point (m) de vue	[pwɛ̃ də vy]
opinion (viewpoint)	opinion (f)	[ɔpinjɔ̃]
speech (talk)	discours (m)	[diskur]

discussion (of report, etc.)	discussion (f)	[diskysjɔ̃]
to discuss (vt)	discuter (vt)	[diskyte]
talk (conversation)	conversation (f)	[kɔ̃vɛrsasjɔ̃]
to talk (vi)	converser (vi)	[kɔ̃vɛrse]
meeting	rencontre (f)	[rɑ̃kɔ̃tr]
to meet (vi, vt)	se rencontrer (vp)	[sə rɑ̃kɔ̃tre]

proverb	proverbe (m)	[prɔvɛrb]
saying	dicton (m)	[diktɔ̃]
riddle (poser)	devinette (f)	[dəvinɛt]
to ask a riddle	poser une devinette	[poze yn dəvinɛt]
password	mot (m) de passe	[mo də pɑs]
secret	secret (m)	[səkrɛ]

oath (vow)	serment (m)	[sɛrmɑ̃]
to swear (an oath)	jurer (vi)	[ʒyre]
promise	promesse (f)	[prɔmɛs]
to promise (vt)	promettre (vt)	[prɔmɛtr]

advice (counsel)	conseil (m)	[kɔ̃sɛj]
to advise (vt)	conseiller (vt)	[kɔ̃seje]
to follow one's advice	suivre le conseil	[sɥivr lə kɔ̃sɛj]
to listen to ... (obey)	écouter (vt)	[ekute]

news	nouvelle (f)	[nuvɛl]
sensation (news)	sensation (f)	[sɑ̃sasjɔ̃]
information (data)	renseignements (m pl)	[rɑ̃sɛɲəmɑ̃]
conclusion (decision)	conclusion (f)	[kɔ̃klyzjɔ̃]
voice	voix (f)	[vwa]
compliment	compliment (m)	[kɔ̃plimɑ̃]
kind (nice)	aimable (adj)	[ɛmabl]

| word | mot (m) | [mo] |
| phrase | phrase (f) | [fraz] |

answer	réponse (f)	[repõs]
truth	vérité (f)	[verite]
lie	mensonge (m)	[mãsõʒ]

thought	pensée (f)	[pãse]
idea (inspiration)	idée (f)	[ide]
fantasy	fantaisie (f)	[fãtezi]

66. Discussion, conversation. Part 2

respected (adj)	respecté (adj)	[rɛspɛkte]
to respect (vt)	respecter (vt)	[rɛspɛkte]
respect	respect (m)	[rɛspɛ]
Dear ... (letter)	Cher ...	[ʃɛr ...]

| to introduce (present) | présenter (vt) | [prezãte] |
| to make acquaintance | faire la connaissance | [fɛr la kɔnɛsãs] |

intention	intention (f)	[ɛ̃tãsjõ]
to intend (have in mind)	avoir l'intention	[avwar lɛ̃tãsjõ]
wish	souhait (m)	[swɛ]
to wish (~ good luck)	souhaiter (vt)	[swete]

surprise (astonishment)	étonnement (m)	[etɔnmã]
to surprise (amaze)	étonner (vt)	[etɔne]
to be surprised	s'étonner (vp)	[setɔne]

to give (vt)	donner (vt)	[dɔne]
to take (get hold of)	prendre (vt)	[prãdr]
to give back	rendre (vt)	[rãdr]
to return (give back)	retourner (vt)	[rəturne]

to apologize (vi)	s'excuser (vp)	[sɛkskyze]
apology	excuse (f)	[ɛkskyz]
to forgive (vt)	pardonner (vt)	[pardɔne]

to talk (speak)	parler (vi)	[parle]
to listen (vi)	écouter (vt)	[ekute]
to hear out	écouter jusqu'au bout	[ekute ʒyskə bu]
to understand (vt)	comprendre (vt)	[kõprãdr]

to show (display)	montrer (vt)	[mõtre]
to look at ...	regarder (vt)	[rəgarde]
to call (with one's voice)	appeler (vt)	[aple]
to distract (disturb)	distraire (vt)	[distrɛr]
to disturb (vt)	ennuyer (vt)	[ãnɥije]
to pass (to hand sth)	passer (vt)	[pɑse]

| demand (request) | prière (f) | [prijɛr] |
| to request (ask) | demander (vt) | [dəmãde] |

demand (firm request)	**exigence** (f)	[ɛgziʒɑ̃s]
to demand (request firmly)	**exiger** (vt)	[ɛgziʒe]
to tease (nickname)	**taquiner** (vt)	[takine]
to mock (make fun of)	**se moquer** (vp)	[sə mɔke]
mockery, derision	**moquerie** (f)	[mɔkri]
nickname	**surnom** (m)	[syrnɔ̃]
allusion	**allusion** (f)	[alyzjɔ̃]
to allude (vi)	**faire allusion**	[fɛr alyzjɔ̃]
to imply (vt)	**sous-entendre** (vt)	[suzɑ̃tɑ̃dr]
description	**description** (f)	[dɛskripsjɔ̃]
to describe (vt)	**décrire** (vt)	[dekrir]
praise (compliments)	**éloge** (m)	[elɔʒ]
to praise (vt)	**louer** (vt)	[lwe]
disappointment	**déception** (f)	[desɛpsjɔ̃]
to disappoint (vt)	**décevoir** (vt)	[desəvwar]
to be disappointed	**être déçu**	[ɛtr desy]
supposition	**supposition** (f)	[sypozisjɔ̃]
to suppose (assume)	**supposer** (vt)	[sypoze]
warning (caution)	**avertissement** (m)	[avɛrtismɑ̃]
to warn (vt)	**prévenir** (vt)	[prevnir]

67. Discussion, conversation. Part 3

to talk into (convince)	**convaincre** (vt)	[kɔ̃vɛ̃kr]
to calm down (vt)	**calmer** (vt)	[kalme]
silence (~ is golden)	**silence** (m)	[silɑ̃s]
to keep silent	**rester silencieux**	[rɛste silɑ̃sjø]
to whisper (vi, vt)	**chuchoter** (vi, vt)	[ʃyʃɔte]
whisper	**chuchotement** (m)	[ʃyʃɔtmɑ̃]
frankly, sincerely (adv)	**sincèrement** (adv)	[sɛ̃sɛrmɑ̃]
in my opinion ...	**à mon avis ...**	[amɔ̃ avi]
detail (of the story)	**détail** (m)	[detaj]
detailed (adj)	**détaillé** (adj)	[detaje]
in detail (adv)	**en détail** (adv)	[ɑ̃ detaj]
hint, clue	**indice** (m)	[ɛ̃dis]
to give a hint	**donner un indice**	[dɔne ynɛ̃dis]
look (glance)	**regard** (m)	[rəgar]
to have a look	**jeter un coup d'oeil**	[ʒəte œ̃ ku dœj]
fixed (look)	**fixe** (adj)	[fiks]
to blink (vi)	**clignoter** (vi)	[kliɲɔte]

| to wink (vi) | cligner de l'oeil | [kliɲe də lœj] |
| to nod (in assent) | hocher la tête | [ɔʃe la tɛt] |

sigh	soupir (m)	[supir]
to sigh (vi)	soupirer (vi)	[supire]
to shudder (vi)	tressaillir (vi)	[tresajir]
gesture	geste (m)	[ʒɛst]
to touch (one's arm, etc.)	toucher (vt)	[tuʃe]
to seize (by the arm)	saisir (vt)	[sezir]
to tap (on the shoulder)	taper (vt)	[tape]

Look out!	Attention!	[atɑ̃sjɔ̃]
Really?	Vraiment?	[vrɛmɑ̃]
Are you sure?	Tu es sûr?	[ty ɛ syr]
Good luck!	Bonne chance!	[bɔn ʃɑ̃s]
I see!	Compris!	[kɔ̃pri]
It's a pity!	Dommage!	[dɔmaʒ]

68. Agreement. Refusal

consent (agreement)	accord (m)	[akɔr]
to agree (say yes)	être d'accord	[ɛtr dakɔr]
approval	approbation (f)	[aprɔbasjɔ̃]
to approve (vt)	approuver (vt)	[apruve]
refusal	refus (m)	[rəfy]
to refuse (vi, vt)	se refuser (vp)	[sə rəfyze]

Great!	Super!	[sypɛr]
All right!	Bon!	[bɔ̃]
Okay! (I agree)	D'accord!	[dakɔr]

forbidden (adj)	interdit (adj)	[ɛ̃tɛrdi]
it's forbidden	c'est interdit	[sɛtɛ̃tɛrdi]
it's impossible	c'est impossible	[set ɛ̃pɔsibl]
incorrect (adj)	incorrect (adj)	[ɛ̃kɔrɛkt]
to reject (~ a demand)	décliner (vt)	[dekline]
to support (cause, idea)	soutenir (vt)	[sutnir]
to accept (~ an apology)	accepter (vt)	[aksɛpte]

to confirm (vt)	confirmer (vt)	[kɔ̃firme]
confirmation	confirmation (f)	[kɔ̃firmasjɔ̃]
permission	permission (f)	[pɛrmisjɔ̃]
to permit (vt)	permettre (vt)	[pɛrmɛtr]
decision	décision (f)	[desizjɔ̃]
to say nothing	ne pas dire un mot	[nəpɑ dir œ̃ mo]

condition (term)	condition (f)	[kɔ̃disjɔ̃]
excuse (pretext)	excuse (f)	[ɛkskyz]
praise (compliments)	éloge (m)	[elɔʒ]
to praise (vt)	louer (vt)	[lwe]

69. Success. Good luck. Failure

success	succès (m)	[syksɛ]
successfully (adv)	avec succès (adv)	[avɛk syksɛ]
successful (adj)	réussi (adj)	[reysi]
good luck	chance (f)	[ʃãs]
Good luck!	Bonne chance!	[bɔn ʃãs]
lucky (e.g., ~ day)	de chance (adj)	[də ʃãs]
lucky (fortunate)	chanceux (adj)	[ʃãsø]
failure	échec (m)	[eʃɛk]
misfortune	infortune (f)	[ɛ̃fɔrtyn]
bad luck	malchance (f)	[malʃãs]
unsuccessful (adj)	raté (adj)	[rate]
catastrophe	catastrophe (f)	[katastrɔf]
pride	fierté (f)	[fjɛrte]
proud (adj)	fier (adj)	[fjɛr]
to be proud	être fier	[ɛtr fjɛr]
winner	gagnant (m)	[gaɲã]
to win (vi)	gagner (vi)	[gaɲe]
to lose (not win)	perdre (vi)	[pɛrdr]
try	tentative (f)	[tãtativ]
to try (vi)	essayer (vt)	[eseje]
chance (opportunity)	chance (f)	[ʃãs]

70. Quarrels. Negative emotions

shout (scream)	cri (m)	[kri]
to shout (vi)	crier (vi)	[krije]
to start to cry out	se mettre à crier	[sə mɛtr ɑ krije]
quarrel	dispute (f)	[dispyt]
to quarrel (vi)	se disputer (vp)	[sə dispyte]
fight (scandal)	scandale (m)	[skãdal]
to have a fight	faire un scandale	[fɛr œ̃ skãdal]
conflict	conflit (m)	[kɔ̃fli]
misunderstanding	malentendu (m)	[malãtãdy]
insult	insulte (f)	[ɛ̃sylt]
to insult (vt)	insulter (vt)	[ɛ̃sylte]
insulted (adj)	insulté (adj)	[ɛ̃sylte]
resentment	offense (f)	[ɔfãs]
to offend (vt)	offenser (vt)	[ɔfãse]
to take offense	s'offenser (vp)	[sɔfãse]
indignation	indignation (f)	[ɛ̃diɲasjɔ̃]
to be indignant	s'indigner (vp)	[sɛ̃diɲe]

complaint	**plainte** (f)	[plɛ̃t]
to complain (vi, vt)	**se plaindre** (vp)	[sə plɛ̃dr]
apology	**excuse** (f)	[ɛkskyz]
to apologize (vi)	**s'excuser** (vp)	[sɛkskyze]
to beg pardon	**demander pardon**	[dəmɑ̃de pardɔ̃]
criticism	**critique** (f)	[kritik]
to criticize (vt)	**critiquer** (vt)	[kritike]
accusation	**accusation** (f)	[akyzasjɔ̃]
to accuse (vt)	**accuser** (vt)	[akyze]
revenge	**vengeance** (f)	[vɑ̃ʒɑ̃s]
to revenge (vt)	**se venger** (vp)	[sə vɑ̃ʒe]
to pay back	**faire payer**	[fɛr peje]
disdain	**mépris** (m)	[mepri]
to despise (vt)	**mépriser** (vt)	[meprize]
hatred, hate	**haine** (f)	[ɛn]
to hate (vt)	**haïr** (vt)	[air]
nervous (adj)	**nerveux** (adj)	[nɛrvø]
to be nervous	**s'énerver** (vp)	[senɛrve]
angry (mad)	**fâché** (adj)	[faʃe]
to make angry	**fâcher** (vt)	[faʃe]
humiliation	**humiliation** (f)	[ymiljasjɔ̃]
to humiliate (vt)	**humilier** (vt)	[ymilje]
to humiliate oneself	**s'humilier** (vp)	[symilje]
shock	**choc** (m)	[ʃɔk]
to shock (vt)	**choquer** (vt)	[ʃɔke]
trouble (annoyance)	**ennui** (m)	[ɑ̃ɥi]
unpleasant (adj)	**désagréable** (adj)	[dezagreabl]
fear (dread)	**peur** (f)	[pœr]
terrible (storm, heat)	**terrible** (adj)	[tɛribl]
scary (e.g., ~ story)	**effrayant** (adj)	[efrɛjɑ̃]
horror	**horreur** (f)	[ɔrœr]
awful (crime, news)	**horrible** (adj)	[ɔribl]
to begin to tremble	**commencer à trembler**	[kɔmɑ̃se a trɑ̃ble]
to cry (weep)	**pleurer** (vi)	[plœre]
to start crying	**se mettre à pleurer**	[sə mɛtr ɑ plœre]
tear	**larme** (f)	[larm]
fault	**faute** (f)	[fot]
guilt (feeling)	**culpabilité** (f)	[kylpabilite]
dishonor (disgrace)	**déshonneur** (m)	[dezɔnœr]
protest	**protestation** (f)	[prɔtɛstasjɔ̃]
stress	**stress** (m)	[strɛs]

to disturb (vt)	**déranger** (vt)	[derɑ̃ʒe]
to be furious	**être furieux**	[ɛtr fyrjø]
mad, angry (adj)	**en colère, fâché** (adj)	[ɑ̃ kɔlɛr], [faʃe]
to end (~ a relationship)	**rompre** (vt)	[rɔ̃pr]
to swear (at sb)	**réprimander** (vt)	[reprimɑ̃de]
to be scared	**prendre peur**	[prɑ̃dr pœr]
to hit (strike with hand)	**frapper** (vt)	[frape]
to fight (vi)	**se battre** (vp)	[sə batr]
to settle (a conflict)	**régler** (vt)	[regle]
discontented (adj)	**mécontent** (adj)	[mekɔ̃tɑ̃]
furious (adj)	**enragé** (adj)	[ɑ̃raʒe]
It's not good!	**Ce n'est pas bien!**	[sə nɛpɑ bjɛ̃]
It's bad!	**C'est mal!**	[sɛ mal]

Medicine

71. Diseases

sickness	**maladie** (f)	[maladi]
to be sick	**être malade**	[ɛtr malad]
health	**santé** (f)	[sɑ̃te]
runny nose (coryza)	**rhume** (m)	[rym]
angina	**angine** (f)	[ɑ̃ʒin]
cold (illness)	**refroidissement** (m)	[rəfrwadismɑ̃]
to catch a cold	**prendre froid**	[prɑ̃dr frwa]
bronchitis	**bronchite** (f)	[brɔ̃ʃit]
pneumonia	**pneumonie** (f)	[pnømɔni]
flu, influenza	**grippe** (f)	[grip]
near-sighted (adj)	**myope** (adj)	[mjɔp]
far-sighted (adj)	**presbyte** (adj)	[prɛsbit]
strabismus (crossed eyes)	**strabisme** (m)	[strabism]
cross-eyed (adj)	**strabique** (adj)	[strabik]
cataract	**cataracte** (f)	[katarakt]
glaucoma	**glaucome** (m)	[glokom]
stroke	**insulte** (f)	[ɛ̃sylt]
heart attack	**crise** (f) **cardiaque**	[kriz kardjak]
myocardial infarction	**infarctus** (m) **de myocarde**	[ɛ̃farktys də mjɔkard]
paralysis	**paralysie** (f)	[paralizi]
to paralyze (vt)	**paralyser** (vt)	[paralize]
allergy	**allergie** (f)	[alɛrʒi]
asthma	**asthme** (m)	[asm]
diabetes	**diabète** (m)	[djabɛt]
toothache	**mal** (m) **de dents**	[mal də dɑ̃]
caries	**carie** (f)	[kari]
diarrhea	**diarrhée** (f)	[djare]
constipation	**constipation** (f)	[kɔ̃stipasjɔ̃]
stomach upset	**estomac** (m) **barbouillé**	[ɛstɔma barbuje]
food poisoning	**intoxication** (f) **alimentaire**	[ɛ̃tɔksikasjɔn alimɑ̃tɛr]
to have a food poisoning	**être intoxiqué**	[ɛtr ɛ̃tɔksike]
arthritis	**arthrite** (f)	[artrit]
rickets	**rachitisme** (m)	[raʃitism]

| rheumatism | rhumatisme (m) | [rymatism] |
| atherosclerosis | athérosclérose (f) | [ateroskleroz] |

gastritis	gastrite (f)	[gastrit]
appendicitis	appendicite (f)	[apɛ̃disit]
cholecystitis	cholécystite (f)	[kɔlesistit]
ulcer	ulcère (m)	[ylsɛr]

measles	rougeole (f)	[ruʒɔl]
German measles	rubéole (f)	[rybeɔl]
jaundice	jaunisse (f)	[ʒɔnis]
hepatitis	hépatite (f)	[epatit]

schizophrenia	schizophrénie (f)	[skizɔfreni]
rabies (hydrophobia)	rage (f)	[raʒ]
neurosis	névrose (f)	[nevroz]
concussion	commotion (f) cérébrale	[kɔmɔsjɔ̃ serebral]

cancer	cancer (m)	[kɑ̃sɛr]
sclerosis	sclérose (f)	[skleroz]
multiple sclerosis	sclérose (f) en plaques	[skleroz ɑ̃ plak]

alcoholism	alcoolisme (m)	[alkɔlism]
alcoholic (n)	alcoolique (m)	[alkɔlik]
syphilis	syphilis (f)	[sifilis]
AIDS	SIDA (m)	[sida]

tumor	tumeur (f)	[tymœr]
malignant (adj)	maligne (adj)	[maliɲ]
benign (adj)	bénigne (adj)	[beniɲ]

fever	fièvre (f)	[fjɛvr]
malaria	malaria (f)	[malarja]
gangrene	gangrène (f)	[gɑ̃grɛn]
seasickness	mal (m) de mer	[mal də mɛr]
epilepsy	épilepsie (f)	[epilɛpsi]

epidemic	épidémie (f)	[epidemi]
typhus	typhus (m)	[tifys]
tuberculosis	tuberculose (f)	[tybɛrkyloz]
cholera	choléra (m)	[kɔlera]
plague (bubonic ~)	peste (f)	[pɛst]

72. Symptoms. Treatments. Part 1

symptom	symptôme (m)	[sɛ̃ptom]
temperature	température (f)	[tɑ̃peratyr]
high temperature	fièvre (f)	[fjɛvr]
pulse	pouls (m)	[pu]

giddiness	**vertige** (m)	[vɛrtiʒ]
hot (adj)	**chaud** (adj)	[ʃo]
shivering	**frisson** (m)	[frisɔ̃]
pale (e.g., ~ face)	**pâle** (adj)	[pɑl]

cough	**toux** (f)	[tu]
to cough (vi)	**tousser** (vi)	[tuse]
to sneeze (vi)	**éternuer** (vi)	[etɛrnɥe]
faint	**évanouissement** (m)	[evanwismɑ̃]
to faint (vi)	**s'évanouir** (vp)	[sevanwir]

bruise (hématome)	**bleu** (m)	[blø]
bump (lump)	**bosse** (f)	[bɔs]
to bruise oneself	**se heurter** (vp)	[sə œrte]
bruise (contusion)	**meurtrissure** (f)	[mœrtrisyr]
to get bruised	**se faire mal**	[sə fɛr mal]

to limp (vi)	**boiter** (vi)	[bwate]
dislocation	**foulure** (f)	[fulyr]
to dislocate (vt)	**se démettre** (vp)	[sə demɛtr]
fracture	**fracture** (f)	[fraktyr]
to have a fracture	**avoir une fracture**	[avwar yn fraktyr]

cut (e.g., paper ~)	**coupure** (f)	[kupyr]
to cut oneself	**se couper** (vp)	[sə kupe]
bleeding	**hémorragie** (f)	[emɔraʒi]

| burn (injury) | **brûlure** (f) | [brylyr] |
| to scald oneself | **se brûler** (vp) | [sə bryle] |

to prick (vt)	**se piquer** (vp)	[sə pike]
to prick oneself	**se piquer** (vp)	[sə pike]
to injure (vt)	**blesser** (vt)	[blese]
injury	**blessure** (f)	[blesyr]
wound	**blessure** (f)	[blesyr]
trauma	**trauma** (m)	[troma]

to be delirious	**délirer** (vi)	[delire]
to stutter (vi)	**bégayer** (vi)	[begeje]
sunstroke	**insolation** (f)	[ɛ̃sɔlasjɔ̃]

73. Symptoms. Treatments. Part 2

| pain | **douleur** (f) | [dulœr] |
| splinter (in foot, etc.) | **écharde** (f) | [eʃard] |

sweat (perspiration)	**sueur** (f)	[sɥœr]
to sweat (perspire)	**suer** (vi)	[sɥe]
vomiting	**vomissement** (m)	[vɔmismɑ̃]
convulsions	**spasmes** (m pl)	[spasm]

pregnant (adj)	**enceinte** (adj)	[ɑ̃sɛt]
to be born	**naître** (vi)	[nɛtr]
delivery, labor	**accouchement** (m)	[akuʃmɑ̃]
to deliver (~ a baby)	**accoucher** (vt)	[akuʃe]
abortion	**avortement** (m)	[avɔrtəmɑ̃]

breathing, respiration	**respiration** (f)	[rɛspirasjɔ̃]
inhalation	**inhalation** (f)	[inalasjɔ̃]
exhalation	**expiration** (f)	[ɛkspirasjɔ̃]
to exhale (vi)	**expirer** (vi)	[ɛkspire]
to inhale (vi)	**inspirer** (vi)	[inale]

disabled person	**invalide** (m)	[ɛ̃valid]
cripple	**handicapé** (m)	[ɑ̃dikape]
drug addict	**drogué** (m)	[drɔge]

deaf (adj)	**sourd** (adj)	[sur]
dumb, mute	**muet** (adj)	[mɥɛ]
deaf-and-dumb (adj)	**sourd-muet** (adj)	[surmɥɛ]

mad, insane (adj)	**fou** (adj)	[fu]
madman	**fou** (m)	[fu]
madwoman	**folle** (f)	[fɔl]
to go insane	**devenir fou**	[dəvnir fu]

gene	**gène** (m)	[ʒɛn]
immunity	**immunité** (f)	[imynite]
hereditary (adj)	**héréditaire** (adj)	[ereditɛr]
congenital (adj)	**congénital** (adj)	[kɔ̃ʒenital]

virus	**virus** (m)	[virys]
microbe	**microbe** (m)	[mikrɔb]
bacterium	**bactérie** (f)	[bakteri]
infection	**infection** (f)	[ɛ̃fɛksjɔ̃]

74. Symptoms. Treatments. Part 3

hospital	**hôpital** (m)	[ɔpital]
patient	**patient** (m)	[pasjɑ̃]

diagnosis	**diagnostic** (m)	[djagnɔstik]
cure	**cure** (f)	[kyr]
medical treatment	**traitement** (m)	[trɛtmɑ̃]
to get treatment	**se faire soigner**	[sə fɛr swaɲe]
to treat (vt)	**traiter** (vt)	[trete]
to nurse (look after)	**soigner** (vt)	[swaɲe]
care (nursing ~)	**soins** (m pl)	[swɛ̃]

operation, surgery	**opération** (f)	[ɔperasjɔ̃]
to bandage (head, limb)	**panser** (vt)	[pɑ̃se]

bandaging	**pansement** (m)	[pɑ̃smɑ̃]
vaccination	**vaccination** (f)	[vaksinasjɔ̃]
to vaccinate (vt)	**vacciner** (vt)	[vaksine]
injection, shot	**piqûre** (f)	[pikyr]
to give an injection	**faire une piqûre**	[fɛr yn pikyr]

attack	**crise, attaque** (f)	[kriz], [atak]
amputation	**amputation** (f)	[ɑ̃pytasjɔ̃]
to amputate (vt)	**amputer** (vt)	[ɑ̃pyte]
coma	**coma** (m)	[kɔma]
to be in a coma	**être dans le coma**	[ɛtr dɑ̃ lə kɔma]
intensive care	**réanimation** (f)	[reanimasjɔ̃]

to recover (~ from flu)	**se rétablir** (vp)	[sə retablir]
state (patient's ~)	**état** (m)	[eta]
consciousness	**conscience** (f)	[kɔ̃sjɑ̃s]
memory (faculty)	**mémoire** (f)	[memwar]

to extract (tooth)	**arracher** (vt)	[araʃe]
filling	**plombage** (m)	[plɔ̃baʒ]
to fill (a tooth)	**plomber** (vt)	[plɔ̃be]

| hypnosis | **hypnose** (f) | [ipnoz] |
| to hypnotize (vt) | **hypnotiser** (vt) | [ipnɔtize] |

75. Doctors

doctor	**médecin** (m)	[medsɛ̃]
nurse	**infirmière** (f)	[ɛ̃firmjɛr]
private physician	**médecin** (m) **personnel**	[medsɛ̃ pɛrsɔnɛl]

dentist	**dentiste** (m)	[dɑ̃tist]
ophthalmologist	**ophtalmologiste** (m)	[ɔftalmɔlɔʒist]
internist	**généraliste** (m)	[ʒeneralist]
surgeon	**chirurgien** (m)	[ʃiryrʒjɛ̃]

psychiatrist	**psychiatre** (m)	[psikjatr]
pediatrician	**pédiatre** (m)	[pedjatr]
psychologist	**psychologue** (m)	[psikɔlɔg]
gynecologist	**gynécologue** (m)	[ʒinekɔlɔg]
cardiologist	**cardiologue** (m)	[kardjɔlɔg]

76. Medicine. Drugs. Accessories

medicine, drug	**médicament** (m)	[medikamɑ̃]
remedy	**remède** (m)	[rəmɛd]
to prescribe (vt)	**prescrire** (vt)	[prɛskrir]
prescription	**ordonnance** (f)	[ɔrdɔnɑ̃s]

tablet, pill	comprimé (m)	[kɔ̃prime]
ointment	onguent (m)	[ɔ̃gɑ̃]
ampule	ampoule (f)	[ɑ̃pul]
mixture	mixture (f)	[mikstyr]
syrup	sirop (m)	[siro]
pill	pilule (f)	[pilyl]
powder	poudre (f)	[pudr]

bandage	bande (f)	[bɑ̃d]
cotton wool	coton (m)	[kɔtɔ̃]
iodine	iode (m)	[jɔd]

Band-Aid	sparadrap (m)	[sparadra]
eyedropper	compte-gouttes (m)	[kɔ̃tgut]
thermometer	thermomètre (m)	[tɛrmɔmɛtr]
syringe	seringue (f)	[sərɛ̃g]

| wheelchair | fauteuil (m) roulant | [fotœj rulɑ̃] |
| crutches | béquilles (f pl) | [bekij] |

painkiller	anesthésique (m)	[anɛstezik]
laxative	purgatif (m)	[pyrgatif]
spirit (ethanol)	alcool (m)	[alkɔl]
medicinal herbs	herbe (f) médicinale	[ɛrb medisinal]
herbal (~ tea)	d'herbes (adj)	[dɛrb]

77. Smoking. Tobacco products

tobacco	tabac (m)	[taba]
cigarette	cigarette (f)	[sigarɛt]
cigar	cigare (f)	[sigar]
pipe	pipe (f)	[pip]
pack (of cigarettes)	paquet (m)	[pakɛ]

matches	allumettes (f pl)	[alymɛt]
matchbox	boîte (f) d'allumettes	[bwat dalymɛt]
lighter	briquet (m)	[brikɛ]
ashtray	cendrier (m)	[sɑ̃drije]
cigarette case	étui (m) à cigarettes	[etɥi ɑ sigarɛt]
cigarette holder	fume-cigarette (m)	[fymsigarɛt]
filter (cigarette tip)	filtre (m)	[filtr]

to smoke (vi, vt)	fumer (vi, vt)	[fyme]
to light a cigarette	allumer une cigarette	[alyme yn sigarɛt]
smoking	tabagisme (m)	[tabaʒism]
smoker	fumeur (m)	[fymœr]

stub, butt (of cigarette)	mégot (m)	[mego]
smoke, fumes	fumée (f)	[fyme]
ash	cendre (f)	[sɑ̃dr]

HUMAN HABITAT

City

78. City. Life in the city

city, town	**ville** (f)	[vil]
capital city	**capitale** (f)	[kapital]
village	**village** (m)	[vilaʒ]
city map	**plan** (m) **de la ville**	[plɑ̃ də la vil]
downtown	**centre-ville** (m)	[sɑ̃trəvil]
suburb	**banlieue** (f)	[bɑ̃ljø]
suburban (adj)	**de banlieue** (adj)	[də bɑ̃ljø]
outskirts	**périphérie** (f)	[periferi]
environs (suburbs)	**alentours** (m pl)	[alɑ̃tur]
city block	**quartier** (m)	[kartje]
residential block	**quartier** (m) **résidentiel**	[kartje rezidɑ̃sjɛl]
traffic	**trafic** (m)	[trafik]
traffic lights	**feux** (m pl) **de circulation**	[fø də sirkylasjɔ̃]
public transportation	**transport** (m) **urbain**	[trɑ̃spɔr yrbɛ̃]
intersection	**carrefour** (m)	[karfur]
crosswalk	**passage** (m) **piéton**	[pɑsaʒ pjetɔ̃]
pedestrian underpass	**passage** (m) **souterrain**	[pɑsaʒ sutɛrɛ̃]
to cross (vt)	**traverser** (vt)	[travɛrse]
pedestrian	**piéton** (m)	[pjetɔ̃]
sidewalk	**trottoir** (m)	[trɔtwar]
bridge	**pont** (m)	[pɔ̃]
bank (riverbank)	**quai** (m)	[kɛ]
fountain	**fontaine** (f)	[fɔ̃tɛn]
allée	**allée** (f)	[ale]
park	**parc** (m)	[park]
boulevard	**boulevard** (m)	[bulvar]
square	**place** (f)	[plas]
avenue (wide street)	**avenue** (f)	[avny]
street	**rue** (f)	[ry]
side street	**ruelle** (f)	[rɥɛl]
dead end	**impasse** (f)	[ɛ̃pas]
house	**maison** (f)	[mɛzɔ̃]
building	**édifice** (m)	[edifis]

skyscraper	**gratte-ciel** (m)	[gratsjɛl]
facade	**façade** (f)	[fasad]
roof	**toit** (m)	[twa]
window	**fenêtre** (f)	[fənɛtr]
arch	**arc** (m)	[ark]
column	**colonne** (f)	[kɔlɔn]
corner	**coin** (m)	[kwɛ̃]
store window	**vitrine** (f)	[vitrin]
store sign	**enseigne** (f)	[ɑ̃sɛɲ]
poster	**affiche** (f)	[afiʃ]
advertising poster	**affiche** (f) **publicitaire**	[afiʃ pyblisitɛr]
billboard	**panneau-réclame** (m)	[pano reklam]
garbage, trash	**ordures** (f pl)	[ɔrdyr]
garbage can	**poubelle** (f)	[pubɛl]
to litter (vi)	**jeter ... à terre**	[ʒəte ... ɑ tɛr]
garbage dump	**décharge** (f)	[deʃarʒ]
phone booth	**cabine** (f) **téléphonique**	[kabin telefɔnik]
lamppost	**réverbère** (m)	[revɛrbɛr]
bench (park ~)	**banc** (m)	[bɑ̃]
police officer	**policier** (m)	[pɔlisje]
police	**police** (f)	[pɔlis]
beggar	**clochard** (m)	[klɔʃar]
homeless, bum	**sans-abri** (m)	[sɑ̃zabri]

79. Urban institutions

store	**magasin** (m)	[magazɛ̃]
drugstore, pharmacy	**pharmacie** (f)	[farmasi]
optical store	**opticien** (m)	[ɔptisjɛ̃]
shopping mall	**centre** (m) **commercial**	[sɑ̃tr kɔmɛrsjal]
supermarket	**supermarché** (m)	[sypɛrmarʃe]
bakery	**boulangerie** (f)	[bulɑ̃ʒri]
baker	**boulanger** (m)	[bulɑ̃ʒe]
candy store	**pâtisserie** (f)	[pɑtisri]
grocery store	**épicerie** (f)	[episri]
butcher shop	**boucherie** (f)	[buʃri]
produce store	**magasin** (m) **de légumes**	[magazɛ̃ də legym]
market	**marché** (m)	[marʃe]
coffee house	**salon** (m) **de café**	[salɔ̃ də kafe]
restaurant	**restaurant** (m)	[rɛstɔrɑ̃]
pub	**brasserie** (f)	[brasri]
pizzeria	**pizzeria** (f)	[pidzerja]
hair salon	**salon** (m) **de coiffure**	[salɔ̃ də kwafyr]

post office	**poste** (f)	[pɔst]
dry cleaners	**pressing** (m)	[presiŋ]
photo studio	**atelier** (m) **de photo**	[atəlje də fɔto]

shoe store	**magasin** (m) **de chaussures**	[magazɛ̃ də ʃosyr]
bookstore	**librairie** (f)	[librɛri]
sporting goods store	**magasin** (m) **d'articles de sport**	[magazɛ̃ dartikl də spɔr]

clothes repair	**atelier** (m) **de retouche**	[atəlje də rətuʃ]
formal wear rental	**location** (f) **de vêtements**	[lɔkasjɔ̃ də vɛtmɑ̃]
movie rental store	**location** (f) **de films**	[lɔkasjɔ̃ də film]

circus	**cirque** (m)	[sirk]
zoo	**zoo** (m)	[zoo]
movie theater	**cinéma** (m)	[sinema]
museum	**musée** (m)	[myze]
library	**bibliothèque** (f)	[biblijɔtɛk]

theater	**théâtre** (m)	[teɑtr]
opera	**opéra** (m)	[ɔpera]
nightclub	**boîte** (f) **de nuit**	[bwat də nɥi]
casino	**casino** (m)	[kazino]

mosque	**mosquée** (f)	[mɔske]
synagogue	**synagogue** (f)	[sinagɔg]
cathedral	**cathédrale** (f)	[katedral]
temple	**temple** (m)	[tɑ̃pl]
church	**église** (f)	[egliz]

college	**institut** (m)	[ɛ̃stity]
university	**université** (f)	[ynivɛrsite]
school	**école** (f)	[ekɔl]

prefecture	**préfecture** (f)	[prefɛktyr]
city hall	**mairie** (f)	[meri]
hotel	**hôtel** (m)	[otɛl]
bank	**banque** (f)	[bɑ̃k]

| embassy | **ambassade** (f) | [ɑ̃basad] |
| travel agency | **agence** (f) **de voyages** | [aʒɑ̃s də vwajaʒ] |

| information office | **bureau** (m) **d'information** | [byro dɛ̃fɔrmasjɔ̃] |
| money exchange | **bureau** (m) **de change** | [byro də ʃɑ̃ʒ] |

| subway | **métro** (m) | [metro] |
| hospital | **hôpital** (m) | [ɔpital] |

| gas station | **station-service** (f) | [stasjɔ̃sɛrvis] |
| parking lot | **parking** (m) | [parkiŋ] |

80. Signs

store sign	enseigne (f)	[ɑ̃sɛɲ]
notice (written text)	pancarte (f)	[pɑ̃kart]
poster	poster (m)	[pɔstɛr]
direction sign	indicateur (m) de direction	[ɛ̃dikatœr də dirɛksjɔ̃]
arrow (sign)	flèche (f)	[flɛʃ]
caution	avertissement (m)	[avɛrtismɑ̃]
warning sign	panneau (m) d'avertissement	[pano davɛrtismɑ̃]
to warn (vt)	avertir (vt)	[avɛrtir]
day off	jour (m) de repos	[ʒur də rəpo]
timetable (schedule)	horaire (m)	[ɔrɛr]
opening hours	heures (f pl) d'ouverture	[zœr duvɛrtyr]
WELCOME!	BIENVENUE!	[bjɛ̃vny]
ENTRANCE	ENTRÉE	[ɑ̃tre]
EXIT	SORTIE	[sɔrti]
PUSH	POUSSER	[puse]
PULL	TIRER	[tire]
OPEN	OUVERT	[uvɛr]
CLOSED	FERMÉ	[fɛrme]
WOMEN	FEMMES	[fam]
MEN	HOMMES	[ɔm]
DISCOUNTS	RABAIS	[sɔld]
SALE	SOLDES	[rabɛ]
NEW!	NOUVEAU!	[nuvo]
FREE	GRATUIT	[gratɥi]
ATTENTION!	ATTENTION!	[atɑ̃sjɔ̃]
NO VACANCIES	COMPLET	[kɔ̃plɛ]
RESERVED	RÉSERVÉ	[rezɛrve]
ADMINISTRATION	ADMINISTRATION	[administrasjɔ̃]
STAFF ONLY	RÉSERVÉ AU PERSONNEL	[rezɛrve o pɛrsɔnɛl]
BEWARE OF THE DOG!	ATTENTION CHIEN MÉCHANT	[atɑ̃sjɔ̃ ʃjɛ̃ meʃɑ̃]
NO SMOKING	DÉFENSE DE FUMER	[defɑ̃s də fyme]
DO NOT TOUCH!	PRIERE DE NE PAS TOUCHER	[prijɛr dənəpa tuʃe]
DANGEROUS	DANGEREUX	[dɑ̃ʒrø]
DANGER	DANGER	[dɑ̃ʒe]

HIGH TENSION	**HAUTE TENSION**	[ot tɑ̃sjɔ̃]
NO SWIMMING!	**BAIGNADE**	[bɛɲad
	INTERDITE	ɛ̃tɛrdit]
OUT OF ORDER	**HORS SERVICE**	[ɔr sɛrvis]
FLAMMABLE	**INFLAMMABLE**	[ɛ̃flamabl]
FORBIDDEN	**INTERDIT**	[ɛ̃tɛrdi]
NO TRESPASSING!	**PASSAGE INTERDIT**	[pɑsaʒ ɛ̃tɛrdi]
WET PAINT	**PEINTURE FRAÎCHE**	[pɛ̃tyr frɛʃ]

81. Urban transportation

bus	**autobus** (m)	[otobys]
streetcar	**tramway** (m)	[tramwɛ]
trolley	**trolleybus** (m)	[trɔlɛbys]
route (of bus)	**itinéraire** (m)	[itinerɛr]
number (e.g., bus ~)	**numéro** (m)	[nymero]
to go by ...	**prendre ...**	[prɑ̃dr]
to get on (~ the bus)	**monter** (vi)	[mɔ̃te]
to get off ...	**descendre de ...**	[desɑ̃dr də]
stop (e.g., bus ~)	**arrêt** (m)	[arɛ]
next stop	**arrêt** (m) **prochain**	[arɛt prɔʃɛ̃]
terminus	**terminus** (m)	[tɛrminys]
schedule	**horaire** (m)	[ɔrɛr]
to wait (vt)	**attendre** (vt)	[atɑ̃dr]
ticket	**ticket** (m)	[tikɛ]
fare	**prix** (m) **du ticket**	[pri dy tikɛ]
cashier (ticket seller)	**caissier** (m)	[kesje]
ticket inspection	**contrôle** (m) **des tickets**	[kɔ̃trol de tikɛ]
conductor	**contrôleur** (m)	[kɔ̃trolœr]
to be late (for ...)	**être en retard**	[ɛtr ɑ̃ rətar]
to miss (~ the train, etc.)	**rater** (vt)	[rate]
to be in a hurry	**se dépêcher**	[sə depeʃe]
taxi, cab	**taxi** (m)	[taksi]
taxi driver	**chauffeur** (m) **de taxi**	[ʃofœr də taksi]
by taxi	**en taxi**	[ɑ̃ taksi]
taxi stand	**arrêt** (m) **de taxi**	[arɛ də taksi]
to call a taxi	**appeler un taxi**	[aple œ̃ taksi]
to take a taxi	**prendre un taxi**	[prɑ̃dr œ̃ taksi]
traffic	**trafic** (m)	[trafik]
traffic jam	**embouteillage** (m)	[ɑ̃butɛjaʒ]
rush hour	**heures** (f pl) **de pointe**	[œr də pwɛ̃t]
to park (vi)	**se garer** (vp)	[sə gare]

| to park (vt) | garer (vt) | [gare] |
| parking lot | parking (m) | [parkiŋ] |

subway	métro (m)	[metro]
station	station (f)	[stasjɔ̃]
to take the subway	prendre le métro	[prɑ̃dr lə metro]
train	train (m)	[trɛ̃]
train station	gare (f)	[gar]

82. Sightseeing

monument	monument (m)	[mɔnymɑ̃]
fortress	forteresse (f)	[fortərɛs]
palace	palais (m)	[palɛ]
castle	château (m)	[ʃato]
tower	tour (f)	[tur]
mausoleum	mausolée (m)	[mozɔle]

architecture	architecture (f)	[arʃitɛktyr]
medieval (adj)	médiéval (adj)	[medjeval]
ancient (adj)	ancien (adj)	[ɑ̃sjɛ̃]
national (adj)	national (adj)	[nasjɔnal]
well-known (adj)	connu (adj)	[kɔny]

tourist	touriste (m)	[turist]
guide (person)	guide (m)	[gid]
excursion, guided tour	excursion (f)	[ɛkskyrsjɔ̃]
to show (vt)	montrer (vt)	[mɔ̃tre]
to tell (vt)	raconter (vt)	[rakɔ̃te]

to find (vt)	trouver (vt)	[truve]
to get lost (lose one's way)	se perdre (vp)	[sə pɛrdr]
map (e.g., subway ~)	plan (m)	[plɑ̃]
map (e.g., city ~)	carte (f)	[kart]

souvenir, gift	souvenir (m)	[suvnir]
gift shop	boutique (f) de souvenirs	[butik də suvnir]
to take pictures	prendre en photo	[prɑ̃dr ɑ̃ foto]
to be photographed	se faire prendre en photo	[sə fɛr prɑ̃dr ɑ̃ foto]

83. Shopping

to buy (purchase)	acheter (vt)	[aʃte]
purchase	achat (m)	[aʃa]
to go shopping	faire des achats	[fɛr dezaʃa]
shopping	shopping (m)	[ʃopiŋ]
to be open (ab. store)	être ouvert	[ɛtr uvɛr]

to be closed	**être fermé**	[ɛtr fɛrme]
footwear	**chaussures** (f pl)	[ʃosyr]
clothes, clothing	**vêtement** (m)	[vɛtmɑ̃]
cosmetics	**produits** (m pl) **de beauté**	[prɔdyi də bote]
food products	**produits** (m pl) **alimentaires**	[prɔdyi alimɑ̃tɛr]
gift, present	**cadeau** (m)	[kado]
salesman	**vendeur** (m)	[vɑ̃dœr]
saleswoman	**vendeuse** (f)	[vɑ̃døz]
check out, cash desk	**caisse** (f)	[kɛs]
mirror	**miroir** (m)	[mirwar]
counter (in shop)	**comptoir** (m)	[kɔ̃twar]
fitting room	**cabine** (f) **d'essayage**	[kabin desɛjaʒ]
to try on	**essayer** (vt)	[eseje]
to fit (ab. dress, etc.)	**aller bien**	[ale bjɛ̃]
to like (I like ...)	**plaire à ...**	[plɛr ɑ]
price	**prix** (m)	[pri]
price tag	**étiquette** (f) **de prix**	[etikɛt də pri]
to cost (vt)	**coûter** (vi, vt)	[kute]
How much?	**Combien?**	[kɔ̃bjɛ̃]
discount	**rabais** (m)	[rabɛ]
inexpensive (adj)	**pas cher** (adj)	[pɑ ʃɛr]
cheap (adj)	**bon marché** (adj)	[bɔ̃ marʃe]
expensive (adj)	**cher** (adj)	[ʃɛr]
It's expensive	**C'est cher**	[sɛ ʃɛr]
rental (n)	**location** (f)	[lɔkasjɔ̃]
to rent (~ a tuxedo)	**louer** (vt)	[lwe]
credit	**crédit** (m)	[kredi]
on credit (adv)	**à crédit** (adv)	[ɑkredi]

84. Money

money	**argent** (m)	[arʒɑ̃]
currency exchange	**échange** (m)	[eʃɑ̃ʒ]
exchange rate	**cours** (m) **de change**	[kur də ʃɑ̃ʒ]
ATM	**distributeur** (m)	[distribytœr]
coin	**monnaie** (f)	[mɔnɛ]
dollar	**dollar** (m)	[dɔlar]
euro	**euro** (m)	[øro]
lira	**lire** (f)	[lir]
Deutschmark	**mark** (m) **allemand**	[mark almɑ̃]
franc	**franc** (m)	[frɑ̃]

pound sterling	**livre sterling** (f)	[livr stɛrliŋ]
yen	**yen** (m)	[jɛn]
debt	**dette** (f)	[dɛt]
debtor	**débiteur** (m)	[debitœr]
to lend (money)	**prêter** (vt)	[prete]
to borrow (vi, vt)	**emprunter** (vt)	[ãprœ̃te]
bank	**banque** (f)	[bãk]
account	**compte** (m)	[kɔ̃t]
to deposit (vt)	**verser** (vt)	[vɛrse]
to deposit into the account	**verser dans le compte**	[vɛrse dã lə kɔ̃t]
to withdraw (vt)	**retirer du compte**	[rətire dy kɔ̃t]
credit card	**carte** (f) **de crédit**	[kart də kredi]
cash	**espèces** (f pl)	[ɛspɛs]
check	**chèque** (m)	[ʃɛk]
to write a check	**faire un chèque**	[fɛr œ̃ ʃɛk]
checkbook	**chéquier** (m)	[ʃekje]
wallet	**portefeuille** (m)	[pɔrtəfœj]
change purse	**bourse** (f)	[burs]
billfold	**porte-monnaie** (m)	[pɔrtmɔnɛ]
safe	**coffre fort** (m)	[kɔfr fɔr]
heir	**héritier** (m)	[eritje]
inheritance	**héritage** (m)	[eritaʒ]
fortune (wealth)	**fortune** (f)	[fɔrtyn]
lease, rent	**location** (f)	[lɔkasjɔ̃]
rent money	**loyer** (m)	[lwaje]
to rent (sth from sb)	**louer** (vt)	[lwe]
price	**prix** (m)	[pri]
cost	**coût** (m)	[ku]
sum	**somme** (f)	[sɔm]
to spend (vt)	**dépenser** (vt)	[depãse]
expenses	**dépenses** (f pl)	[depãs]
to economize (vi, vt)	**économiser** (vt)	[ekɔnɔmize]
economical	**économe** (adj)	[ekɔnɔm]
to pay (vi, vt)	**payer** (vi, vt)	[peje]
payment	**paiement** (m)	[pɛmã]
change (give the ~)	**monnaie** (f)	[mɔnɛ]
tax	**impôt** (m)	[ɛ̃po]
fine	**amende** (f)	[amãd]
to fine (vt)	**mettre une amende**	[mɛtr ynamãd]

85. Post. Postal service

post office	**poste** (f)	[pɔst]
mail (letters, etc.)	**courrier** (m)	[kurje]
mailman	**facteur** (m)	[faktœr]
opening hours	**heures** (f pl) **d'ouverture**	[zœr duvɛrtyr]
letter	**lettre** (f)	[lɛtr]
registered letter	**recommandé** (m)	[rəkɔmãde]
postcard	**carte** (f) **postale**	[kart pɔstal]
telegram	**télégramme** (m)	[telegram]
parcel	**colis** (m)	[kɔli]
money transfer	**mandat** (m) **postal**	[mãda pɔstal]
to receive (vt)	**recevoir** (vt)	[rəsəvwar]
to send (vt)	**envoyer** (vt)	[ãvwaje]
sending	**envoi** (m)	[ãvwa]
address	**adresse** (f)	[adrɛs]
ZIP code	**code** (m) **postal**	[kɔd pɔstal]
sender	**expéditeur** (m)	[ɛkspeditœr]
receiver, addressee	**destinataire** (m)	[dɛstinatɛr]
name	**prénom** (m)	[prenɔ̃]
family name	**nom** (m) **de famille**	[nɔ̃ də famij]
rate (of postage)	**tarif** (m)	[tarif]
standard (adj)	**normal** (adj)	[nɔrmal]
economical (adj)	**économique** (adj)	[ekɔnɔmik]
weight	**poids** (m)	[pwa]
to weigh up (vt)	**peser** (vt)	[pəze]
envelope	**enveloppe** (f)	[ãvlɔp]
postage stamp	**timbre** (m)	[tɛ̃br]
to stamp an envelope	**timbrer** (vt)	[tɛ̃bre]

Dwelling. House. Home

86. House. Dwelling

house	maison (f)	[mɛzɔ̃]
at home (adv)	chez soi	[ʃeswa]
courtyard	cour (f)	[kur]
fence	clôture (f)	[klotyr]
brick (n)	brique (f)	[brik]
brick (as adj)	en brique (adj)	[ɑ̃ brik]
stone (n)	pierre (f)	[pjɛr]
stone (as adj)	en pierre (adj)	[ɑ̃ pjɛr]
concrete (n)	béton (m)	[betɔ̃]
concrete (as adj)	en béton (adj)	[ɑ̃ betɔ̃]
new (new-built)	neuf (adj)	[nœf]
old (adj)	vieux (adj)	[vjø]
decrepit (house)	délabré (adj)	[delabre]
modern (adj)	moderne (adj)	[mɔdɛrn]
multistory (adj)	à plusieurs étages	[a plyzjœr zetaʒ]
high (adj)	haut (adj)	[o]
floor, story	étage (m)	[etaʒ]
single-story (adj)	sans étage (adj)	[sɑ̃ zetaʒ]
ground floor	rez-de-chaussée (m)	[redʃose]
top floor	dernier étage (m)	[dɛrnjɛr etaʒ]
roof	toit (m)	[twa]
chimney (stack)	cheminée (f)	[ʃəmine]
roof tiles	tuile (f)	[tɥil]
tiled (adj)	en tuiles (adj)	[ɑ̃ tɥil]
loft (attic)	grenier (m)	[grənje]
window	fenêtre (f)	[fənɛtr]
glass	vitre (f)	[vitr]
window ledge	rebord (m)	[rəbɔr]
shutters	volets (m pl)	[vɔle]
wall	mur (m)	[myr]
balcony	balcon (m)	[balkɔ̃]
downspout	gouttière (f)	[gutjɛr]
upstairs (to be ~)	en haut (adv)	[ɑn o]
to go upstairs	monter (vi)	[mɔ̃te]
to come down	descendre (vi)	[desɑ̃dr]
to move (to new premises)	déménager (vi)	[demenaʒe]

87. House. Entrance. Lift

entrance	entrée (f)	[ãtre]
stairs (stairway)	escalier (m)	[ɛskalje]
steps	marches (f pl)	[marʃ]
banisters	rampe (f)	[rãp]
lobby (hotel ~)	hall (m)	[ol]
mailbox	boîte (f) à lettres	[bwat ɑ lɛtr]
trash container	poubelle (f)	[pubɛl]
trash chute	vide-ordures (m)	[vidɔrdyr]
elevator	ascenseur (m)	[asãsœr]
freight elevator	monte-charge (m)	[mɔ̃tʃarʒ]
elevator cage	cabine (f)	[kabin]
to take the elevator	prendre l'ascenseur	[prãdr lasãsœr]
apartment	appartement (m)	[apartəmã]
residents, inhabitants	locataires (m pl)	[lɔkatɛr]
neighbor (masc.)	voisin (m)	[vwazɛ̃]
neighbor (fem.)	voisine (f)	[vwazin]
neighbors	voisins (m pl)	[vwazɛ̃]

88. House. Electricity

electricity	électricité (f)	[elɛktrisite]
light bulb	ampoule (f)	[ãpul]
switch	interrupteur (m)	[ɛ̃teryptœr]
fuse	plomb, fusible (m)	[plɔ̃], [fyzibl]
cable, wire (electric ~)	fil (m)	[fil]
wiring	installation (f) électrique	[ɛ̃stalasjɔ̃ elɛktrik]
electricity meter	compteur (m) électrique	[kɔ̃tœr elɛktrik]
readings	relevé (m)	[rəlve]

89. House. Doors. Locks

door	porte (f)	[pɔrt]
vehicle gate	portail (m)	[pɔrtaj]
handle, doorknob	poignée (f)	[pwaɲe]
to unlock (unbolt)	déverrouiller (vt)	[devɛruje]
to open (vt)	ouvrir (vt)	[uvrir]
to close (vt)	fermer (vt)	[fɛrme]
key	clé, clef (f)	[kle]
bunch (of keys)	trousseau (m), jeu (m)	[truso], [ʒø]
to creak (door hinge)	grincer (vi)	[grɛ̃se]

creak	**grincement** (m)	[grɛ̃smɑ̃]
hinge (of door)	**gond** (m)	[gɔ̃]
doormat	**paillasson** (m)	[pajasɔ̃]
door lock	**serrure** (f)	[seryr]
keyhole	**trou** (m) **de la serrure**	[tru də la seryr]
bolt (sliding bar)	**verrou** (m)	[veru]
door latch	**loquet** (m)	[lɔkɛ]
padlock	**cadenas** (m)	[kadna]
to ring (~ the door bell)	**sonner** (vi)	[sɔ̃]
ringing (sound)	**sonnerie** (f)	[sɔnri]
doorbell	**sonnette** (f)	[sɔnɛt]
doorbell button	**bouton** (m)	[butɔ̃]
knock (at the door)	**coups** (m pl) **à la porte**	[ku ɑla pɔrt]
to knock (vi)	**frapper** (vi)	[frape]
code	**code** (m)	[kɔd]
code lock	**serrure** (f) **à combinaison**	[seryr a kɔ̃binɛzɔ̃]
door phone	**interphone** (m)	[ɛ̃tɛrfɔn]
number (on the door)	**numéro** (m)	[nymero]
doorplate	**plaque** (f) **de porte**	[plak də pɔrt]
peephole	**judas** (m)	[ʒyda]

90. Country house

village	**village** (m)	[vilaʒ]
vegetable garden	**potager** (m)	[pɔtaʒe]
fence	**palissade** (f)	[palisad]
picket fence	**clôture** (f)	[klotyr]
wicket gate	**portillon** (m)	[pɔrtijɔ̃]
granary	**grange** (f)	[grɑ̃ʒ]
cellar	**cave** (f)	[kav]
shed (in garden)	**abri** (m) **de jardin**	[abri də ʒardɛ̃]
well (water)	**puits** (m)	[pɥi]
stove (wood-fired ~)	**poêle** (m)	[pwal]
to stoke the stove	**chauffer le poêle**	[ʃofe lə pwal]
firewood	**bois** (m) **de chauffage**	[bwa də ʃofaʒ]
log (firewood)	**bûche** (f)	[byʃ]
veranda, stoop	**véranda** (f)	[verɑ̃da]
terrace (patio)	**terrasse** (f)	[tɛras]
front steps	**perron** (m)	[perɔ̃]
swing (hanging seat)	**balançoire** (f)	[balɑ̃swar]

91. Villa. Mansion

country house	**maison** (f) **de campagne**	[mɛzɔ̃ də kɑ̃paɲ]
villa (by sea)	**villa** (f)	[vila]
wing (of building)	**aile** (f)	[ɛl]
garden	**jardin** (m)	[ʒardɛ̃]
park	**parc** (m)	[park]
tropical greenhouse	**serre** (f) **tropicale**	[sɛr trɔpikal]
to look after (garden, etc.)	**s'occuper de ...**	[sɔkype də]
swimming pool	**piscine** (f)	[pisin]
gym	**salle** (f) **de gym**	[sal də ʒim]
tennis court	**court** (m) **de tennis**	[kur də tenis]
home theater room	**salle** (f) **de cinéma**	[sal də sinema]
garage	**garage** (m)	[garaʒ]
private property	**propriété** (f) **privée**	[prɔprijete prive]
private land	**terrain** (m) **privé**	[tɛrɛ̃ prive]
warning (caution)	**avertissement** (m)	[avɛrtismɑ̃]
warning sign	**panneau** (m) **d'avertissement**	[pano davɛrtismɑ̃]
security	**sécurité** (f)	[sekyrite]
security guard	**agent** (m) **de sécurité**	[aʒɑ̃ də sekyrite]
burglar alarm	**alarme** (f) **antivol**	[alarm ɑ̃tivɔl]

92. Castle. Palace

castle	**château** (m)	[ʃato]
palace	**palais** (m)	[palɛ]
fortress	**forteresse** (f)	[fortərɛs]
wall (round castle)	**muraille** (f)	[myrɑj]
tower	**tour** (f)	[tur]
keep, donjon	**donjon** (m)	[dɔ̃ʒɔ̃]
portcullis	**herse** (f)	[ɛrs]
underground passage	**souterrain** (m)	[sutɛrɛ̃]
moat	**douve** (f)	[duv]
chain	**chaîne** (f)	[ʃɛn]
arrow loop	**meurtrière** (f)	[mœrtrijɛr]
magnificent (adj)	**magnifique** (adj)	[maɲifik]
majestic (adj)	**majestueux** (adj)	[maʒɛstɥø]
impregnable (adj)	**inaccessible** (adj)	[inaksesibl]
medieval (adj)	**médiéval** (adj)	[medjeval]

93. Apartment

apartment	**appartement** (m)	[apartəmã]
room	**chambre** (f)	[ʃãbr]
bedroom	**chambre** (f) **à coucher**	[ʃãbr a kuʃe]
dining room	**salle** (f) **à manger**	[sal a mãʒe]
living room	**salon** (m)	[salɔ̃]
study (home office)	**bureau** (m)	[byro]
entry room	**antichambre** (f)	[ãtiʃãbr]
bathroom	**salle** (f) **de bains**	[sal də bɛ̃]
half bath	**toilettes** (f pl)	[twalɛt]
ceiling	**plafond** (m)	[plafɔ̃]
floor	**plancher** (m)	[plãʃe]
corner	**coin** (m)	[kwɛ̃]

94. Apartment. Cleaning

to clean (vi, vt)	**faire le ménage**	[fɛr le menaʒ]
to put away (to stow)	**ranger** (vt)	[rãʒe]
dust	**poussière** (f)	[pusjɛr]
dusty (adj)	**poussiéreux** (adj)	[pusjerø]
to dust (vt)	**essuyer la poussière**	[esɥije la pusjɛr]
vacuum cleaner	**aspirateur** (m)	[aspiratœr]
to vacuum (vt)	**passer l'aspirateur**	[pɑse laspiratœr]
to sweep (vi, vt)	**balayer** (vt)	[baleje]
sweepings	**balayures** (f pl)	[balejyr]
order	**ordre** (m)	[ɔrdr]
disorder, mess	**désordre** (m)	[dezɔrdr]
mop	**balai** (m) **à franges**	[balɛ a frãʒ]
dust cloth	**torchon** (m)	[tɔrʃɔ̃]
broom	**balayette** (f)	[balɛjɛt]
dustpan	**pelle** (f) **à ordures**	[pɛl a ɔrdyr]

95. Furniture. Interior

furniture	**meubles** (m pl)	[mœbl]
table	**table** (f)	[tabl]
chair	**chaise** (f)	[ʃɛz]
bed	**lit** (m)	[li]
couch, sofa	**canapé** (m)	[kanape]
armchair	**fauteuil** (m)	[fotœj]
bookcase	**bibliothèque** (f)	[biblijɔtɛk]
shelf	**rayon** (m)	[rɛjɔ̃]

set of shelves	**étagère** (f)	[etaʒɛr]
wardrobe	**armoire** (f)	[armwar]
coat rack	**patère** (f)	[patɛr]
coat stand	**portemanteau** (m)	[pɔrtmɑ̃to]
dresser	**commode** (f)	[kɔmɔd]
coffee table	**table** (f) **basse**	[tabl bas]
mirror	**miroir** (m)	[mirwar]
carpet	**tapis** (m)	[tapi]
rug, small carpet	**petit tapis** (m)	[pəti tapi]
fireplace	**cheminée** (f)	[ʃəmine]
candle	**bougie** (f)	[buʒi]
candlestick	**chandelier** (m)	[ʃɑ̃dəlje]
drapes	**rideaux** (m pl)	[rido]
wallpaper	**papier** (m) **peint**	[papje pɛ̃]
blinds (jalousie)	**jalousie** (f)	[ʒaluzi]
table lamp	**lampe** (f) **de table**	[lɑ̃p də tabl]
wall lamp (sconce)	**applique** (f)	[aplik]
floor lamp	**lampadaire** (m)	[lɑ̃padɛr]
chandelier	**lustre** (m)	[lystr]
leg (of chair, table)	**pied** (m)	[pje]
armrest	**accoudoir** (m)	[akudwar]
back (backrest)	**dossier** (m)	[dosje]
drawer	**tiroir** (m)	[tirwar]

96. Bedding

bedclothes	**linge** (m) **de lit**	[lɛ̃ʒ də li]
pillow	**oreiller** (m)	[ɔrɛje]
pillowcase	**taie** (f) **d'oreiller**	[tɛ dɔrɛje]
blanket (comforter)	**couverture** (f)	[kuvɛrtyr]
sheet	**drap** (m)	[dra]
bedspread	**couvre-lit** (m)	[kuvrəli]

97. Kitchen

kitchen	**cuisine** (f)	[kɥizin]
gas	**gaz** (m)	[gaz]
gas cooker	**cuisinière** (f) **à gaz**	[kɥizinjɛr ɑ gaz]
electric cooker	**cuisinière** (f) **électrique**	[kɥizinjɛr elɛktrik]
oven	**four** (m)	[fur]
microwave oven	**four** (m) **micro-ondes**	[fur mikrɔɔ̃d]
refrigerator	**réfrigérateur** (m)	[refriʒeratœr]

freezer	**congélateur** (m)	[kɔ̃ʒelatœr]
dishwasher	**lave-vaisselle** (m)	[lavvesɛl]
meat grinder	**hachoir** (m)	[aʃwar]
juicer	**centrifugeuse** (f)	[sãtrifyʒøz]
toaster	**grille-pain** (m)	[grijpɛ̃]
mixer	**batteur** (m)	[batœr]
coffee maker	**machine** (f) **à café**	[maʃin ɑ kafe]
coffee pot	**cafetière** (f)	[kaftjɛr]
coffee grinder	**moulin** (m) **à café**	[mulɛ̃ ɑ kafe]
kettle	**bouilloire** (f)	[bujwar]
teapot	**théière** (f)	[tejɛr]
lid	**couvercle** (m)	[kuvɛrkl]
tea strainer	**passoire** (f) **à thé**	[pɑswar ɑ te]
spoon	**cuillère** (f)	[kɥijɛr]
teaspoon	**petite cuillère** (f)	[pətit kɥijɛr]
tablespoon	**cuillère** (f) **à soupe**	[kɥijɛr ɑ sup]
fork	**fourchette** (f)	[furʃɛt]
knife	**couteau** (m)	[kuto]
tableware (dishes)	**vaisselle** (f)	[vɛsɛl]
plate (dinner ~)	**assiette** (f)	[asjɛt]
saucer	**soucoupe** (f)	[sukup]
shot glass	**verre** (m) **à shot**	[vɛr ɑ ʃot]
glass (~ of water)	**verre** (m)	[vɛr]
cup	**tasse** (f)	[tɑs]
sugar bowl	**sucrier** (m)	[sykrije]
salt shaker	**salière** (f)	[saljɛr]
pepper shaker	**poivrière** (f)	[pwavrijɛr]
butter dish	**beurrier** (m)	[bœrje]
saucepan	**casserole** (f)	[kasrɔl]
frying pan	**poêle** (f)	[pwal]
ladle	**louche** (f)	[luʃ]
colander	**passoire** (f)	[pɑswar]
tray	**plateau** (m)	[plato]
bottle	**bouteille** (f)	[butɛj]
jar (glass)	**bocal** (m)	[bɔkal]
can	**boîte** (f) **en fer-blanc**	[bwat ɑ̃ fɛrblɑ̃]
bottle opener	**ouvre-bouteille** (m)	[uvrəbutɛj]
can opener	**ouvre-boîte** (m)	[uvrəbwat]
corkscrew	**tire-bouchon** (m)	[tirbuʃɔ̃]
filter	**filtre** (m)	[filtr]
to filter (vt)	**filtrer** (vt)	[filtre]
trash	**ordures** (f pl)	[ɔrdyr]
trash can	**poubelle** (f)	[pubɛl]

98. Bathroom

bathroom	salle (f) de bains	[sal də bɛ̃]
water	eau (f)	[o]
tap, faucet	robinet (m)	[rɔbinɛ]
hot water	eau (f) chaude	[o ʃod]
cold water	eau (f) froide	[o frwad]

toothpaste	dentifrice (m)	[dɑ̃tifris]
to brush one's teeth	se brosser les dents	[sə brɔse le dɑ̃]
toothbrush	brosse (f) à dents	[brɔs a dɑ̃]

to shave (vi)	se raser (vp)	[sə raze]
shaving foam	mousse (f) à raser	[mus a raze]
razor	rasoir (m)	[razwar]

to wash (one's hands, etc.)	laver (vt)	[lave]
to take a bath	se laver (vp)	[sə lave]
shower	douche (f)	[duʃ]
to take a shower	prendre une douche	[prɑ̃dr yn duʃ]

bathtub	baignoire (f)	[bɛɲwar]
toilet (toilet bowl)	cuvette (f)	[kyvɛt]
sink (washbasin)	lavabo (m)	[lavabo]

| soap | savon (m) | [savɔ̃] |
| soap dish | porte-savon (m) | [pɔrtsavɔ̃] |

sponge	éponge (f)	[epɔ̃ʒ]
shampoo	shampooing (m)	[ʃɑ̃pwɛ̃]
towel	serviette (f)	[sɛrvjɛt]
bathrobe	peignoir (m) de bain	[pɛɲwar də bɛ̃]

laundry (process)	lessive (f)	[lɛsiv]
washing machine	machine (f) à laver	[maʃin a lave]
to do the laundry	faire la lessive	[fɛr la lɛsiv]
laundry detergent	lessive (f)	[lɛsiv]

99. Household appliances

TV set	télé (f)	[tele]
tape recorder	magnétophone (m)	[maɲetɔfɔn]
video, VCR	magnétoscope (m)	[maɲetɔskɔp]
radio	radio (f)	[radjo]
player (CD, MP3, etc.)	lecteur (m)	[lɛktœr]

video projector	vidéoprojecteur (m)	[videɔprɔʒɛktœr]
home movie theater	home cinéma (m)	[həʊm sinema]
DVD player	lecteur DVD (m)	[lɛktœr devede]

amplifier	amplificateur (m)	[ɑ̃plifikatœr]
video game console	console (f) de jeux	[kõsɔl də ʒø]
video camera	caméscope (m)	[kameskɔp]
camera (photo)	appareil (m) photo	[aparɛj fɔto]
digital camera	appareil (m) photo numérique	[aparɛj fɔto nymerik]

vacuum cleaner	aspirateur (m)	[aspiratœr]
iron (e.g., steam ~)	fer (m) à repasser	[fɛr ɑ rəpase]
ironing board	planche (f) à repasser	[plɑ̃ʃ ɑ rəpase]

telephone	téléphone (m)	[telefɔn]
mobile phone	portable (m)	[pɔrtabl]
typewriter	machine (f) à écrire	[maʃin ɑ ekrir]
sewing machine	machine (f) à coudre	[maʃin ɑ kudr]

microphone	micro (m)	[mikro]
headphones	écouteurs (m pl)	[ekutœr]
remote control (TV)	télécommande (f)	[telekɔmɑ̃d]

CD, compact disc	CD (m)	[sede]
cassette	cassette (f)	[kasɛt]
vinyl record	disque (m) vinyle	[disk vinil]

100. Repairs. Renovation

renovations	rénovation (f)	[renɔvasjõ]
to renovate (vt)	faire la rénovation	[fɛr la renɔvasjõ]
to repair (vt)	réparer (vt)	[repare]
to put in order	remettre en ordre	[rəmɛtr anɔrdr]
to redo (do again)	refaire (vt)	[rəfɛr]

paint	peinture (f)	[pɛ̃tyr]
to paint (~ a wall)	peindre (vt)	[pɛ̃dr]
house painter	peintre (m) en bâtiment	[pɛ̃tr ɑ̃ batimɑ̃]
paintbrush	pinceau (m)	[pɛ̃so]
whitewash	chaux (f)	[ʃo]
to whitewash (vt)	blanchir à la chaux	[blɑ̃ʃir ala ʃo]

wallpaper	papier (m) peint	[papje pɛ̃]
to wallpaper (vt)	tapisser (vt)	[tapise]
varnish	vernis (m)	[vɛrni]
to varnish (vt)	vernir (vt)	[vɛrnir]

101. Plumbing

water	eau (f)	[o]
hot water	eau (f) chaude	[o ʃod]

| cold water | eau (f) froide | [o frwad] |
| tap, faucet | robinet (m) | [rɔbinɛ] |

drop (of water)	goutte (f)	[gut]
to drip (vi)	goutter (vi)	[gute]
to leak (ab. pipe)	fuir (vi)	[fɥir]
leak (pipe ~)	fuite (f)	[fɥit]
puddle	flaque (f)	[flak]

pipe	tuyau (m)	[tɥijo]
stop valve	valve (f)	[valv]
to be clogged up	se boucher (vp)	[sə buʃe]

tools	outils (m pl)	[uti]
adjustable wrench	clé (f) réglable	[kle reglabl]
to unscrew, untwist (vt)	dévisser (vt)	[devise]
to screw (tighten)	visser (vt)	[vise]

to unclog (vt)	déboucher (vt)	[debuʃe]
plumber	plombier (m)	[plɔ̃bje]
basement	sous-sol (m)	[susɔl]
sewerage (system)	égouts (m pl)	[egu]

102. Fire. Conflagration

fire (to catch ~)	feu (m)	[fø]
flame	flamme (f)	[flam]
spark	étincelle (f)	[etɛ̃sɛl]
smoke (from fire)	fumée (f)	[fyme]
torch (flaming stick)	flambeau (m)	[flɑ̃bo]
campfire	feu (m) de bois	[fø də bwa]

gas, gasoline	essence (f)	[esɑ̃s]
kerosene (for aircraft)	kérosène (m)	[kerɔzɛn]
flammable (adj)	inflammable (adj)	[ɛ̃flamabl]
explosive (adj)	explosif (adj)	[ɛksplozif]
NO SMOKING	DÉFENSE DE FUMER	[defɑ̃s də fyme]

safety	sécurité (f)	[sekyrite]
danger	danger (m)	[dɑ̃ʒe]
dangerous (adj)	dangereux (adj)	[dɑ̃ʒrø]

to catch fire	prendre feu	[prɑ̃dr fø]
explosion	explosion (f)	[ɛksplozjɔ̃]
to set fire	mettre feu	[mɛtr fø]
incendiary (arsonist)	incendiaire (m)	[ɛ̃sɑ̃djɛr]
arson	incendie (m) prémédité	[ɛ̃sɑ̃di premedite]

| to blaze (vi) | flamboyer (vi) | [flɑ̃bwaje] |
| to burn (be on fire) | brûler (vi) | [bryle] |

to burn down	**brûler complètement**	[bryle kɔ̃plɛtmɑ̃]
to call the fire department	**appeler les pompiers**	[aple le pɔ̃pje]
fireman	**pompier** (m)	[pɔ̃pje]
fire truck	**voiture** (f) **de pompiers**	[vwatyr də pɔ̃pje]
fire department	**sapeurs-pompiers** (m pl)	[sapœrpɔ̃pje]
fire truck ladder	**échelle** (f) **des pompiers**	[eʃɛl de pɔ̃pje]
fire hose	**tuyau** (m) **d'incendie**	[tɥijo dɛ̃sɑ̃di]
fire extinguisher	**extincteur** (m)	[ɛkstɛ̃ktœr]
helmet	**casque** (m)	[kask]
siren	**sirène** (f)	[sirɛn]
to call out	**crier** (vi)	[krije]
to call for help	**appeler au secours**	[aple o səkur]
rescuer	**secouriste** (m)	[səkurist]
to rescue (vt)	**sauver** (vt)	[sove]
to arrive (vi)	**venir** (vi)	[vənir]
to extinguish (vt)	**éteindre** (vt)	[etɛ̃dr]
water	**eau** (f)	[o]
sand	**sable** (m)	[sabl]
ruins (destruction)	**ruines** (f pl)	[rɥin]
to collapse (building, etc.)	**tomber en ruine**	[tɔ̃be ɑ̃ rɥin]
to fall down (vi)	**s'écrouler** (vp)	[sekrule]
to cave in (ceiling, floor)	**s'effondrer** (vp)	[sefɔ̃dre]
piece of wreckage	**morceau** (m)	[mɔrso]
ash	**cendre** (f)	[sɑ̃dr]
to suffocate (die)	**mourir étouffé**	[murir etufe]
to be killed (perish)	**périr** (vi)	[perir]

HUMAN ACTIVITIES

Job. Business. Part 1

103. Office. Working in the office

office (of firm)	**bureau** (m)	[byro]
office (of director, etc.)	**bureau** (m)	[byro]
front desk	**accueil** (m)	[akœj]
secretary	**secrétaire** (m)	[səkretɛr]
secretary (fem.)	**secrétaire** (f)	[səkretɛr]
director	**directeur** (m)	[dirɛktœr]
manager	**manager** (m)	[manadʒœr]
accountant	**comptable** (m)	[kõtabl]
employee	**collaborateur** (m)	[kɔlabɔratœr]
furniture	**meubles** (m pl)	[mœbl]
desk	**bureau** (m)	[byro]
desk chair	**fauteuil** (m)	[fotœj]
chest of drawers	**classeur** (m) **à tiroirs**	[klasœr ɑ tirwar]
coat stand	**portemanteau** (m)	[pɔrtmãto]
computer	**ordinateur** (m)	[ɔrdinatœr]
printer	**imprimante** (f)	[ɛ̃primãt]
fax machine	**fax** (m)	[faks]
photocopier	**copieuse** (f)	[kɔpjøz]
paper	**papier** (m)	[papje]
office supplies	**papeterie** (f)	[papɛtri]
mouse pad	**tapis** (m) **de souris**	[tapi də suri]
sheet (of paper)	**feuille** (f)	[fœj]
folder, binder	**classeur** (m)	[klasœr]
catalog	**catalogue** (m)	[katalɔg]
phone book (directory)	**annuaire** (m)	[anɥɛr]
documentation	**documents** (m pl)	[dɔkymã]
brochure	**brochure** (f)	[brɔʃyr]
(e.g., 12 pages ~)		
leaflet	**prospectus** (m)	[prɔspɛktys]
sample	**échantillon** (m)	[eʃãtijõ]
training meeting	**formation** (f)	[fɔrmasjõ]
meeting (of managers)	**réunion** (f)	[reynjõ]
lunch time	**pause** (f) **déjeuner**	[poz deʒœne]

to make a copy	faire une copie	[fɛr yn kɔpi]
to make copies	faire des copies	[fɛr de kɔpi]
to receive a fax	recevoir un fax	[rəsəvwar œ̃ faks]
to send a fax	envoyer un fax	[ɑ̃vwaje œ̃ faks]

to call (by phone)	téléphoner, appeler	[telefɔne], [aple]
to answer (vt)	répondre (vi, vt)	[repɔ̃dr]
to put through	passer (vt)	[pɑse]

to arrange, to set up	fixer (vt)	[fikse]
to demonstrate (vt)	montrer (vt)	[mɔ̃tre]
to be absent	être absent	[ɛtr apsɑ̃]
absence	absence (f)	[apsɑ̃s]

104. Business processes. Part 1

| business | affaire (f) | [afɛr] |
| occupation | métier (m) | [metje] |

firm	firme (f), société (f)	[firm], [sɔsjete]
company	compagnie (f)	[kɔ̃paɲi]
corporation	corporation (f)	[kɔrpɔrasjɔ̃]
enterprise	entreprise (f)	[ɑ̃trœpriz]
agency	agence (f)	[aʒɑ̃s]

agreement (contract)	accord (m)	[akɔr]
contract	contrat (m)	[kɔ̃tra]
deal	marché (m)	[marʃe]
order (to place an ~)	commande (f)	[kɔmɑ̃d]
term (of contract)	terme (m)	[tɛrm]

wholesale (adv)	en gros (adv)	[ɑ̃ gro]
wholesale (adj)	en gros (adj)	[ɑ̃ gro]
wholesale (n)	vente (f) en gros	[vɑ̃t ɑ̃ gro]
retail (adj)	au détail (adj)	[odetaj]
retail (n)	vente (f) au détail	[vɑ̃t o detaj]

competitor	concurrent (m)	[kɔ̃kyrɑ̃]
competition	concurrence (f)	[kɔ̃kyrɑ̃s]
to compete (vi)	concurrencer (vt)	[kɔ̃kyrɑ̃se]

| partner (associate) | associć (m) | [asɔsje] |
| partnership | partenariat (m) | [partənarja] |

crisis	crise (f)	[kriz]
bankruptcy	faillite (f)	[fajit]
to go bankrupt	faire faillite	[fɛr fajit]
difficulty	difficulté (f)	[difikylte]
problem	problème (m)	[prɔblɛm]
catastrophe	catastrophe (f)	[katastrɔf]

economy	**économie** (f)	[ekɔnɔmi]
economic (~ growth)	**économique** (adj)	[ekɔnɔmik]
economic recession	**baisse** (f) **économique**	[bɛs ekɔnɔmik]

goal (aim)	**but** (m)	[byt]
task	**objectif** (m)	[ɔbʒɛktif]

to trade (vi)	**faire du commerce**	[fɛr dy kɔmɛrs]
network (distribution ~)	**réseau** (m)	[rezo]
inventory (stock)	**inventaire** (m)	[ɛ̃vɑ̃tɛr]
assortment	**assortiment** (m)	[asɔrtimɑ̃]

leader (leading company)	**leader** (m)	[lidœr]
large (~ company)	**grand, grande** (adj)	[grɑ̃, grɑ̃d]
monopoly	**monopole** (m)	[mɔnɔpɔl]

theory	**théorie** (f)	[teɔri]
practice	**pratique** (f)	[pratik]
experience (in my ~)	**expérience** (f)	[ɛksperjɑ̃s]
trend (tendency)	**tendance** (f)	[tɑ̃dɑ̃s]
development	**développement** (m)	[devlɔpmɑ̃]

105. Business processes. Part 2

benefit, profit	**rentabilité** (m)	[rɑ̃tabilite]
profitable (adj)	**rentable** (adj)	[rɑ̃tabl]

delegation (group)	**délégation** (f)	[delegasjɔ̃]
salary	**salaire** (m)	[salɛr]
to correct (an error)	**corriger** (vt)	[kɔriʒe]
business trip	**voyage** (m) **d'affaires**	[vwajaʒ dafɛr]
commission	**commission** (f)	[kɔmisjɔ̃]

to control (vt)	**contrôler** (vt)	[kɔ̃trole]
conference	**conférence** (f)	[kɔ̃ferɑ̃s]
license	**licence** (f)	[lisɑ̃s]
reliable (~ partner)	**fiable** (adj)	[fjabl]

initiative (undertaking)	**initiative** (f)	[inisjativ]
norm (standard)	**norme** (f)	[nɔrm]
circumstance	**circonstance** (f)	[sirkɔ̃stɑ̃s]
duty (of employee)	**fonction** (f)	[fɔ̃ksjɔ̃]

organization (company)	**entreprise** (f)	[ɑ̃trœpriz]
organization (process)	**organisation** (f)	[ɔrganizasjɔ̃]
organized (adj)	**organisé** (adj)	[ɔrganize]
cancellation	**annulation** (f)	[anylasjɔ̃]
to cancel (call off)	**annuler** (vt)	[anyle]
report (official ~)	**rapport** (m)	[rapɔr]
patent	**brevet** (m)	[brəvɛ]

to patent (obtain patent)	**breveter** (vt)	[brəvte]
to plan (vt)	**planifier** (vt)	[planifje]
bonus (money)	**prime** (f)	[prim]
professional (adj)	**professionnel** (adj)	[prɔfɛsjɔnɛl]
procedure	**procédure** (f)	[prɔsedyr]
to examine (contract, etc.)	**examiner** (vt)	[ɛgzamine]
calculation	**calcul** (m)	[kalkyl]
reputation	**réputation** (f)	[repytasjɔ̃]
risk	**risque** (m)	[risk]
to manage, to run	**diriger** (vt)	[diriʒe]
information	**renseignements** (m pl)	[rɑ̃sɛɲəmɑ̃]
property	**propriété** (f)	[prɔprijete]
union	**union** (f)	[ynjɔ̃]
life insurance	**assurance vie** (f)	[asyrɑ̃s vi]
to insure (vt)	**assurer** (vt)	[asyre]
insurance	**assurance** (f)	[asyrɑ̃s]
auction (~ sale)	**enchères** (f pl)	[ɑ̃ʃɛr]
to notify (inform)	**notifier** (vt)	[nɔtifje]
management (process)	**gestion** (f)	[ʒɛstjɔ̃]
service (~ industry)	**service** (m)	[sɛrvis]
forum	**forum** (m)	[fɔrɔm]
to function (vi)	**fonctionner** (vi)	[fɔ̃ksjɔne]
stage (phase)	**étape** (f)	[etap]
legal (~ services)	**juridique** (adj)	[ʒyridik]
lawyer (legal expert)	**juriste** (m)	[ʒyrist]

106. Production. Works

plant	**usine** (f)	[yzin]
factory	**fabrique** (f)	[fabrik]
workshop	**atelier** (m)	[atəlje]
works, production site	**site** (m) **de production**	[sit də prɔdyksjɔ̃]
industry	**industrie** (f)	[ɛ̃dystri]
industrial (adj)	**industriel** (adj)	[ɛ̃dystrijɛl]
heavy industry	**industrie** (f) **lourde**	[ɛ̃dystri lurd]
light industry	**industrie** (f) **légère**	[ɛ̃dystri leʒɛr]
products	**produit** (m)	[prɔdyi]
to produce (vt)	**produire** (vt)	[prɔdyir]
raw materials	**matières** (f pl) **premières**	[matjɛr prəmjɛr]
foreman	**chef** (m) **d'équipe**	[ʃɛf dekip]
workers team	**équipe** (f) **d'ouvriers**	[ekip duvrije]

worker	**ouvrier** (m)	[uvrije]
working day	**jour** (m) **ouvrable**	[ʒur uvrabl]
pause	**pause** (f)	[poz]
meeting	**réunion** (f)	[reynjɔ̃]
to discuss (vt)	**discuter** (vt)	[diskyte]

plan	**plan** (m)	[plɑ̃]
to fulfill the plan	**accomplir le plan**	[akɔ̃plir lə plɑ̃]
rate of output	**norme** (f) **de production**	[nɔrm də prɔdyksjɔ̃]
quality	**qualité** (f)	[kalite]
checking (control)	**contrôle** (m)	[kɔ̃trol]
quality control	**contrôle** (m) **qualité**	[kɔ̃trol kalite]

work safety	**sécurité** (f) **de travail**	[sekyrite də travaj]
discipline	**discipline** (f)	[disiplin]
violation	**infraction** (f)	[ɛ̃fraksjɔ̃]
(of safety rules, etc.)		
to violate (rules)	**violer** (vt)	[vjɔle]
strike	**grève** (f)	[grɛv]
striker	**gréviste** (m)	[grevist]
to be on strike	**faire grève**	[fɛr grɛv]
labor union	**syndicat** (m)	[sɛ̃dika]

to invent (machine, etc.)	**inventer** (vt)	[ɛ̃vɑ̃te]
invention	**invention** (f)	[ɛ̃vɑ̃sjɔ̃]
research	**recherche** (f)	[rəʃɛrʃ]
to improve (make better)	**améliorer** (vt)	[ameljɔre]
technology	**technologie** (f)	[tɛknɔlɔʒi]
technical drawing	**dessin** (m) **technique**	[desɛ̃ tɛknik]

load, cargo	**charge** (f)	[ʃarʒ]
loader (person)	**chargeur** (m)	[ʃarʒœr]
to load (vehicle, etc.)	**charger** (vt)	[ʃarʒe]
loading (process)	**chargement** (m)	[ʃarʒəmɑ̃]
to unload (vi, vt)	**décharger** (vt)	[deʃarʒe]
unloading	**déchargement** (m)	[deʃarʒəmɑ̃]

transportation	**transport** (m)	[trɑ̃spɔr]
transportation company	**compagnie** (f)	[kɔ̃paɲi
	de transport	də trɑ̃spɔr]
to transport (vt)	**transporter** (vt)	[trɑ̃spɔrte]

freight car	**wagon de marchandise**	[vagɔ̃ də marʃɑ̃diz]
cistern	**citerne** (f)	[sitɛrn]
truck	**camion** (m)	[kamjɔ̃]

| machine tool | **machine-outil** (f) | [maʃinuti] |
| mechanism | **mécanisme** (m) | [mekanism] |

industrial waste	**déchets** (m pl)	[deʃɛ]
packing (process)	**emballage** (m)	[ɑ̃balaʒ]
to pack (vt)	**emballer** (vt)	[ɑ̃bale]

107. Contract. Agreement

contract	contrat (m)	[kɔ̃tra]
agreement	accord (m)	[akɔr]
addendum	annexe (f)	[anɛks]
to sign a contract	signer un contrat	[siɲe œ̃ kɔ̃tra]
signature	signature (f)	[siɲatyr]
to sign (vt)	signer (vt)	[siɲe]
stamp (seal)	cachet (m)	[kaʃe]
subject of contract	objet (m) du contrat	[ɔbʒɛ dy kɔ̃tra]
clause	clause (f)	[kloz]
parties (in contract)	côtés (m pl)	[kote]
legal address	adresse (f) légale	[adrɛs legal]
to break the contract	violer l'accord	[vjɔle lakɔr]
commitment	obligation (f)	[ɔbligasjɔ̃]
responsibility	responsabilité (f)	[rɛspɔ̃sabilite]
force majeure	force (f) majeure	[fɔrs maʒœr]
dispute	litige (m)	[litiʒ]
penalties	pénalités (f pl)	[penalite]

108. Import & Export

import	importation (f)	[ɛ̃pɔrtasjɔ̃]
importer	importateur (m)	[ɛ̃pɔrtatœr]
to import (vt)	importer (vt)	[ɛ̃pɔrte]
import (e.g., ~ goods)	d'importation	[dɛ̃pɔrtasjɔ̃]
export	exportation (f)	[ɛkspɔrtasjɔ̃]
exporter	exportateur (m)	[ɛkspɔrtatœr]
to export (vi, vt)	exporter (vt)	[ɛkspɔrte]
export (e.g., ~ goods)	à l'export	[a lɛkspɔr]
goods	marchandise (f)	[marʃɑ̃diz]
consignment, lot	lot (m) de marchandises	[lo də marʃɑ̃diz]
weight	poids (m)	[pwa]
volume	volume (m)	[vɔlym]
cubic meter	mètre (m) cube	[mɛtr kyb]
manufacturer	producteur (m)	[prɔdyktœr]
transportation company	compagnie (f) de transport	[kɔ̃paɲi də trɑ̃spɔr]
container	container (m)	[kɔ̃tɛnɛr]
border	frontière (f)	[frɔ̃tjɛr]
customs	douane (f)	[dwan]

customs duty	**droit** (m) **de douane**	[drwa də dwan]
customs officer	**douanier** (m)	[dwanje]
smuggling	**contrebande** (f)	[kɔ̃trəbɑ̃d]
contraband (goods)	**contrebande** (f)	[kɔ̃trəbɑ̃d]

109. Finances

stock (share)	**action** (f)	[aksjɔ̃]
bond (certificate)	**obligation** (f)	[ɔbligasjɔ̃]
bill of exchange	**lettre** (f) **de change**	[lɛtr də ʃɑ̃ʒ]

| stock exchange | **bourse** (f) | [burs] |
| stock price | **cours** (m) **d'actions** | [kur daksjɔ̃] |

| to go down | **baisser** (vi) | [bese] |
| to go up | **augmenter** (vi) | [ogmɑ̃te] |

| shareholding | **part** (f) | [par] |
| controlling interest | **participation** (f) **de contrôle** | [partisipasjɔ̃ də kɔ̃trol] |

investment	**investissements** (m pl)	[ɛ̃vɛstismɑ̃]
to invest (vt)	**investir** (vt)	[ɛ̃vɛstir]
percent	**pour-cent** (m)	[pursɑ̃]
interest (on investment)	**intérêts** (m pl)	[ɛ̃terɛ]
profit	**profit** (m)	[prɔfi]
profitable (adj)	**profitable** (adj)	[prɔfitabl]
tax	**impôt** (m)	[ɛ̃po]

currency (foreign ~)	**devise** (f)	[dəviz]
national (adj)	**national** (adj)	[nasjɔnal]
exchange (currency ~)	**échange** (m)	[eʃɑ̃ʒ]

| accountant | **comptable** (m) | [kɔ̃tabl] |
| accounting | **comptabilité** (f) | [kɔ̃tabilite] |

bankruptcy	**faillite** (f)	[fajit]
collapse, crash	**krach** (m)	[krak]
ruin	**ruine** (f)	[rɥin]
to be ruined	**se ruiner** (vp)	[sə rɥine]
inflation	**inflation** (f)	[ɛ̃flasjɔ̃]
devaluation	**dévaluation** (f)	[devalɥasjɔ̃]

capital	**capital** (m)	[kapital]
income	**revenu** (m)	[rəvəny]
turnover	**chiffre** (m) **d'affaires**	[ʃifr dafɛr]
resources	**ressources** (f pl)	[rəsurs]
monetary resources	**moyens** (m pl) **financiers**	[mwajɛ̃ finɑ̃sje]
overhead	**frais** (m pl) **généraux**	[frɛ ʒenerø]
to reduce (expenses)	**réduire** (vt)	[redɥir]

110. Marketing

marketing	**marketing** (m)	[marketiŋ]
market	**marché** (m)	[marʃe]
market segment	**segment** (m) **du marché**	[sɛgmɑ̃ dy marʃe]
product	**produit** (m)	[prɔdyi]
goods	**marchandise** (f)	[marʃɑ̃diz]
brand	**marque** (f) **de fabrique**	[mark də fabrik]
trademark	**marque** (f) **déposée**	[mark depoze]
logotype	**logotype** (m)	[lɔgɔtip]
logo	**logo** (m)	[logo]
demand	**demande** (f)	[dəmɑ̃d]
supply	**offre** (f)	[ɔfr]
need	**besoin** (m)	[bəzwɛ̃]
consumer	**consommateur** (m)	[kɔ̃sɔmatœr]
analysis	**analyse** (f)	[analiz]
to analyze (vt)	**analyser** (vt)	[analize]
positioning	**positionnement** (m)	[pozisjɔnmɑ̃]
to position (vt)	**positionner** (vt)	[pozisjɔne]
price	**prix** (m)	[pri]
pricing policy	**politique** (f) **des prix**	[pɔlitik de pri]
formation of price	**formation** (f) **des prix**	[fɔrmasjɔ̃ de pri]

111. Advertising

advertising	**publicité** (f), **pub** (f)	[pyblisite], [pyb]
to advertise (vt)	**faire de la publicité**	[fɛr də la pyblisite]
budget	**budget** (m)	[bydʒɛ]
ad, advertisement	**annonce** (f), **pub** (f)	[anɔ̃s], [pyb]
TV advertising	**publicité** (f) **à la télévision**	[pyblisite ɑla televizjɔ̃]
radio advertising	**publicité** (f) **à la radio**	[pyblisite ɑla radjo]
outdoor advertising	**publicité** (f) **extérieure**	[pyblisite ɛksterjœr]
mass media	**mass média** (m pl)	[masmedja]
periodical (n)	**périodique** (m)	[perjɔdik]
image (public appearance)	**image** (f)	[imaʒ]
slogan	**slogan** (m)	[slɔgɑ̃]
motto (maxim)	**devise** (f)	[dəviz]
campaign	**campagne** (f)	[kɑ̃paɲ]
advertising campaign	**campagne** (f) **publicitaire**	[kɑ̃paɲ pyblisitɛr]
target group	**public** (m) **cible**	[pyblik sibl]

business card	carte (f) de visite	[kart də vizit]
leaflet	prospectus (m)	[prɔspɛktys]
brochure	brochure (f)	[brɔʃyr]
(e.g., 12 pages ~)		
pamphlet	dépliant (m)	[deplijã]
newsletter	bulletin (m)	[byltɛ̃]
store sign	enseigne (f)	[ãsɛɲ]
poster	poster (m)	[pɔstɛr]
billboard	panneau-réclame (m)	[pano reklam]

112. Banking

bank	banque (f)	[bãk]
branch (of bank, etc.)	agence (f) bancaire	[aʒãs bãkɛr]
bank clerk, consultant	conseiller (m)	[kõseje]
manager (director)	gérant (m)	[ʒerã]
banking account	compte (m)	[kõt]
account number	numéro (m) du compte	[nymero dy kõt]
checking account	compte (m) courant	[kõt kurã]
savings account	compte (m) sur livret	[kõt syr livrɛ]
to open an account	ouvrir un compte	[uvrir œ̃ kõt]
to close the account	clôturer le compte	[klotyre lə kõt]
to deposit into the account	verser dans le compte	[vɛrse dã lə kõt]
to withdraw (vt)	retirer du compte	[rətire dy kõt]
deposit	dépôt (m)	[depo]
to make a deposit	faire un dépôt	[fɛr œ̃ depo]
wire transfer	virement (m) bancaire	[virmã bãkɛr]
to wire, to transfer	faire un transfert	[fɛr œ̃ trãsfɛr]
sum	somme (f)	[sɔm]
How much?	Combien?	[kõbjɛ̃]
signature	signature (f)	[siɲatyr]
to sign (vt)	signer (vt)	[siɲe]
credit card	carte (f) de crédit	[kart də kredi]
code	code (m)	[kɔd]
credit card number	numéro (m) de carte	[nymero də kart
	de crédit	də kredi]
ATM	distributeur (m)	[distribytœr]
check	chèque (m)	[ʃɛk]
to write a check	faire un chèque	[fɛr œ̃ ʃɛk]
checkbook	chéquier (m)	[ʃekje]
loan (bank ~)	crédit (m)	[kredi]

to apply for a loan	demander un crédit	[dəmɑ̃de œ̃ kredi]
to get a loan	prendre un crédit	[prɑ̃dr œ̃ kredi]
to give a loan	accorder un crédit	[akɔrde œ̃ kredi]
guarantee	gage (m)	[gaʒ]

113. Telephone. Phone conversation

telephone	téléphone (m)	[telefɔn]
mobile phone	portable (m)	[pɔrtabl]
answering machine	répondeur (m)	[repɔ̃dœr]

| to call (telephone) | téléphoner, appeler | [telefɔne], [aple] |
| phone call | appel (m) | [apɛl] |

to dial a number	composer le numéro	[kɔ̃poze lə nymero]
Hello!	Allô!	[alo]
to ask (vt)	demander (vt)	[dəmɑ̃de]
to answer (vi, vt)	répondre (vi, vt)	[repɔ̃dr]

to hear (vt)	entendre (vt)	[ɑ̃tɑ̃dr]
well (adv)	bien (adv)	[bjɛ̃]
not well (adv)	mal (adv)	[mal]
noises (interference)	bruits (m pl)	[brɥi]

receiver	récepteur (m)	[resɛptœr]
to pick up (~ the phone)	décrocher (vt)	[dekrɔʃe]
to hang up (~ the phone)	raccrocher (vi)	[rakrɔʃe]

busy (adj)	occupé (adj)	[ɔkype]
to ring (ab. phone)	sonner (vi)	[sɔ̃]
telephone book	carnet (m) de téléphone	[karnɛ də telefɔn]

local (adj)	local (adj)	[lɔkal]
local call	appel (m) local	[apɛl lɔkal]
long distance (~ call)	interurbain (adj)	[ɛ̃tɛryrbɛ̃]
long-distance call	appel (m) interurbain	[apɛl ɛ̃tɛryrbɛ̃]
international (adj)	international (adj)	[ɛ̃tɛrnasjɔnal]
international call	appel (m) international	[apɛl ɛ̃tɛrnasjɔnal]

114. Mobile telephone

mobile phone	portable (m)	[pɔrtabl]
display	écran (m)	[ekrɑ̃]
button	bouton (m)	[butɔ̃]
SIM card	carte SIM (f)	[kart sim]

| battery | pile (f) | [pil] |
| to be dead (battery) | être déchargé | [ɛtr deʃarʒe] |

charger	chargeur (m)	[ʃarʒœr]
menu	menu (m)	[məny]
settings	réglages (m pl)	[reglaʒ]
tune (melody)	mélodie (f)	[melɔdi]
to select (vt)	sélectionner (vt)	[selɛksjɔne]

calculator	calculatrice (f)	[kalkylatris]
voice mail	répondeur (m)	[repɔ̃dœr]
alarm clock	réveil (m)	[revɛj]
contacts	contacts (m pl)	[kɔ̃takt]

| SMS (text message) | SMS (m) | [esemes] |
| subscriber | abonné (m) | [abɔne] |

115. Stationery

| ballpoint pen | stylo (m) à bille | [stilo ɑ bij] |
| fountain pen | stylo (m) à plume | [stilo ɑ plym] |

pencil	crayon (m)	[krɛjɔ̃]
highlighter	marqueur (m)	[markœr]
felt-tip pen	feutre (m)	[føtr]

| notepad | bloc-notes (m) | [blɔknɔt] |
| agenda (diary) | agenda (m) | [aʒɛ̃da] |

ruler	règle (f)	[rɛgl]
calculator	calculatrice (f)	[kalkylatris]
eraser	gomme (f)	[gɔm]
thumbtack	punaise (f)	[pynɛz]
paper clip	trombone (m)	[trɔ̃bɔn]

glue	colle (f)	[kɔl]
stapler	agrafeuse (f)	[agraføz]
hole punch	perforateur (m)	[pɛrfɔratœr]
pencil sharpener	taille-crayon (m)	[tajkrɛjɔ̃]

116. Various kinds of documents

account (report)	rapport (m)	[rapɔr]
agreement	accord (m)	[akɔr]
application form	formulaire (m) d'inscription	[fɔrmylɛr dɛ̃skripsjɔ̃]
authentic (adj)	authentique (adj)	[otɑ̃tik]
badge (identity tag)	badge (m)	[badʒ]
business card	carte (f) de visite	[kart də vizit]
certificate (~ of quality)	certificat (m)	[sɛrtifika]
check (e.g., draw a ~)	chèque (m) de banque	[ʃɛk də bɑ̃k]

| check (in restaurant) | addition (f) | [adisjɔ̃] |
| constitution | constitution (f) | [kɔ̃stitysjɔ̃] |

contract	contrat (m)	[kɔ̃tra]
copy	copie (f)	[kɔpi]
copy (of contract, etc.)	exemplaire (m)	[ɛgzɑ̃plɛr]

customs declaration	déclaration (f) de douane	[deklarasjɔ̃ də dwan]
document	document (m)	[dɔkymɑ̃]
driver's license	permis (m) de conduire	[pɛrmi də kɔ̃dɥir]
addendum	annexe (f)	[anɛks]
form	questionnaire (m)	[kɛstjɔnɛr]

identity card, ID	carte (f) d'identité	[kart didɑ̃tite]
inquiry (request)	demande (f) de renseignements	[dəmɑ̃d də rɑ̃sɛɲəmɑ̃]
invitation card	lettre (f) d'invitation	[lɛtr dɛ̃vitasjɔ̃]
invoice	facture (f)	[faktyr]

law	loi (f)	[lwa]
letter (mail)	lettre (f)	[lɛtr]
letterhead	papier (m) à en-tête	[papje ɑ ɑ̃tɛt]
list (of names, etc.)	liste (f)	[list]
manuscript	manuscrit (m)	[manyskri]
newsletter	bulletin (m)	[byltɛ̃]
note (short message)	mot (m)	[mo]

pass (for worker, visitor)	laissez-passer (m)	[lese pɑse]
passport	passeport (m)	[pɑspɔr]
permit	permis (m)	[pɛrmi]
résumé	C.V. (m)	[seve]
debt note, IOU	reconnaissance (f) de dette	[rəkɔnɛsɑ̃s də dɛt]

| receipt (for purchase) | reçu (m) | [rəsy] |

| sales slip, receipt | ticket (m) de caisse | [tikɛ də kɛs] |
| report | rapport (m) | [rapɔr] |

to show (ID, etc.)	présenter (vt)	[prezɑ̃te]
to sign (vt)	signer (vt)	[siɲe]
signature	signature (f)	[siɲatyr]
stamp (seal)	cachet (m)	[kaʃe]

| text | texte (m) | [tɛkst] |
| ticket (for entry) | ticket (m) | [tikɛ] |

| to cross out | rayer (vt) | [rɛje] |
| to fill out (~ a form) | remplir (vt) | [rɑ̃plir] |

| waybill | bordereau (m) de transport | [bɔrdəro də trɑ̃spɔr] |
| will (testament) | testament (m) | [tɛstamɑ̃] |

117. Kinds of business

accounting services	services (m pl) comptables	[sɛrvis kɔ̃tabl]
advertising	publicité (f), pub (f)	[pyblisite], [pyb]
advertising agency	agence (f) publicitaire	[aʒɑ̃s pyblisitɛr]
air-conditioners	climatisation (m)	[klimatizasjɔ̃]
airline	compagnie (f) aérienne	[kɔ̃paɲi aerjɛn]
alcoholic drinks	boissons (f pl) alcoolisées	[bwasɔ̃ alkɔlize]
antiquities	antiquités (f pl)	[ɑ̃tikite]
art gallery	galerie (f) d'art	[galri dar]
audit services	services (m pl) d'audition	[sɛrvis dodisjɔ̃]
banks	banques (f pl)	[bɑ̃k]
bar	bar (m)	[bar]
beauty parlor	salon (m) de beauté	[salɔ̃ də bote]
bookstore	librairie (f)	[librɛri]
brewery	brasserie (f)	[brasri]
business center	centre (m) d'affaires	[sɑ̃tr dafɛr]
business school	école (f) de commerce	[ekɔl də kɔmɛrs]
casino	casino (m)	[kazino]
construction	bâtiment (m)	[batimɑ̃]
consulting	conseil (m)	[kɔ̃sɛj]
dental clinic	dentistes (pl)	[dɑ̃tists]
design	design (m)	[dizajn]
drugstore, pharmacy	pharmacie (f)	[farmasi]
dry cleaners	pressing (m)	[presiŋ]
employment agency	agence (f) de recrutement	[aʒɑ̃s də rəkrytmɑ̃]
financial services	service (m) financier	[sɛrvis finɑ̃sje]
food products	produits (m pl) alimentaires	[prɔdyi alimɑ̃tɛr]
funeral home	maison (f) funéraire	[mɛzɔ̃ fynerɛr]
furniture (e.g., house ~)	meubles (m pl)	[mœbl]
garment	vêtement (m)	[vɛtmɑ̃]
hotel	hôtel (m)	[otɛl]
ice-cream	glace (f)	[glas]
industry	industrie (f)	[ɛ̃dystri]
insurance	assurance (f)	[asyrɑ̃s]
Internet	Internet (m)	[ɛ̃tɛrnɛt]
investment	investissements (m pl)	[ɛ̃vɛstismɑ̃]
jeweler	bijoutier (m)	[biʒutje]
jewelry	bijouterie (f)	[biʒutri]
laundry (shop)	blanchisserie (f)	[blɑ̃ʃisri]

| legal advisor | **service** (m) **juridique** | [sɛrvis ʒyridik] |
| light industry | **industrie** (f) **légère** | [ɛ̃dystri leʒɛr] |

magazine	**revue** (f)	[rəvy]
mail-order selling	**vente** (f) **par catalogue**	[vɑ̃t par katalɔg]
medicine	**médecine** (f)	[medsin]
movie theater	**cinéma** (m)	[sinema]
museum	**musée** (m)	[myze]

news agency	**agence** (f) **d'information**	[aʒɑ̃s dɛ̃fɔrmasjɔ̃]
newspaper	**journal** (m)	[ʒurnal]
nightclub	**boîte** (f) **de nuit**	[bwat də nɥi]

oil (petroleum)	**pétrole** (m)	[petrɔl]
parcels service	**coursiers** (m pl)	[kursje]
pharmaceuticals	**industrie** (f) **pharmaceutique**	[ɛ̃dystri farmasøtik]
printing (industry)	**imprimerie** (f)	[ɛ̃primri]
publishing house	**maison** (f) **d'édition**	[mɛzɔ̃ dedisjɔ̃]

radio (~ station)	**radio** (f)	[radjo]
real estate	**immobilier** (m)	[imɔbilje, -ɛr]
restaurant	**restaurant** (m)	[rɛstɔrɑ̃]

security agency	**agence** (f) **de sécurité**	[aʒɑ̃s də sekyrite]
sports	**sport** (m)	[spɔr]
stock exchange	**bourse** (f)	[burs]
store	**magasin** (m)	[magazɛ̃]
supermarket	**supermarché** (m)	[sypɛrmarʃe]
swimming pool	**piscine** (f)	[pisin]

tailors	**atelier** (m) **de couture**	[atəlje də kutyr]
television	**télévision** (f)	[televizjɔ̃]
theater	**théâtre** (m)	[teɑtr]
trade	**commerce** (m)	[kɔmɛrs]
transportation	**sociétés de transport**	[sɔsjete trɑ̃spɔr]
travel	**tourisme** (m)	[turism]

veterinarian	**vétérinaire** (m)	[veterinɛr]
warehouse	**entrepôt** (m)	[ɑ̃trəpo]
waste collection	**récupération** (f) **des déchets**	[rekyperasjɔ̃ də deʃɛ]

Job. Business. Part 2

118. Show. Exhibition

exhibition, show	salon (m)	[salɔ̃]
trade show	salon (m) commercial	[salɔ̃ kɔmɛrsjal]
participation	participation (f)	[partisipɑsjɔ̃]
to participate (vi)	participer à ...	[partisipe a]
participant (exhibitor)	participant (m)	[partisipɑ̃]
director	directeur (m)	[dirɛktœr]
organizer's office	direction (f)	[dirɛksjɔ̃]
organizer	organisateur (m)	[ɔrganizatœr]
to organize (vt)	organiser (vt)	[ɔrganize]
participation form	demande (f)	[dəmɑ̃d
	de participation	də partisipɑsjɔ̃]
to fill out (vt)	remplir (vt)	[rɑ̃plir]
details	détails (m pl)	[detaj]
information	information (f)	[ɛ̃fɔrmasjɔ̃]
price	prix (m)	[pri]
including	y compris	[i kɔ̃pri]
to include (vt)	inclure (vt)	[ɛ̃klyr]
to pay (vi, vt)	payer (vi, vt)	[peje]
registration fee	droits (m pl) d'inscription	[drwa dɛ̃skripsjɔ̃]
entrance	entrée (f)	[ɑ̃tre]
pavilion, hall	pavillon (m)	[pavijɔ̃]
to register (vt)	enregistrer (vt)	[ɑ̃rəʒistre]
badge (identity tag)	badge (m)	[badʒ]
booth, stand	stand (m)	[stɑ̃d]
to reserve, to book	réserver (vt)	[rezɛrve]
display case	vitrine (f)	[vitrin]
spotlight	lampe (f)	[lɑ̃p]
design	design (m)	[dizajn]
to place (put, set)	mettre, placer	[mɛtr], [plase]
to be placed	être placé	[ɛtr plase]
distributor	distributeur (m)	[distribytœr]
supplier	fournisseur (m)	[furnisœr]
to supply (vt)	fournir (vt)	[furnir]
country	pays (m)	[pei]

foreign (adj)	**étranger** (adj)	[etrɑ̃ʒe]
product	**produit** (m)	[prɔdyi]

association	**association** (f)	[asɔsjasjɔ̃]
conference hall	**salle** (f) **de conférences**	[sal də kɔ̃ferɑ̃s]
congress	**congrès** (m)	[kɔ̃grɛ]
contest (competition)	**concours** (m)	[kɔ̃kur]

visitor	**visiteur** (m)	[vizitœr]
to visit (attend)	**visiter** (vt)	[vizite]
customer	**client** (m)	[klijɑ̃]

119. Mass Media

newspaper	**journal** (m)	[ʒurnal]
magazine	**revue** (f)	[rəvy]
press (printed media)	**presse** (f)	[prɛs]
radio	**radio** (f)	[radjo]
radio station	**station** (f) **de radio**	[stasjɔ̃ də radjo]
television	**télévision** (f)	[televizjɔ̃]

presenter, host	**animateur** (m)	[animatœr]
newscaster	**présentateur** (m)	[prezɑ̃tatœr]
commentator	**commentateur** (m)	[kɔmɑ̃tatœr]

journalist	**journaliste** (m)	[ʒurnalist]
correspondent (reporter)	**correspondant** (m)	[kɔrɛspɔ̃dɑ̃]
press photographer	**reporter photographe** (m)	[rəpɔrtœr fɔtɔgraf]
reporter	**reporter** (m)	[rəpɔrtɛr]

editor	**rédacteur** (m)	[redaktœr]
editor-in-chief	**rédacteur** (m) **en chef**	[redaktœr ɑ̃ ʃɛf]

to subscribe (to ...)	**s'abonner** (vp)	[sabɔne]
subscription	**abonnement** (m)	[abɔnmɑ̃]
subscriber	**abonné** (m)	[abɔne]
to read (vi, vt)	**lire** (vi, vt)	[lir]
reader	**lecteur** (m)	[lɛktœr]

circulation (of newspaper)	**tirage** (m)	[tiraʒ]
monthly (adj)	**mensuel** (adj)	[mɑ̃sɥɛl]
weekly (adj)	**hebdomadaire** (adj)	[ɛbdɔmadɛr]
issue (edition)	**numéro** (m)	[nymero]
new (~ issue)	**nouveau** (adj)	[nuvo]

headline	**titre** (m)	[titr]
short article	**entrefilet** (m)	[ɑ̃trəfilɛ]
column (regular article)	**rubrique** (f)	[rybrik]
article	**article** (m)	[artikl]
page	**page** (f)	[paʒ]

reportage, report	**reportage** (m)	[rəpɔrtaʒ]
event (happening)	**événement** (m)	[evɛnmã]
sensation (news)	**sensation** (f)	[sãsasjõ]
scandal	**scandale** (m)	[skãdal]
scandalous (adj)	**scandaleux**	[skãdalø]
great (~ scandal)	**grand** (adj)	[grã]
program	**émission** (f)	[emisjõ]
interview	**interview** (f)	[ɛ̃tɛrvju]
live broadcast	**émission** (f) **en direct**	[emisjõ ã dirɛkt]
channel	**chaîne** (f)	[ʃɛn]

120. Agriculture

agriculture	**agriculture** (f)	[agrikyltyr]
peasant (masc.)	**paysan** (m)	[peizã]
peasant (fem.)	**paysanne** (f)	[peizan]
farmer	**fermier** (m)	[fɛrmje]
tractor	**tracteur** (m)	[traktœr]
combine, harvester	**moissonneuse-batteuse**	[mwasɔnøzbatøz]
plow	**charrue** (f)	[ʃary]
to plow (vi, vt)	**labourer** (vt)	[labure]
plowland	**champ** (m) **labouré**	[ʃã labure]
furrow (in field)	**sillon** (m)	[sijõ]
to sow (vi, vt)	**semer** (vt)	[səme]
seeder	**semeuse** (f)	[səmøz]
sowing (process)	**semailles** (f pl)	[səmaj]
scythe	**faux** (f)	[fo]
to mow, to scythe	**faucher** (vt)	[foʃe]
spade (tool)	**pelle** (f)	[pɛl]
to dig (to till)	**bêcher** (vt)	[beʃe]
hoe	**couperet** (m)	[kuprɛ]
to hoe, to weed	**sarcler** (vt)	[sarkle]
weed (plant)	**mauvaise herbe** (f)	[movɛz ɛrb]
watering can	**arrosoir** (m)	[arozwar]
to water (plants)	**arroser** (vt)	[aroze]
watering (act)	**arrosage** (m)	[arozaʒ]
pitchfork	**fourche** (f)	[furʃ]
rake	**râteau** (m)	[rɑto]
fertilizer	**engrais** (m)	[ãgrɛ]
to fertilize (vt)	**engraisser** (vt)	[ãgrese]

manure (fertilizer)	**fumier** (m)	[fymje]
field	**champ** (m)	[ʃɑ̃]
meadow	**pré** (m)	[pre]
vegetable garden	**potager** (m)	[pɔtaʒe]
orchard (e.g., apple ~)	**jardin** (m)	[ʒardɛ̃]

to pasture (vt)	**faire paître**	[fɛr pɛtr]
herdsman	**berger** (m)	[bɛrʒe]
pastureland	**pâturage** (m)	[pɑtyraʒ]

cattle breeding	**élevage** (m)	[ɛlvaʒ]
sheep farming	**élevage** (m) **de moutons**	[ɛlvaʒ də mutɔ̃]

plantation	**plantation** (f)	[plɑ̃tasjɔ̃]
row (garden bed ~s)	**plate-bande** (f)	[platbɑ̃d]
hothouse	**serre** (f)	[sɛr]

drought (lack of rain)	**sécheresse** (f)	[seʃrɛs]
dry (~ summer)	**sec** (adj)	[sɛk]

grain	**grains** (m pl)	[grɛ̃]
cereal crops	**céréales** (f pl)	[sereal]
to harvest, to gather	**récolter** (vt)	[rekɔlte]

miller (person)	**meunier** (m)	[mønje]
mill (e.g., gristmill)	**moulin** (m)	[mulɛ̃]
to grind (grain)	**moudre** (vt)	[mudr]
flour	**farine** (f)	[farin]
straw	**paille** (f)	[paj]

121. Building. Building process

construction site	**chantier** (m)	[ʃɑ̃tje]
to build (vt)	**construire** (vt)	[kɔ̃struir]
construction worker	**ouvrier** (m) **du bâtiment**	[uvrije dy batimɑ̃]

project	**projet** (m)	[prɔʒɛ]
architect	**architecte** (m)	[arʃitɛkt]
worker	**ouvrier** (m)	[uvrije]

foundation (of building)	**fondations** (f pl)	[fɔ̃dasjɔ̃]
roof	**toit** (m)	[twa]
foundation plle	**pieu** (m) **de fondation**	[pjø də fɔ̃dasjɔ̃]
wall	**mur** (m)	[myr]

reinforcing bars	**ferraillage** (m)	[fɛrajaʒ]
scaffolding	**échafaudage** (m)	[eʃafodaʒ]

concrete	**béton** (m)	[betɔ̃]
granite	**granit** (m)	[grani]

| stone | **pierre** (f) | [pjɛr] |
| brick | **brique** (f) | [brik] |

sand	**sable** (m)	[sabl]
cement	**ciment** (m)	[simɑ̃]
plaster (for walls)	**plâtre** (m)	[plɑtr]
to plaster (vt)	**plâtrer** (vt)	[plɑtre]
paint	**peinture** (f)	[pɛ̃tyr]
to paint (~ a wall)	**peindre** (vt)	[pɛ̃dr]
barrel	**tonneau** (m)	[tɔno]

crane	**grue** (f)	[gry]
to lift (vt)	**monter** (vt)	[mɔ̃te]
to lower (vt)	**abaisser** (vt)	[abese]

bulldozer	**bulldozer** (m)	[byldozɛr]
excavator	**excavateur** (m)	[ɛkskavatœr]
scoop, bucket	**godet** (m)	[gɔdɛ]
to dig (excavate)	**creuser** (vt)	[krøze]
hard hat	**casque** (m)	[kask]

122. Science. Research. Scientists

science	**science** (f)	[sjɑ̃s]
scientific (adj)	**scientifique** (adj)	[sjɑ̃tifik]
scientist	**savant** (m)	[savɑ̃]
theory	**théorie** (f)	[teɔri]

axiom	**axiome** (m)	[aksjom]
analysis	**analyse** (f)	[analiz]
to analyze (vt)	**analyser** (vt)	[analize]
argument (strong ~)	**argument** (m)	[argymɑ̃]
substance (matter)	**substance** (f)	[sypstɑ̃s]

hypothesis	**hypothèse** (f)	[ipɔtɛz]
dilemma	**dilemme** (m)	[dilɛm]
dissertation	**thèse** (f)	[tɛz]
dogma	**dogme** (m)	[dɔgm]

doctrine	**doctrine** (f)	[dɔktrin]
research	**recherche** (f)	[rəʃɛrʃ]
to do research	**rechercher** (vt)	[rəʃɛrʃe]
testing	**test** (m)	[tɛst]
laboratory	**laboratoire** (m)	[labɔratwar]

method	**méthode** (f)	[metɔd]
molecule	**molécule** (f)	[mɔlekyl]
monitoring	**monitoring** (m)	[mɔnitɔriŋ]
discovery (act, event)	**découverte** (f)	[dekuvɛrt]
postulate	**postulat** (m)	[pɔstyla]

principle	**principe** (m)	[prɛ̃sip]
forecast	**prévision** (f)	[previzjɔ̃]
prognosticate (vt)	**prévoir** (vt)	[prevwar]

synthesis	**synthèse** (f)	[sɛ̃tɛz]
trend (tendency)	**tendance** (f)	[tɑ̃dɑ̃s]
theorem	**théorème** (m)	[teɔrɛm]

teachings	**enseignements** (m pl)	[ɑ̃sɛɲmɑ̃]
fact	**fait** (m)	[fɛ]
expedition	**expédition** (f)	[ɛkspedisjɔ̃]
experiment	**expérience** (f)	[ɛksperjɑ̃s]

academician	**académicien** (m)	[akademisjɛn]
bachelor (e.g., ~ of Arts)	**bachelier** (m)	[baʃəlje]
doctor (PhD)	**docteur** (m)	[dɔktœr]
Associate Professor	**chargé** (m) **de cours**	[ʃarʒe də kur]
Master (e.g., ~ of Arts)	**magistère** (m)	[maʒistɛr]
professor	**professeur** (m)	[prɔfɛsœr]

Professions and occupations

123. Job search. Dismissal

job	**travail** (m)	[travaj]
staff (work force)	**employés** (pl)	[ãplwaje]
personnel	**personnel** (m)	[pɛrsɔnɛl]
career	**carrière** (f)	[karjɛr]
prospects	**perspective** (f)	[pɛrspɛktiv]
skills (mastery)	**maîtrise** (f)	[metriz]
selection (screening)	**sélection** (f)	[selɛksjõ]
employment agency	**agence** (f)	[aʒãs
	de recrutement	də rəkrytmã]
résumé	**C.V.** (m)	[seve]
interview (for job)	**entretien** (m)	[ãtrətjɛ̃]
vacancy, opening	**emploi** (m) **vacant**	[ãplwa vakã]
salary, pay	**salaire** (m)	[salɛr]
fixed salary	**salaire** (m) **fixe**	[salɛr fiks]
pay, compensation	**rémunération** (f)	[remynerasjõ]
position (job)	**poste** (m)	[pɔst]
duty (of employee)	**fonction** (f)	[fõksjõ]
range of duties	**liste** (f) **des fonctions**	[list de fõksjõ]
busy (I'm ~)	**occupé** (adj)	[ɔkype]
to fire (dismiss)	**licencier** (vt)	[lisãsje]
dismissal	**licenciement** (m)	[lisãsimã]
unemployment	**chômage** (m)	[ʃomaʒ]
unemployed (n)	**chômeur** (m)	[ʃomœr]
retirement	**retraite** (f)	[rətrɛt]
to retire (from job)	**prendre sa retraite**	[prãdr sa rətrɛt]

124. Business people

director	**directeur** (m)	[dirɛktœr]
manager (director)	**gérant** (m)	[ʒerã]
boss	**patron** (m)	[patrõ]
superior	**supérieur** (m)	[syperjœr]
superiors	**supérieurs** (m pl)	[syperjœr]

| president | **président** (m) | [prezidɑ̃] |
| chairman | **président** (m) | [prezidɑ̃] |

deputy (substitute)	**adjoint** (m)	[adʒwɛ̃]
assistant	**assistant** (m)	[asistɑ̃]
secretary	**secrétaire** (m, f)	[səkretɛr]
personal assistant	**secrétaire** (m, f) **personnel**	[səkretɛr pɛrsɔnɛl]

businessman	**homme** (m) **d'affaires**	[ɔm dafɛr]
entrepreneur	**entrepreneur** (m)	[ɑ̃trəprənœr]
founder	**fondateur** (m)	[fɔ̃datœr]
to found (vt)	**fonder** (vt)	[fɔ̃de]

incorporator	**fondateur** (m)	[fɔ̃datœr]
partner	**partenaire** (m)	[partənɛr]
stockholder	**actionnaire** (m)	[aksjɔnɛr]

millionaire	**millionnaire** (m)	[miljɔnɛr]
billionaire	**milliardaire** (m)	[miljardɛr]
owner, proprietor	**propriétaire** (m)	[prɔprijetɛr]
landowner	**propriétaire** (m) **foncier**	[prɔprijetɛr fɔ̃sje]

| client | **client** (m) | [klijɑ̃] |
| regular client | **client** (m) **régulier** | [klijɑ̃ regylje] |

| buyer (customer) | **acheteur** (m) | [aʃtœr] |
| visitor | **visiteur** (m) | [vizitœr] |

professional (n)	**professionnel** (m)	[prɔfɛsjɔnɛl]
expert	**expert** (m)	[ɛkspɛr]
specialist	**spécialiste** (m)	[spesjalist]

| banker | **banquier** (m) | [bɑ̃kje] |
| broker | **courtier** (m) | [kurtje] |

cashier, teller	**caissier** (m)	[kesje]
accountant	**comptable** (m)	[kɔ̃tabl]
security guard	**agent** (m) **de sécurité**	[aʒɑ̃ də sekyrite]

| investor | **investisseur** (m) | [ɛ̃vɛstisœr] |
| debtor | **débiteur** (m) | [debitœr] |

| creditor | **créancier** (m) | [kreɑ̃sje] |
| borrower | **emprunteur** (m) | [ɑ̃prœ̃tœr] |

| importer | **importateur** (m) | [ɛ̃pɔrtatœr] |
| exporter | **exportateur** (m) | [ɛkspɔrtatœr] |

manufacturer	**producteur** (m)	[prɔdyktœr]
distributor	**distributeur** (m)	[distribytœr]
middleman	**intermédiaire** (m)	[ɛ̃tɛrmedjɛr]
consultant	**conseiller** (m)	[kɔ̃seje]

sales representative	représentant (m)	[rəprezãtã]
agent	agent (m)	[aʒã]
insurance agent	agent (m) d'assurances	[aʒã dasyrãs]

125. Service professions

cook	cuisinier (m)	[kɥizinje]
chef (kitchen chef)	cuisinier (m) en chef	[kɥizinje ã ʃɛf]
baker	boulanger (m)	[bulãʒe]

bartender	barman (m)	[barman]
waiter	serveur (m)	[sɛrvœr]
waitress	serveuse (f)	[sɛrvøz]

lawyer, attorney	avocat (m)	[avɔka]
lawyer (legal expert)	juriste (m)	[ʒyrist]
notary	notaire (m)	[nɔtɛr]

electrician	électricien (m)	[elɛktrisjɛ̃]
plumber	plombier (m)	[plɔ̃bje]
carpenter	charpentier (m)	[ʃarpãtje]

masseur	masseur (m)	[masœr]
masseuse	masseuse (f)	[masøz]
doctor	médecin (m)	[medsɛ̃]

taxi driver	chauffeur (m) de taxi	[ʃofœr də taksi]
driver	chauffeur (m)	[ʃofœr]
delivery man	livreur (m)	[livrœr]

chambermaid	femme (f) de chambre	[fam də ʃãbr]
security guard	agent (m) de sécurité	[aʒã də sekyrite]
flight attendant	hôtesse (f) de l'air	[otɛs də lɛr]

teacher (in primary school)	professeur (m)	[prɔfɛsœr]
librarian	bibliothécaire (m)	[biblijɔtekɛr]
translator	traducteur (m)	[tradyktœr]

| interpreter | interprète (m) | [ɛ̃tɛrprɛt] |
| guide | guide (m) | [gid] |

hairdresser	coiffeur (m)	[kwafœr]
mailman	facteur (m)	[faktœr]
salesman (store staff)	vendeur (m)	[vãdœr]

| gardener | jardinier (m) | [ʒardinje] |
| domestic servant | serviteur (m) | [sɛrvitœr] |

| maid | servante (f) | [sɛrvãt] |
| cleaner (cleaning lady) | femme (f) de ménage | [fam də menaʒ] |

126. Military professions and ranks

private	soldat (m)	[sɔlda]
sergeant	sergent (m)	[sɛrʒɑ̃]
lieutenant	lieutenant (m)	[ljøtnɑ̃]
captain	capitaine (m)	[kapitɛn]

major	commandant (m)	[kɔmɑ̃dɑ̃]
colonel	colonel (m)	[kɔlɔnɛl]
general	général (m)	[ʒeneral]
marshal	maréchal (m)	[mareʃal]
admiral	amiral (m)	[amiral]

military man	militaire (m)	[militɛr]
soldier	soldat (m)	[sɔlda]
officer	officier (m)	[ɔfisje]
commander	commandant (m)	[kɔmɑ̃dɑ̃]

border guard	garde-frontière (m)	[gardəfrɔ̃tjɛr]
radio operator	opérateur (m) radio	[ɔperatœr radjo]
scout (searcher)	éclaireur (m)	[eklɛrœr]
pioneer (sapper)	démineur (m)	[deminœr]
marksman	tireur (m)	[tirœr]
navigator	navigateur (m)	[navigatœr]

127. Officials. Priests

king	roi (m)	[rwa]
queen	reine (f)	[rɛn]

prince	prince (m)	[prɛ̃s]
princess	princesse (f)	[prɛ̃sɛs]

tsar, czar	tsar (m)	[tsar]
czarina	tsarine (f)	[tsarin]

president	président (m)	[prezidɑ̃]
Secretary (~ of State)	ministre (m)	[ministr]
prime minister	premier ministre (m)	[prəmje ministɛr]
senator	sénateur (m)	[senatœr]

diplomat	diplomate (m)	[diplɔmat]
consul	consul (m)	[kɔ̃syl]
ambassador	ambassadeur (m)	[ɑ̃basadœr]
advisor (military ~)	conseiller (m)	[kɔ̃seje]

official (civil servant)	fonctionnaire (m)	[fɔ̃ksjɔnɛr]
prefect	préfet (m)	[prefɛ]
mayor	maire (m)	[mɛr]

| judge | **juge** (m) | [ʒyʒ] |
| district attorney (prosecutor) | **procureur** (m) | [prɔkyrœr] |

missionary	**missionnaire** (m)	[misjɔnɛr]
monk	**moine** (m)	[mwan]
abbot	**abbé** (m)	[abe]
rabbi	**rabbin** (m)	[rabɛ̃]

vizier	**vizir** (m)	[vizir]
shah	**shah** (m)	[ʃa]
sheikh	**cheik** (m)	[ʃɛjk]

128. Agricultural professions

beekeeper	**apiculteur** (m)	[apikyltœr]
herder, shepherd	**berger** (m)	[bɛrʒe]
agronomist	**agronome** (m)	[agrɔnɔm]
cattle breeder	**éleveur** (m)	[elvœr]
veterinarian	**vétérinaire** (m)	[veterinɛr]

farmer	**fermier** (m)	[fɛrmje]
winemaker	**vinificateur** (m)	[vinifikatœr]
zoologist	**zoologiste** (m)	[zɔɔlɔʒist]
cowboy	**cow-boy** (m)	[kɔbɔj]

129. Art professions

| actor | **acteur** (m) | [aktœr] |
| actress | **actrice** (f) | [aktris] |

| singer (masc.) | **chanteur** (m) | [ʃɑ̃tœr] |
| singer (fem.) | **cantatrice** (f) | [kɑ̃tatris] |

| dancer (masc.) | **danseur** (m) | [dɑ̃sœr] |
| dancer (fem.) | **danseuse** (f) | [dɑ̃søz] |

| performing artist (masc.) | **artiste** (m) | [artist] |
| performing artist (fem.) | **artiste** (f) | [artist] |

musician	**musicien** (m)	[myzisjɛ̃]
pianist	**pianiste** (m)	[pjanist]
guitar player	**guitariste** (m)	[gitarist]

conductor (orchestra ~)	**chef** (m) **d'orchestre**	[ʃɛf dɔrkɛstr]
composer	**compositeur** (m)	[kɔ̃pozitœr]
impresario	**imprésario** (m)	[ɛ̃presarjo]
movie director	**metteur** (m) **en scène**	[mɛtœr ɑ̃ sɛn]

producer	producteur (m)	[prɔdyktœr]
scriptwriter	scénariste (m)	[senarist]
critic	critique (m)	[kritik]

writer	écrivain (m)	[ekrivɛ̃]
poet	poète (m)	[pɔɛt]
sculptor	sculpteur (m)	[skyltœr]
artist (painter)	peintre (m)	[pɛ̃tr]

juggler	jongleur (m)	[ʒɔ̃glœr]
clown	clown (m)	[klun]
acrobat	acrobate (m)	[akrɔbat]
magician	magicien (m)	[maʒisjɛ̃]

130. Various professions

doctor	médecin (m)	[medsɛ̃]
nurse	infirmière (f)	[ɛ̃firmjɛr]
psychiatrist	psychiatre (m)	[psikjatr]
dentist	stomatologue (m)	[stomatɔlɔg]
surgeon	chirurgien (m)	[ʃiryrʒjɛ̃]

astronaut	astronaute (m)	[astrɔnot]
astronomer	astronome (m)	[astrɔnɔm]
pilot	pilote (m)	[pilɔt]

driver (of taxi, etc.)	chauffeur (m)	[ʃofœr]
engineer (train driver)	conducteur (m) de train	[kɔ̃dyktœr də trɛ̃]
mechanic	mécanicien (m)	[mekanisjɛ̃]

miner	mineur (m)	[minœr]
worker	ouvrier (m)	[uvrije]
metalworker	serrurier (m)	[seryrje]
joiner (carpenter)	menuisier (m)	[mənɥizje]
turner	tourneur (m)	[turnœr]
construction worker	ouvrier (m) du bâtiment	[uvrije dy batimɑ̃]
welder	soudeur (m)	[sudœr]

professor (title)	professeur (m)	[prɔfɛsœr]
architect	architecte (m)	[arʃitɛkt]
historian	historien (m)	[istɔrjɛ̃]
scientist	savant (m)	[savɑ̃]
physicist	physicien (m)	[fizisjɛ̃]
chemist (scientist)	chimiste (m)	[ʃimist]

archeologist	archéologue (m)	[arkeɔlɔg]
geologist	géologue (m)	[ʒeɔlɔg]
researcher	chercheur (m)	[ʃɛrʃœr]
babysitter	baby-sitter (m, f)	[bebisitœr]
teacher, educator	pédagogue (m, f)	[pedagɔg]

editor	**rédacteur** (m)	[redaktœr]
editor-in-chief	**rédacteur** (m) **en chef**	[redaktœr ɑ̃ ʃɛf]
correspondent	**correspondant** (m)	[kɔrɛspɔ̃dɑ̃]
typist (fem.)	**dactylographe** (f)	[daktilɔgraf]
designer	**designer** (m)	[dizajnœr]
computer expert	**informaticien** (m)	[ɛ̃fɔrmatisjɛ̃]
programmer	**programmeur** (m)	[prɔgramœr]
engineer (designer)	**ingénieur** (m)	[ɛ̃ʒenjœr]
sailor	**marin** (m)	[marɛ̃]
seaman	**matelot** (m)	[matlo]
rescuer	**secouriste** (m)	[səkurist]
fireman	**pompier** (m)	[pɔ̃pje]
policeman	**policier** (m)	[pɔlisje]
watchman	**veilleur** (m) **de nuit**	[vejœr də nɥi]
detective	**détective** (m)	[detɛktiv]
customs officer	**douanier** (m)	[dwanje]
bodyguard	**garde** (m) **du corps**	[gard dy kɔr]
prison guard	**gardien** (m) **de prison**	[gardjɛ̃ də prizɔ̃]
inspector	**inspecteur** (m)	[ɛ̃spɛktœr]
sportsman	**sportif** (m)	[spɔrtif]
trainer, coach	**entraîneur** (m)	[ɑ̃trɛnœr]
butcher	**boucher** (m)	[buʃe]
cobbler	**cordonnier** (m)	[kɔrdɔnje]
merchant	**commerçant** (m)	[kɔmɛrsɑ̃]
loader (person)	**chargeur** (m)	[ʃarʒœr]
fashion designer	**couturier** (m)	[kutyrje]
model (fem.)	**modèle** (f)	[mɔdɛl]

131. Occupations. Social status

schoolboy	**écolier** (m)	[ekɔlje]
student (college ~)	**étudiant** (m)	[etydjɑ̃]
philosopher	**philosophe** (m)	[filɔzɔf]
economist	**économiste** (m)	[ekɔnɔmist]
inventor	**inventeur** (m)	[ɛ̃vɑ̃tœr]
unemployed (n)	**chômeur** (m)	[ʃomœr]
retiree	**retraité** (m)	[rətrɛte]
spy, secret agent	**espion** (m)	[ɛspjɔ̃]
prisoner	**prisonnier** (m)	[prizɔnje]
striker	**gréviste** (m)	[grevist]
bureaucrat	**bureaucrate** (m)	[byrokrat]

traveler	**voyageur** (m)	[vwajaʒœr]
homosexual	**homosexuel** (m)	[ɔmɔsɛksɥɛl]
hacker	**hacker** (m)	[akeːr]
hippie	**hippie** (m, f)	[ipi]

bandit	**bandit** (m)	[bɑ̃di]
hit man, killer	**tueur** (m) **à gages**	[tɥœr ɑ gaʒ]
drug addict	**drogué** (m)	[drɔge]
drug dealer	**trafiquant** (m) **de drogue**	[trafikɑ̃ də drɔg]
prostitute (fem.)	**prostituée** (f)	[prɔstitɥe]
pimp	**souteneur** (m)	[sutnœr]

sorcerer	**sorcier** (m)	[sɔrsje]
sorceress	**sorcière** (f)	[sɔrsjɛr]
pirate	**pirate** (m)	[pirat]
slave	**esclave** (m)	[ɛsklav]
samurai	**samouraï** (m)	[samuraj]
savage (primitive)	**sauvage** (m)	[sovaʒ]

Sports

132. Kinds of sports. Sportspersons

sportsman	**sportif** (m)	[spɔrtif]
kind of sports	**type** (m) **de sport**	[tip də spɔr]
basketball	**basket-ball** (m)	[baskɛtbol]
basketball player	**basketteur** (m)	[baskɛtœr]
baseball	**base-ball** (m)	[bɛzbol]
baseball player	**joueur** (m) **de base-ball**	[ʒwœr də bɛzbol]
soccer	**football** (m)	[futbol]
soccer player	**joueur** (m) **de football**	[ʒwœr də futbol]
goalkeeper	**gardien** (m) **de but**	[gardjɛ̃ də byt]
hockey	**hockey** (m)	[ɔkɛ]
hockey player	**hockeyeur** (m)	[ɔkɛjœr]
volleyball	**volley-ball** (m)	[vɔlɛbol]
volleyball player	**joueur** (m) **de volley-ball**	[ʒwœr də vɔlɛbol]
boxing	**boxe** (f)	[bɔks]
boxer	**boxeur** (m)	[bɔksœr]
wrestling	**lutte** (f)	[lyt]
wrestler	**lutteur** (m)	[lytœr]
karate	**karaté** (m)	[karate]
karate fighter	**karatéka** (m)	[karateka]
judo	**judo** (m)	[ʒydo]
judo athlete	**judoka** (m)	[ʒydɔka]
tennis	**tennis** (m)	[tenis]
tennis player	**joueur** (m) **de tennis**	[ʒwœr də tenis]
swimming	**natation** (f)	[natasjɔ̃]
swimmer	**nageur** (m)	[naʒœr]
fencing	**escrime** (f)	[ɛskrim]
fencer	**escrimeur** (m)	[ɛskrimœr]
chess	**échecs** (m pl)	[eʃɛk]
chess player	**joueur** (m) **d'échecs**	[ʒwœr deʃɛk]

alpinism	**alpinisme** (m)	[alpinism]
alpinist	**alpiniste** (m)	[alpinist]
running	**course** (f)	[kurs]
runner	**coureur** (m)	[kurœr]
athletics	**athlétisme** (m)	[atletism]
athlete	**athlète** (m)	[atlɛt]
horseback riding	**équitation** (f)	[ekitasjɔ̃]
horse rider	**cavalier** (m)	[kavalje]
figure skating	**patinage** (m) **artistique**	[patinaʒ artistik]
figure skater (masc.)	**patineur** (m)	[patinœr]
figure skater (fem.)	**patineuse** (f)	[patinøz]
weightlifting	**haltérophilie** (f)	[alterɔfili]
weightlifter	**haltérophile** (m)	[alterɔfil]
car racing	**course** (f) **automobile**	[kurs otomɔbil]
racing driver	**pilote** (m)	[pilɔt]
cycling	**cyclisme** (m)	[siklism]
cyclist	**cycliste** (m)	[siklist]
broad jump	**sauts** (m pl) **en longueur**	[le so ɑ̃ lɔ̃gœr]
pole vault	**sauts** (m pl) **à la perche**	[le so ɑla pɛrʃ]
jumper	**sauteur** (m)	[sotœr]

133. Kinds of sports. Miscellaneous

football	**football** (m) **américain**	[futbol amerikɛ̃]
badminton	**badminton** (m)	[badmintɔn]
biathlon	**biathlon** (m)	[biatlɔ̃]
billiards	**billard** (m)	[bijar]
bobsled	**bobsleigh** (m)	[bɔbslɛg]
bodybuilding	**bodybuilding** (m)	[bɔdibildiŋ]
water polo	**water-polo** (m)	[watɛrpolo]
handball	**handball** (m)	[ɑ̃dbal]
golf	**golf** (m)	[gɔlf]
rowing	**aviron** (m)	[avirɔ̃]
scuba diving	**plongée** (f)	[plɔ̃ʒe]
cross-country skiing	**course** (f) **à skis**	[kurs ɑ ski]
ping-pong	**tennis** (m) **de table**	[tenis də tabl]
sailing	**voile** (f)	[vwal]
rally racing	**rallye** (m)	[rali]
rugby	**rugby** (m)	[rygbi]

| snowboarding | snowboard (m) | [snəubɔːd] |
| archery | tir (m) à l'arc | [tir ɑ lark] |

134. Gym

| barbell | barre (f) à disques | [bar ɑ disk] |
| dumbbells | haltères (m pl) | [altɛr] |

training machine	appareil (m) d'entraînement	[aparɛj dɑ̃trɛnmɑ̃]
bicycle trainer	vélo (m) d'exercice	[velo dɛgzɛrsis]
treadmill	tapis (m) roulant	[tapi rulɑ̃]

horizontal bar	barre (f) fixe	[bar fiks]
parallel bars	barres (pl) parallèles	[le bar paralɛl]
vaulting horse	cheval (m) d'Arçons	[ʃeval darsɔ̃]
mat (in gym)	tapis (m) gymnastique	[tapi ʒimnastik]

jump rope	corde (f) à sauter	[kɔrd a sote]
aerobics	aérobic (m)	[aerobik]
yoga	yoga (m)	[jɔga]

135. Hockey

hockey	hockey (m)	[ɔkɛ]
hockey player	hockeyeur (m)	[ɔkɛjœr]
to play hockey	jouer au hockey	[ʒew o ɔkɛ]
ice	glace (f)	[glas]

puck	palet (m)	[palɛ]
hockey stick	crosse (f)	[krɔs]
ice skates	patins (m pl)	[patɛ̃]
board	rebord (m)	[rəbɔr]
shot	tir (m)	[tir]
goaltender	gardien (m) de but	[gardjɛ̃ də byt]
goal (score)	but (m)	[byt]
to score a goal	marquer un but	[marke œ̃ byt]

period	période (f)	[perjɔd]
second period	deuxième période (f)	[døzjɛm perjɔd]
substitutes bench	banc (m) des remplaçants	[bɑ̃ de rɑ̃plasɑ̃]

136. Football

| soccer | football (m) | [futbol] |
| soccer player | joueur (m) de football | [ʒwœr də futbol] |

to play soccer	**jouer au football**	[ʒwe o futbɔl]
major league	**ligue** (f) **supérieure**	[lig syperjœr]
soccer club	**club** (m) **de football**	[klœb də futbɔl]
coach	**entraîneur** (m)	[ɑ̃trɛnœr]
owner, proprietor	**propriétaire** (m)	[prɔprijetɛr]
team	**équipe** (f)	[ekip]
team captain	**capitaine** (m) **de l'équipe**	[kapitɛn də lekip]
player	**joueur** (m)	[ʒwœr]
substitute	**remplaçant** (m)	[rɑ̃plasɑ̃]
forward	**attaquant** (m)	[atakɑ̃]
center forward	**avant-centre** (m)	[avɑ̃sɑ̃tr]
striker, scorer	**butteur** (m)	[bytœr]
defender, back	**arrière** (m)	[arjɛr]
halfback	**demi** (m)	[dəmi]
match	**match** (m)	[matʃ]
to meet (vi, vt)	**se rencontrer** (vp)	[sə rɑ̃kɔ̃tre]
final	**finale** (f)	[final]
semi-final	**demi-finale** (f)	[dəmifinal]
championship	**championnat** (m)	[ʃɑ̃pjɔna]
period, half	**mi-temps** (f)	[mitɑ̃]
first period	**première mi-temps** (f)	[prəmjɛr mitɑ̃]
half-time	**mi-temps** (f)	[mitɑ̃]
goal	**but** (m)	[byt]
goalkeeper	**gardien** (m) **de but**	[gardjɛ̃ də byt]
goalpost	**poteau** (m)	[pɔto]
crossbar	**barre** (f)	[bar]
net	**filet** (m)	[filɛ]
to concede a goal	**encaisser un but**	[ɑ̃kese ɑ̃ byt]
ball	**ballon** (m)	[balɔ̃]
pass	**passe** (f)	[pɑs]
kick	**coup** (m)	[ku]
to kick (~ the ball)	**porter un coup**	[pɔrte œ̃ ku]
free kick	**coup** (m) **franc**	[ku frɑ̃]
corner kick	**corner** (m)	[kɔrnɛr]
attack	**attaque** (f)	[atak]
counterattack	**contre-attaque** (f)	[kɔ̃tratak]
combination	**combinaison** (f)	[kɔ̃binɛzɔ̃]
referee	**arbitre** (m)	[arbitr]
to whistle (vi)	**siffler** (vi)	[sifle]
whistle (sound)	**sifflet** (m)	[sifle]
foul, misconduct	**faute** (f)	[fot]
to commit a foul	**commettre un foul**	[kɔmɛtr œ̃ ful]
to send off	**expulser du terrain**	[ɛkspylse dy tɛrɛ̃]
yellow card	**carton** (m) **jaune**	[kartɔ̃ ʒon]

red card	carton (m) rouge	[kartɔ̃ ruʒ]
disqualification	disqualification (f)	[diskalifikasjɔ̃]
to disqualify (vt)	disqualifier (vt)	[diskalifje]

penalty kick	penalty (m)	[penalti]
wall	mur (m)	[myr]
to score (vi, vt)	marquer (vt)	[marke]
goal (score)	but (m)	[byt]
to score a goal	marquer un but	[marke œ̃ byt]

substitution	remplacement (m)	[rɑ̃plasmɑ̃]
to replace (vt)	remplacer (vt)	[rɑ̃plase]
rules	règles (f pl)	[rɛgl]
tactics	tactique (f)	[taktik]

stadium	stade (m)	[stad]
stand (bleachers)	tribune (f)	[tribyn]
fan, supporter	supporteur (m)	[sypɔrtœr]
to shout (vi)	crier (vi)	[krije]

| scoreboard | tableau (m) | [tablo] |
| score | score (m) | [skɔr] |

defeat	défaite (f)	[defɛt]
to lose (not win)	perdre (vi)	[pɛrdr]
draw	match (m) nul	[matʃ nyl]
to draw (vi)	faire match nul	[fɛr matʃ nyl]

| victory | victoire (f) | [viktwar] |
| to win (vi, vt) | gagner (vi, vt) | [gaɲe] |

champion	champion (m)	[ʃɑ̃pjɔ̃]
best (adj)	meilleur (adj)	[mɛjœr]
to congratulate (vt)	féliciter (vt)	[felisite]

commentator	commentateur (m)	[kɔmɑ̃tatœr]
to commentate (vt)	commenter (vt)	[kɔmɑ̃te]
broadcast	retransmission (f)	[rətrɑ̃smisjɔ̃]

137. Alpine skiing

| skis | skis (m pl) | [ski] |
| to ski (vi) | faire du ski | [fɛr dy ski] |

| mountain-ski resort | station (f) de ski | [stasjɔ̃ də ski] |
| ski lift | remontée (f) mécanique | [rəmɔ̃te mekanik] |

ski poles	bâtons (m pl)	[batɔ̃]
slope	pente (f)	[pɑ̃t]
slalom	slalom (m)	[slalɔm]

138. Tennis. Golf

golf	**golf** (m)	[gɔlf]
golf club	**club** (m) **de golf**	[klœb də gɔlf]
golfer	**joueur** (m) **au golf**	[ʒwœr o gɔlf]
hole	**trou** (m)	[tru]
club	**club** (m)	[klœb]
golf trolley	**chariot** (m) **de golf**	[ʃarjo də gɔlf]
tennis	**tennis** (m)	[tenis]
tennis court	**court** (m) **de tennis**	[kur də tenis]
serve	**service** (m)	[sɛrvis]
to serve (vt)	**servir** (vi)	[sɛrvir]
racket	**raquette** (f)	[rakɛt]
net	**filet** (m)	[filɛ]
ball	**balle** (f)	[bal]

139. Chess

chess	**échecs** (m pl)	[eʃɛk]
chessmen	**pièces** (f pl)	[pjɛs]
chess player	**joueur** (m) **d'échecs**	[ʒwœr deʃɛk]
chessboard	**échiquier** (m)	[eʃikje]
chessman	**pièce** (f)	[pjɛs]
White (white pieces)	**blancs** (m pl)	[blɑ̃]
Black (black pieces)	**noirs** (m pl)	[nwar]
pawn	**pion** (m)	[pjɔ̃]
bishop	**fou** (m)	[fu]
knight	**cavalier** (m)	[kavalje]
rook (castle)	**tour** (f)	[tur]
queen	**reine** (f)	[rɛn]
king	**roi** (m)	[rwa]
move	**coup** (m)	[ku]
to move (vi, vt)	**jouer** (vt)	[ʒwe]
to sacrifice (vt)	**sacrifier** (vt)	[sakrifje]
castling	**roque** (m)	[rɔk]
check	**échec** (m)	[eʃɛk]
checkmate	**tapis** (m)	[tapi]
chess tournament	**tournoi** (m) **d'échecs**	[turnwa deʃɛk]
Grand Master	**grand maître** (m)	[grɑ̃ mɛtr]
combination	**combinaison** (f)	[kɔ̃binɛzɔ̃]
game (in chess)	**partie** (f)	[parti]
checkers	**dames** (f pl)	[dam]

140. Boxing

boxing	**boxe** (f)	[bɔks]
fight (bout)	**combat** (m)	[kɔ̃ba]
boxing match	**match** (m)	[matʃ]
round (in boxing)	**round** (m)	[rawnd, rund]
ring	**ring** (m)	[riŋ]
gong	**gong** (m)	[gɔ̃g]
punch	**coup** (m)	[ku]
knock-down	**knock-down** (m)	[nɔkdawn]
knockout	**knock-out** (m)	[nɔkaut]
to knock out	**mettre KO**	[mɛtr kao]
boxing glove	**gant** (m) **de boxe**	[gɑ̃ də bɔks]
referee	**arbitre** (m)	[arbitr]
lightweight	**poids** (m) **léger**	[pwa leʒe]
middleweight	**poids** (m) **moyen**	[pwa mwajɛ̃]
heavyweight	**poids** (m) **lourd**	[pwa lur]

141. Sports. Miscellaneous

Olympic Games	**Jeux** (m pl) **olympiques**	[ʒø zɔlɛ̃pik]
winner	**gagnant** (m)	[gaɲɑ̃]
to be winning	**remporter** (vt)	[rɑ̃pɔrte]
to win (vi)	**gagner** (vi)	[gaɲe]
leader	**leader** (m)	[lidœr]
to lead (vi)	**prendre la tête**	[prɑ̃dr la tɛt]
first place	**première place** (f)	[prəmjɛr plas]
second place	**deuxième place** (f)	[døzjɛm plas]
third place	**troisième place** (f)	[trwazjɛm plas]
medal	**médaille** (f)	[medaj]
trophy	**trophée** (m)	[trɔfe]
prize cup (trophy)	**coupe** (f)	[kup]
prize (in game)	**prix** (m)	[pri]
main prize	**prix** (m) **principal**	[pri prɛ̃sipal]
record	**record** (m)	[rəkɔr]
to set a record	**établir un record**	[etablir œ̃ rəkɔr]
final	**finale** (f)	[final]
final (adj)	**final** (adj)	[final]
champion	**champion** (m)	[ʃɑ̃pjɔ̃]
championship	**championnat** (m)	[ʃɑ̃pjɔna]

stadium	**stade** (m)	[stad]
stand (bleachers)	**tribune** (f)	[tribyn]
fan, supporter	**supporteur** (m)	[sypɔrtœr]
opponent, rival	**adversaire** (m)	[advɛrsɛr]
start	**départ** (m)	[depar]
finish line	**ligne** (f) **d'arrivée**	[liɲ darive]
defeat	**défaite** (f)	[defɛt]
to lose (not win)	**perdre** (vi)	[pɛrdr]
referee	**arbitre** (m)	[arbitr]
jury	**jury** (m)	[ʒyri]
score	**score** (m)	[skɔr]
draw	**match** (m) **nul**	[matʃ nyl]
to draw (vi)	**faire match nul**	[fɛr matʃ nyl]
point	**point** (m)	[pwɛ̃]
result (final score)	**résultat** (m)	[rezylta]
period	**période** (f)	[perjɔd]
half-time	**mi-temps** (f)	[mitɑ̃]
doping	**dopage** (m)	[dɔpaʒ]
to penalize (vt)	**pénaliser** (vt)	[penalize]
to disqualify (vt)	**disqualifier** (vt)	[diskalifje]
apparatus	**agrès** (m)	[agrɛ]
javelin	**lance** (f)	[lɑ̃s]
shot put ball	**poids** (m)	[pwa]
ball (snooker, etc.)	**bille** (f)	[bij]
aim (target)	**cible** (f)	[sibl]
target	**cible** (f)	[sibl]
to shoot (vi)	**tirer** (vi)	[tire]
precise (~ shot)	**précis** (adj)	[presi]
trainer, coach	**entraîneur** (m)	[ɑ̃trɛnœr]
to train (sb)	**entraîner** (vt)	[ɑ̃trene]
to train (vi)	**s'entraîner** (vp)	[sɑ̃trene]
training	**entraînement** (m)	[ɑ̃trɛnmɑ̃]
gym	**salle** (f) **de gym**	[sal də ʒim]
exercise (physical)	**exercice** (m)	[ɛgzɛrsis]
warm-up (of athlete)	**échauffement** (m)	[eʃofmɑ̃]

Education

142. School

school	**école** (f)	[ekɔl]
headmaster	**directeur** (m) **d'école**	[dirɛktœr dekɔl]
pupil (boy)	**élève** (m)	[elɛv]
pupil (girl)	**élève** (f)	[elɛv]
schoolboy	**écolier** (m)	[ekɔlje]
schoolgirl	**écolière** (f)	[ekɔljɛr]
to teach (sb)	**enseigner** (vt)	[ɑ̃seɲe]
to learn (language, etc.)	**apprendre** (vt)	[aprɑ̃dr]
to learn by heart	**apprendre par cœur**	[aprɑ̃dr par kœr]
to study (work to learn)	**apprendre** (vi)	[aprɑ̃dr]
to be in school	**être étudiant, -e**	[ɛtr etydjɑ̃, -ɑ̃t]
to go to school	**aller à l'école**	[ale ɑ lekɔl]
alphabet	**alphabet** (m)	[alfabɛ]
subject (at school)	**matière** (f)	[matjɛr]
classroom	**salle** (f) **de classe**	[sal də klas]
lesson	**leçon** (f)	[ləsɔ̃]
recess	**récréation** (f)	[rekreasjɔ̃]
school bell	**sonnerie** (f)	[sɔnri]
school desk	**pupitre** (m)	[pypitr]
chalkboard	**tableau** (m)	[tablo]
grade	**note** (f)	[nɔt]
good grade	**bonne note** (f)	[bɔnnɔt]
bad grade	**mauvaise note** (f)	[movɛz nɔt]
to give a grade	**donner une note**	[dɔne yn nɔt]
mistake, error	**faute** (f)	[fot]
to make mistakes	**faire des fautes**	[fɛr de fot]
to correct (an error)	**corriger** (vt)	[kɔriʒe]
cheat sheet	**antisèche** (f)	[ɑ̃tisɛʃ]
homework	**devoir** (m)	[dəvwar]
exercise (in education)	**exercice** (m)	[ɛgzɛrsis]
to be present	**être présent**	[ɛtr prezɑ̃]
to be absent	**être absent**	[ɛtr apsɑ̃]
to miss school	**manquer l'école**	[mɑ̃ke lekɔl]

to punish (vt)	**punir** (vt)	[pynir]
punishment	**punition** (f)	[pynisjɔ̃]
conduct (behavior)	**conduite** (f)	[kɔ̃dɥit]

report card	**carnet** (m) **de notes**	[karnɛ də nɔt]
pencil	**crayon** (m)	[krɛjɔ̃]
eraser	**gomme** (f)	[gɔm]
chalk	**craie** (f)	[krɛ]
pencil case	**plumier** (m)	[plymje]

schoolbag	**cartable** (m)	[kartabl]
pen	**stylo** (m)	[stilo]
school notebook	**cahier** (m)	[kaje]
textbook	**manuel** (m)	[manɥɛl]
compasses	**compas** (m)	[kɔ̃pa]

| to draw (a blueprint, etc.) | **dessiner** (vt) | [desine] |
| technical drawing | **dessin** (m) **technique** | [desɛ̃ tɛknik] |

poem	**poésie** (f)	[pɔezi]
by heart (adv)	**par cœur** (adv)	[par kœr]
to learn by heart	**apprendre par cœur**	[aprɑ̃dr par kœr]

school vacation	**vacances** (f pl)	[vakɑ̃s]
to be on vacation	**être en vacances**	[ɛtr ɑ̃ vakɑ̃s]
to spend one's vacation	**passer les vacances**	[pɑse le vakɑ̃s]

test (written math ~)	**interrogation** (f) **écrite**	[ɛ̃terɔgasjɔ̃ ekrit]
essay (composition)	**composition** (f)	[kɔ̃pozisjɔ̃]
dictation	**dictée** (f)	[dikte]
exam	**examen** (m)	[ɛgzamɛ̃]
to take an exam	**passer les examens**	[pɑse lezɛgzamɛ̃]
experiment (chemical ~)	**expérience** (f)	[ɛksperjɑ̃s]

143. College. University

academy	**académie** (f)	[akademi]
university	**université** (f)	[ynivɛrsite]
faculty (section)	**faculté** (f)	[fakylte]

student (masc.)	**étudiant** (m)	[etydjɑ̃]
student (fem.)	**étudiante** (f)	[etydjɑ̃t]
lecturer (teacher)	**enseignant** (m)	[ɑ̃sɛɲɑ̃]

lecture hall, room	**salle** (f)	[sal]
graduate	**licencié** (m)	[lisɑ̃sje]
diploma	**diplôme** (m)	[diplom]
dissertation	**thèse** (f)	[tɛz]
study (report)	**étude** (f)	[etyd]
laboratory	**laboratoire** (m)	[labɔratwar]

lecture	**cours** (m)	[kur]
course mate	**camarade** (m) **de cours**	[kamarad də kur]
scholarship	**bourse** (f)	[burs]
academic degree	**grade** (m) **universitaire**	[grad yniversitɛr]

144. Sciences. Disciplines

mathematics	**mathématiques** (f pl)	[matematik]
algebra	**algèbre** (f)	[alʒɛbr]
geometry	**géométrie** (f)	[ʒeɔmetri]
astronomy	**astronomie** (f)	[astrɔnɔmi]
biology	**biologie** (f)	[bjɔlɔʒi]
geography	**géographie** (f)	[ʒeɔgrafi]
geology	**géologie** (f)	[ʒeɔlɔʒi]
history	**histoire** (f)	[istwar]
medicine	**médecine** (f)	[medsin]
pedagogy	**pédagogie** (f)	[pedagɔʒi]
law	**droit** (m)	[drwa]
physics	**physique** (f)	[fizik]
chemistry	**chimie** (f)	[ʃimi]
philosophy	**philosophie** (f)	[filɔzɔfi]
psychology	**psychologie** (f)	[psikɔlɔʒi]

145. Writing system. Orthography

grammar	**grammaire** (f)	[gramɛr]
vocabulary	**vocabulaire** (m)	[vɔkabylɛr]
phonetics	**phonétique** (f)	[fɔnetik]
noun	**nom** (m)	[nɔ̃]
adjective	**adjectif** (m)	[adʒɛktif]
verb	**verbe** (m)	[vɛrb]
adverb	**adverbe** (m)	[advɛrb]
pronoun	**pronom** (m)	[prɔnɔ̃]
interjection	**interjection** (f)	[ɛ̃tɛrʒɛksjɔ̃]
preposition	**préposition** (f)	[prepozisjɔ̃]
root	**racine** (f)	[rasin]
ending	**terminaison** (f)	[tɛrminɛzɔ̃]
prefix	**préfixe** (m)	[prefiks]
syllable	**syllabe** (f)	[silab]
suffix	**suffixe** (m)	[syfiks]
stress mark	**accent** (m) **tonique**	[aksã tɔnik]
apostrophe	**apostrophe** (f)	[apɔstrɔf]

period, dot	**point** (m)	[pwɛ̃]
comma	**virgule** (f)	[virgyl]
semicolon	**point** (m) **virgule**	[pwɛ̃ virgyl]

| colon | **deux-points** (m) | [døpwɛ̃] |
| ellipsis | **points** (m pl) **de suspension** | [pwɛ̃ də syspɑ̃sjɔ̃] |

| question mark | **point** (m) **d'interrogation** | [pwɛ̃ dɛ̃terɔgasjɔ̃] |
| exclamation point | **point** (m) **d'exclamation** | [pwɛ̃ dɛksklamasjɔ̃] |

| quotation marks | **guillemets** (m pl) | [gijmɛ] |
| in quotation marks | **entre guillemets** | [ɑ̃tr gijmɛ] |

| parenthesis | **parenthèses** (f pl) | [parɑ̃tɛz] |
| in parenthesis | **entre parenthèses** | [ɑ̃tr parɑ̃tɛz] |

hyphen	**trait** (m) **d'union**	[trɛ dynjɔ̃]
dash	**tiret** (m)	[tire]
space (between words)	**blanc** (m)	[blɑ̃]

| letter | **lettre** (f) | [lɛtr] |
| capital letter | **majuscule** (f) | [maʒyskyl] |

| vowel (n) | **voyelle** (f) | [vwajɛl] |
| consonant (n) | **consonne** (f) | [kɔ̃sɔn] |

sentence	**proposition** (f)	[prɔpozisjɔ̃]
subject	**sujet** (m)	[syʒɛ]
predicate	**prédicat** (m)	[predika]

line	**ligne** (f)	[liɲ]
on a new line	**à la ligne**	[ɑlaliɲ]
paragraph	**paragraphe** (m)	[paragraf]

word	**mot** (m)	[mo]
group of words	**groupe** (m) **de mots**	[grup də mo]
expression	**expression** (f)	[ɛkspresjɔ̃]

| synonym | **synonyme** (m) | [sinɔnim] |
| antonym | **antonyme** (m) | [ɑ̃tɔnim] |

rule	**règle** (f)	[rɛgl]
exception	**exception** (f)	[ɛksɛpsjɔ̃]
correct (adj)	**correct** (adj)	[kɔrɛkt]

conjugation	**conjugaison** (f)	[kɔ̃ʒygɛzɔ̃]
declension	**déclinaison** (f)	[deklinɛzɔ̃]
nominal case	**cas** (m)	[ka]
question	**question** (f)	[kɛstjɔ̃]
to underline (vt)	**souligner** (vt)	[suliɲe]
dotted line	**pointillé** (m)	[pwɛ̃tije]

146. Foreign languages

language	**langue** (f)	[lɑ̃g]
foreign language	**langue** (f) **étrangère**	[lɑ̃g etrɑ̃ʒɛr]
to study (vt)	**étudier** (vt)	[etydje]
to learn (language, etc.)	**apprendre** (vt)	[aprɑ̃dr]

to read (vi, vt)	**lire** (vi, vt)	[lir]
to speak (vi, vt)	**parler** (vi)	[parle]
to understand (vt)	**comprendre** (vt)	[kɔ̃prɑ̃dr]
to write (vt)	**écrire** (vt)	[ekrir]

fast (adv)	**vite** (adv)	[vit]
slowly (adv)	**lentement** (adv)	[lɑ̃tmɑ̃]
fluently (adv)	**couramment** (adv)	[kuramɑ̃]

rules	**règles** (f pl)	[rɛgl]
grammar	**grammaire** (f)	[gramɛr]
vocabulary	**vocabulaire** (m)	[vɔkabylɛr]
phonetics	**phonétique** (f)	[fɔnetik]

textbook	**manuel** (m)	[manɥɛl]
dictionary	**dictionnaire** (m)	[diksjɔnɛr]
teach-yourself book	**manuel** (m) **autodidacte**	[manɥɛl otodidakt]
phrasebook	**guide** (m) **de conversation**	[gid də kɔ̃vɛrsasjɔ̃]

cassette	**cassette** (f)	[kasɛt]
videotape	**cassette** (f) **vidéo**	[kasɛt video]
CD, compact disc	**CD** (m)	[sede]
DVD	**DVD** (m)	[devede]

alphabet	**alphabet** (m)	[alfabɛ]
to spell (vt)	**épeler** (vt)	[eple]
pronunciation	**prononciation** (f)	[prɔnɔ̃sjasjɔ̃]

accent	**accent** (m)	[aksɑ̃]
with an accent	**avec un accent**	[avɛk œn aksɑ̃]
without an accent	**sans accent**	[sɑ̃ zaksɑ̃]

word	**mot** (m)	[mo]
meaning	**sens** (m)	[sɑ̃s]

course (e.g., a French ~)	**cours** (m pl)	[kur]
to sign up	**s'inscrire** (vp)	[sɛ̃skrir]
teacher	**professeur** (m)	[prɔfɛsœr]

translation (process)	**traduction** (f)	[tradyksjɔ̃]
translation (text, etc.)	**traduction** (f)	[tradyksjɔ̃]
translator	**traducteur** (m)	[tradyktœr]
interpreter	**interprète** (m)	[ɛ̃tɛrprɛt]

polyglot	**polyglotte** (m)	[pɔliglɔt]
memory	**mémoire** (f)	[memwar]

147. Fairy tale characters

Santa Claus	**Père Noël** (m)	[pɛr nɔɛl]
Cinderella	**Cendrillon** (f)	[sãdrijõ]
mermaid	**sirène** (f)	[sirɛn]
Neptune	**Neptune** (m)	[nɛptyn]
magician, wizard	**magicien** (m)	[maʒisjɛ̃]
fairy	**fée** (f)	[fe]
magic (adj)	**magique** (adj)	[maʒik]
magic wand	**baguette** (f) **magique**	[bagɛt maʒik]
fairy tale	**conte** (m) **de fées**	[kõt də fe]
miracle	**miracle** (m)	[mirakl]
dwarf	**gnome** (m)	[gnom]
to turn into ...	**se transformer en ...**	[sə trãsfɔrme ã]
ghost	**esprit** (m)	[ɛspri]
phantom	**fantôme** (m)	[fãtom]
monster	**monstre** (m)	[mõstr]
dragon	**dragon** (m)	[dragõ]
giant	**géant** (m)	[ʒeã]

148. Zodiac Signs

Aries	**Bélier** (m)	[belje]
Taurus	**Taureau** (m)	[tɔro]
Gemini	**Gémeaux** (m pl)	[ʒemo]
Cancer	**Cancer** (m)	[kãsɛr]
Leo	**Lion** (m)	[ljõ]
Virgo	**Vierge** (f)	[vjɛrʒ]
Libra	**Balance** (f)	[balãs]
Scorpio	**Scorpion** (m)	[skɔrpjõ]
Sagittarius	**Sagittaire** (m)	[saʒitɛr]
Capricorn	**Capricorne** (m)	[kaprikɔrn]
Aquarius	**Verseau** (m)	[vɛrso]
Pisces	**Poissons** (m pl)	[pwasõ]
character	**caractère** (m)	[karaktɛr]
features of character	**traits** (m pl) **du caractère**	[trɛ dy karaktɛr]
behavior	**conduite** (f)	[kõdµit]
to tell fortunes	**dire la bonne aventure**	[dir la bɔnavãtyr]
fortune-teller	**diseuse** (f) **de bonne aventure**	[dizøz də bɔnavãtyr]
horoscope	**horoscope** (m)	[ɔrɔskɔp]

Arts

theater	**théâtre** (m)	[teɑtr]
opera	**opéra** (m)	[ɔpera]
operetta	**opérette** (f)	[ɔpɛrɛt]
ballet	**ballet** (m)	[balɛ]
theater poster	**affiche** (f)	[afiʃ]
theatrical company	**troupe** (f)	[trup]
tour	**tournée** (f)	[turne]
to be on tour	**être en tournée**	[ɛtr ɑ̃ turne]
to rehearse (vi, vt)	**répéter** (vt)	[repete]
rehearsal	**répétition** (f)	[repetisjɔ̃]
repertoire	**répertoire** (m)	[repɛrtwar]
performance	**représentation** (f)	[rəprezɑ̃tasjɔ̃]
theatrical show	**spectacle** (m)	[spɛktakl]
play	**pièce** (f) **de théâtre**	[pjɛs də teɑtr]
ticket	**billet** (m)	[bijɛ]
Box office	**billetterie** (f pl)	[bijɛtri]
lobby, foyer	**hall** (m)	[ol]
coat check	**vestiaire** (m)	[vɛstjɛr]
coat check tag	**jeton** (m)	[ʒətɔ̃]
binoculars	**jumelles** (f pl)	[ʒymɛl]
usher	**placeur** (m)	[plasœr]
orchestra seats	**parterre** (m)	[partɛr]
balcony	**balcon** (m)	[balkɔ̃]
dress circle	**premier** (m) **balcon**	[prəmje balkɔ̃]
box	**loge** (f)	[lɔʒ]
row	**rang** (m)	[rɑ̃]
seat	**place** (f)	[plas]
audience	**public** (m)	[pyblik]
spectator	**spectateur** (m)	[spɛktatœr]
to clap (vi, vt)	**applaudir** (vi)	[aplodir]
applause	**applaudissements** (m pl)	[aplodismɑ̃]
ovation	**ovation** (f)	[ɔvasjɔ̃]
stage	**scène** (f)	[sɛn]
curtain	**rideau** (m)	[rido]
scenery	**décor** (m)	[dekɔr]
backstage	**coulisses** (f pl)	[kulis]

scene (e.g., the last ~)	scène (f)	[sɛn]
act	acte (m)	[akt]
intermission	entracte (m)	[ãtrakt]

150. Cinema

actor	acteur (m)	[aktœr]
actress	actrice (f)	[aktris]

movies (industry)	cinéma (m)	[sinema]
movie	film (m)	[film]
episode	épisode (m)	[epizɔd]

detective	film (m) policier	[film polisje]
action movie	film (m) d'action	[film daksjõ]
adventure movie	film (m) d'aventures	[film davãtyr]
science fiction movie	film (m) de science-fiction	[film də sjãsfiksjõ]
horror movie	film (m) d'horreur	[film dɔrœr]

comedy movie	comédie (f)	[kɔmedi]
melodrama	mélodrame (m)	[melɔdram]
drama	drame (m)	[dram]

fictional movie	film (m) de fiction	[film də fiksjõ]
documentary	documentaire (m)	[dɔkymãtɛr]
cartoon	dessin (m) animé	[desɛn anime]
silent movies	cinéma (m) muet	[sinema mɥɛ]

role (part)	rôle (m)	[rol]
leading role	rôle (m) principal	[rəʊl prɛ̃sipal]
to play (vi, vt)	jouer (vt)	[ʒwe]

movie star	vedette (f)	[vədɛt]
well-known (adj)	connu (adj)	[kɔny]
famous (adj)	célèbre (adj)	[selɛbr]
popular (adj)	populaire (adj)	[pɔpylɛr]

script (screenplay)	scénario (m)	[senarjo]
scriptwriter	scénariste (m)	[senarist]
movie director	metteur (m) en scène	[mɛtœr ã sɛn]
producer	producteur (m)	[prɔdyktœr]
assistant	assistant (m)	[asistã]
cameraman	opérateur (m)	[ɔperatœr]
stuntman	cascadeur (m)	[kaskadœr]
double	doublure (f)	[dublyr]

to shoot a movie	tourner un film	[turne œ̃ film]
audition, screen test	audition (f)	[odisjõ]
shooting	tournage (m)	[turnaʒ]

movie crew	équipe (f) de tournage	[ekip də turnaʒ]
movie set	plateau (m) de tournage	[plato də turnaʒ]
camera	caméra (f)	[kamera]

movie theater	cinéma (m)	[sinema]
screen (e.g., big ~)	écran (m)	[ekrɑ̃]
to show a movie	donner un film	[dɔne œ̃ film]

soundtrack	piste (f) sonore	[pist sɔnɔr]
special effects	effets (m pl) spéciaux	[efɛ spesjø]
subtitles	sous-titres (m pl)	[sutitr]
credits	générique (m)	[ʒenerik]
translation	traduction (f)	[tradyksjɔ̃]

151. Painting

art	art (m)	[ar]
fine arts	beaux-arts (m pl)	[bozar]
art gallery	galerie (f) d'art	[galri dar]
art exhibition	exposition (f) d'art	[ɛkspozisjɔ̃ dar]

painting (art)	peinture (f)	[pɛ̃tyr]
graphic art	graphique (f)	[grafik]
abstract art	art (m) abstrait	[ar apstrɛ]
impressionism	impressionnisme (m)	[ɛ̃presjɔnism]

picture (painting)	tableau (m)	[tablo]
drawing	dessin (m)	[desɛ̃]
poster	poster (m)	[pɔstɛr]

illustration (picture)	illustration (f)	[ilystrasjɔ̃]
miniature	miniature (f)	[minjatyr]
copy (of painting, etc.)	copie (f)	[kɔpi]
reproduction	reproduction (f)	[rəprɔdyksjɔ̃]

mosaic	mosaïque (f)	[mɔzaik]
stained glass	vitrail (m)	[vitraj]
fresco	fresque (f)	[frɛsk]
engraving	gravure (f)	[gravyr]

bust (sculpture)	buste (m)	[byst]
sculpture	sculpture (f)	[skyltyr]
statue	statue (f)	[staty]
plaster of Paris	plâtre (m)	[plɑtr]
plaster (as adj)	en plâtre	[ɑ̃ plɑtr]

portrait	portrait (m)	[pɔrtrɛ]
self-portrait	autoportrait (m)	[otopɔrtrɛ]
landscape painting	paysage (m)	[peizaʒ]
still life	nature (f) morte	[natyr mɔrt]

caricature	**caricature** (f)	[karikatyr]
sketch	**croquis** (m)	[krɔki]
paint	**peinture** (f)	[pɛ̃tyr]
watercolor	**aquarelle** (f)	[akwarɛl]
oil (paint)	**huile** (f)	[ɥil]
pencil	**crayon** (m)	[krɛjɔ̃]
Indian ink	**encre** (f) **de Chine**	[ɑ̃kr də ʃin]
charcoal	**fusain** (m)	[fyzɛ̃]
to draw (vi, vt)	**dessiner** (vi, vt)	[desine]
to paint (vi, vt)	**peindre** (vi, vt)	[pɛ̃dr]
to pose (vi)	**poser** (vi)	[poze]
artist's model (masc.)	**modèle** (m)	[mɔdɛl]
artist's model (fem.)	**modèle** (f)	[mɔdɛl]
artist (painter)	**peintre** (m)	[pɛ̃tr]
work of art	**œuvre** (f) **d'art**	[œvr dar]
masterpiece	**chef** (m) **d'œuvre**	[ʃɛdœvr]
artist's workshop	**atelier** (m) **d'artiste**	[atəlje dartist]
canvas (cloth)	**toile** (f)	[twal]
easel	**chevalet** (m)	[ʃəvalɛ]
palette	**palette** (f)	[palɛt]
frame (of picture, etc.)	**encadrement** (m)	[ɑ̃kadrəmɑ̃]
restoration	**restauration** (f)	[rɛstɔrasjɔ̃]
to restore (vt)	**restaurer** (vt)	[rɛstɔre]

152. Literature & Poetry

literature	**littérature** (f)	[literatyr]
author (writer)	**auteur** (m)	[otœr]
pseudonym	**pseudonyme** (m)	[psødɔnim]
book	**livre** (m)	[livr]
volume	**volume** (m)	[vɔlym]
table of contents	**table** (f) **des matières**	[tabl de matjɛr]
page	**page** (f)	[paʒ]
main character	**protagoniste** (m)	[prɔtagɔnist]
autograph	**autographe** (m)	[otograf]
short story	**récit** (m)	[resi]
story (novella)	**nouvelle** (f)	[nuvɛl]
novel	**roman** (m)	[rɔmɑ̃]
work (writing)	**œuvre** (f) **littéraire**	[œvr literɛr]
fable	**fable** (f)	[fabl]
detective novel	**roman** (m) **policier**	[rɔmɑ̃ pɔlisje]
poem (verse)	**vers** (m)	[vɛr]

poetry	**poésie** (f)	[pɔezi]
poem (epic, ballad)	**poème** (m)	[pɔɛm]
poet	**poète** (m)	[pɔɛt]

fiction	**belles-lettres** (f pl)	[bɛllɛtr]
science fiction	**science-fiction** (f)	[sjɑ̃sfiksjɔ̃]
adventures	**aventures** (f pl)	[avɑ̃tyr]
educational literature	**littérature** (f) **didactique**	[literatyr didaktik]
children's literature	**littérature** (f) **pour enfants**	[literatyr pur ɑ̃fɑ̃]

153. Circus

circus	**cirque** (m)	[sirk]
chapiteau circus	**chapiteau** (m)	[ʃapito]
program	**programme** (m)	[prɔgram]
performance	**représentation** (f)	[rəprezɑ̃tasjɔ̃]

| act (circus ~) | **numéro** (m) | [nymero] |
| circus ring | **arène** (f) | [arɛn] |

| pantomime (act) | **pantomime** (f) | [pɑ̃tɔmim] |
| clown | **clown** (m) | [klun] |

acrobat	**acrobate** (m)	[akrɔbat]
acrobatics	**acrobatie** (f)	[akrɔbasi]
gymnast	**gymnaste** (m)	[ʒimnast]
gymnastics	**gymnastique** (f)	[ʒimnastik]
somersault	**salto** (m)	[salto]

athlete (strongman)	**hercule** (m)	[ɛrkyl]
animal-tamer	**dompteur** (m)	[dɔ̃tœr]
equestrian	**écuyer** (m)	[ekɥije]
assistant	**assistant** (m)	[asistɑ̃]

stunt	**truc** (m)	[tryk]
magic trick	**tour** (m) **de passe-passe**	[tur də pɑspɑs]
conjurer, magician	**magicien** (m)	[maʒisjɛ̃]

juggler	**jongleur** (m)	[ʒɔ̃glœr]
to juggle (vi, vt)	**jongler** (vi)	[ʒɔ̃gle]
animal trainer	**dresseur** (m)	[drɛsœr]
animal training	**dressage** (m)	[drɛsaʒ]
to train (animals)	**dresser** (vt)	[drese]

154. Music. Pop music

| music | **musique** (f) | [myzik] |
| musician | **musicien** (m) | [myzisjɛ̃] |

musical instrument	**instrument** (m) **de musique**	[ɛ̃strymɑ̃ də myzik]
to play …	**jouer de …**	[ʒwe də]
guitar	**guitare** (f)	[gitar]
violin	**violon** (m)	[vjɔlɔ̃]
cello	**violoncelle** (m)	[vjɔlɔ̃sɛl]
double bass	**contrebasse** (f)	[kɔ̃trəbas]
harp	**harpe** (f)	[arp]
piano	**piano** (m)	[pjano]
grand piano	**piano** (m) **à queue**	[pjano ɑ kø]
organ	**orgue** (m)	[ɔrg]
wind instruments	**instruments** (m pl) **à vent**	[ɛ̃strymɑ̃ ɑ vɑ̃]
oboe	**hautbois** (m)	[obwa]
saxophone	**saxophone** (m)	[saksɔfon]
clarinet	**clarinette** (f)	[klarinɛt]
flute	**flûte** (f)	[flyt]
trumpet	**trompette** (f)	[trɔ̃pɛt]
accordion	**accordéon** (m)	[akɔrdeɔ̃]
drum	**tambour** (m)	[tɑ̃bur]
duo	**duo** (m)	[dyo]
trio	**trio** (m)	[trijo]
quartet	**quartette** (m)	[kwartɛt]
choir	**chœur** (m)	[kœr]
orchestra	**orchestre** (m)	[ɔrkɛstr]
pop music	**musique** (f) **pop**	[myzik pɔp]
rock music	**musique** (f) **rock**	[myzik rɔk]
rock group	**groupe** (m) **de rock**	[grup də rɔk]
jazz	**jazz** (m)	[dʒaz]
idol	**idole** (f)	[idɔl]
admirer, fan	**admirateur** (m)	[admiratœr]
concert	**concert** (m)	[kɔ̃sɛr]
symphony	**symphonie** (f)	[sɛ̃foni]
composition	**œuvre** (f) **musicale**	[œvr myzikal]
to compose (write)	**composer** (vt)	[kɔ̃poze]
singing	**chant** (m)	[ʃɑ̃]
song	**chanson** (f)	[ʃɑ̃sɔ̃]
tune (melody)	**mélodie** (f)	[melɔdi]
rhythm	**rythme** (m)	[ritm]
blues	**blues** (m)	[bluz]
sheet music	**notes** (f pl)	[nɔt]
baton	**baguette** (f)	[bagɛt]
bow	**archet** (m)	[arʃɛ]

| string | **corde** (f) | [kɔrd] |
| case (e.g., guitar ~) | **étui** (m) | [etɥi] |

Rest. Entertainment. Travel

155. Trip. Travel

tourism	tourisme (m)	[turism]
tourist	touriste (m)	[turist]
trip, voyage	voyage (m)	[vwajaʒ]
adventure	aventure (f)	[avɑ̃tyr]
trip, journey	voyage (m)	[vwajaʒ]
vacation	vacances (f pl)	[vakɑ̃s]
to be on vacation	être en vacances	[ɛtr ɑ̃ vakɑ̃s]
rest	repos (m)	[rəpo]
train	train (m)	[trɛ̃]
by train	en train	[ɑ̃ trɛ̃]
airplane	avion (m)	[avjɔ̃]
by airplane	en avion	[ɑn avjɔ̃]
by car	en voiture	[ɑ̃ vwatyr]
by ship	en bateau	[ɑ̃ bato]
luggage	bagage (m)	[bagaʒ]
suitcase, luggage	malle (f)	[mal]
luggage cart	chariot (m)	[ʃarjo]
passport	passeport (m)	[pɑspɔr]
visa	visa (m)	[viza]
ticket	ticket (m)	[tikɛ]
air ticket	billet (m) d'avion	[bijɛ davjɔ̃]
guidebook	guide (m)	[gid]
map	carte (f)	[kart]
area (rural ~)	région (f)	[reʒjɔ̃]
place, site	endroit (m)	[ɑ̃drwa]
exotic (n)	exotisme (m)	[ɛgzɔtism]
exotic (adj)	exotique (adj)	[ɛgzɔtik]
amazing (adj)	étonnant (adj)	[etɔnɑ̃]
group	groupe (m)	[grup]
excursion	excursion (f)	[ɛkskyrsjɔ̃]
guide (person)	guide (m)	[gid]

156. Hotel

| hotel | hôtel (m) | [otɛl] |
| motel | motel (m) | [mɔtɛl] |

three-star	3 étoiles	[trwa zetwal]
five-star	5 étoiles	[sɛ̃k etwal]
to stay (in hotel, etc.)	descendre (vi)	[desɑ̃dr]

room	chambre (f)	[ʃɑ̃br]
single room	chambre (f) simple	[ʃɑ̃br sɛ̃pl]
double room	chambre (f) double	[ʃɑ̃br dubl]
to book a room	réserver une chambre	[rezɛrve yn ʃɑ̃br]

| half board | demi-pension (f) | [dəmipɑ̃sjɔ̃] |
| full board | pension (f) complète | [pɑ̃sjɔ̃ kɔ̃plɛt] |

with bath	avec une salle de bain	[avɛk yn saldəbɛ̃]
with shower	avec une douche	[avɛk yn duʃ]
satellite television	télévision (f) par satellite	[televizjɔ̃ par satelit]
air-conditioner	climatiseur (m)	[klimatizœr]
towel	serviette (f)	[sɛrvjɛt]
key	clé, clef (f)	[kle]

administrator	administrateur (m)	[administratœr]
chambermaid	femme (f) de chambre	[fam də ʃɑ̃br]
porter, bellboy	porteur (m)	[pɔrtœr]
doorman	portier (m)	[pɔrtje]

restaurant	restaurant (m)	[rɛstɔrɑ̃]
pub, bar	bar (m)	[bar]
breakfast	petit déjeuner (m)	[pəti deʒœne]
dinner	dîner (m)	[dine]
buffet	buffet (m)	[byfɛ]

| lobby | hall (m) | [ol] |
| elevator | ascenseur (m) | [asɑ̃sœr] |

| DO NOT DISTURB | PRIÈRE DE NE PAS DÉRANGER | [prijɛr dənəpa derɑ̃ʒe] |
| NO SMOKING | DÉFENSE DE FUMER | [defɑ̃s də fyme] |

157. Books. Reading

book	livre (m)	[livr]
author	auteur (m)	[otœr]
writer	écrivain (m)	[ekrivɛ̃]
to write (~ a book)	écrire (vt)	[ekrir]
reader	lecteur (m)	[lɛktœr]

to read (vi, vt)	**lire** (vi, vt)	[lir]
reading (activity)	**lecture** (f)	[lɛktyr]
silently (to oneself)	**à part soi**	[ɑ par swa]
aloud (adv)	**à haute voix**	[ɑ ot vwa]
to publish (vt)	**éditer** (vt)	[edite]
publishing (process)	**édition** (f)	[edisjɔ̃]
publisher	**éditeur** (m)	[editœr]
publishing house	**maison** (f) **d'édition**	[mɛzɔ̃ dedisjɔ̃]
to come out (be released)	**paraître** (vi)	[parɛtr]
release (of a book)	**sortie** (f)	[sɔrti]
print run	**tirage** (m)	[tiraʒ]
bookstore	**librairie** (f)	[librɛri]
library	**bibliothèque** (f)	[biblijɔtɛk]
story (novella)	**nouvelle** (f)	[nuvɛl]
short story	**récit** (m)	[resi]
novel	**roman** (m)	[rɔmɑ̃]
detective novel	**roman** (m) **policier**	[rɔmɑ̃ pɔlisje]
memoirs	**mémoires** (m pl)	[memwar]
legend	**légende** (f)	[leʒɑ̃d]
myth	**mythe** (m)	[mit]
poetry, poems	**vers** (m pl)	[vɛr]
autobiography	**autobiographie** (f)	[otobjɔgrafi]
selected works	**les œuvres choisies**	[lezœvr ʃwazi]
science fiction	**science-fiction** (f)	[sjɑ̃sfiksjɔ̃]
title	**titre** (m)	[titr]
introduction	**introduction** (f)	[ɛ̃trɔdyksjɔ̃]
title page	**page** (f) **de titre**	[paʒ də titr]
chapter	**chapitre** (m)	[ʃapitr]
extract	**extrait** (m)	[ɛkstrɛ]
episode	**épisode** (m)	[epizɔd]
plot (storyline)	**sujet** (m)	[syʒɛ]
contents	**sommaire** (m)	[sɔmɛr]
table of contents	**table** (f) **des matières**	[tabl de matjɛr]
main character	**protagoniste** (m)	[prɔtagɔnist]
volume	**volume** (m)	[vɔlym]
cover	**couverture** (f)	[kuvɛrtyr]
binding	**reliure** (f)	[rəljyr]
bookmark	**marque-page** (m)	[markpaʒ]
page	**page** (f)	[paʒ]
to flick through	**feuilleter** (vt)	[fœjte]

margins	marges (f pl)	[marʒ]
annotation	annotation (f)	[anɔtasjɔ̃]
footnote	note (f) de bas de page	[nɔt dəba dəpaʒ]

text	texte (m)	[tɛkst]
type, font	police (f)	[pɔlis]
misprint, typo	faute (f) d'impression	[fot dɛ̃presjɔ̃]

translation	traduction (f)	[tradyksjɔ̃]
to translate (vt)	traduire (vt)	[traduir]
original (n)	original (m)	[ɔriʒinal]

famous (adj)	célèbre (adj)	[selɛbr]
unknown (adj)	inconnu (adj)	[ɛ̃kɔny]
interesting (adj)	intéressant (adj)	[ɛ̃terɛsɑ̃]
bestseller	best-seller (m)	[bɛstsɛlœr]

dictionary	dictionnaire (m)	[diksjɔnɛr]
textbook	manuel (m)	[manɥɛl]
encyclopedia	encyclopédie (f)	[ɑ̃siklɔpedi]

158. Hunting. Fishing

hunting	chasse (f)	[ʃas]
to hunt (vi, vt)	chasser (vi, vt)	[ʃase]
hunter	chasseur (m)	[ʃasœr]

to shoot (vi)	tirer (vi)	[tire]
rifle	fusil (m)	[fyzi]
bullet (shell)	cartouche (f)	[kartuʃ]
shot (lead balls)	grains (m pl) de plomb	[grɛ̃ də plɔ̃]

trap (e.g., bear ~)	piège (m) à mâchoires	[pjɛʒ a maʃwar]
snare (for birds, etc.)	piège (m)	[pjɛʒ]
to lay a trap	mettre un piège	[mɛtr œ̃ pjɛʒ]

poacher	braconnier (m)	[brakɔnje]
game (in hunting)	gibier (m)	[ʒibje]
hound dog	chien (m) de chasse	[ʃjɛ̃ də ʃas]
safari	safari (m)	[safari]
mounted animal	animal (m) empaillé	[animal ɑ̃paje]

fisherman	pêcheur (m)	[pɛʃœr]
fishing	pêche (f)	[pɛʃ]
to fish (vi)	pêcher (vi)	[peʃe]

fishing rod	canne (f) à pêche	[kan a pɛʃ]
fishing line	ligne (f) de pêche	[liɲ də pɛʃ]
hook	hameçon (m)	[amsɔ̃]
float	flotteur (m)	[flɔtœr]

bait	amorce (f)	[amɔrs]
to cast a line	lancer la ligne	[lɑ̃se la liɲ]
to bite (ab. fish)	mordre (vt)	[mɔrdr]
catch (of fish)	pêche (f)	[pɛʃ]
ice-hole	trou (m) dans la glace	[tru dɑ̃ la glas]
fishing net	filet (m)	[filɛ]
boat	barque (f)	[bark]
to net (catch with net)	pêcher au filet	[peʃe o filɛ]
to cast the net	jeter un filet	[ʒəte ɑ̃ filɛ]
to haul in the net	retirer le filet	[rətire lə filɛ]
whaler (person)	baleinier (m)	[balenje]
whaleboat	baleinière (f)	[balenjɛr]
harpoon	harpon (m)	[arpɔ̃]

159. Games. Billiards

billiards	billard (m)	[bijar]
billiard room, hall	salle (f) de billard	[sal də bijar]
ball	bille (f) de billard	[bij də bijar]
to pocket a ball	empocher une bille	[ɑ̃pɔʃe yn bij]
cue	queue (f)	[kø]
pocket	poche (f)	[pɔʃ]

160. Games. Playing cards

diamonds	carreau (m)	[karo]
spades	pique (m)	[pik]
hearts	cœur (m)	[kœr]
clubs	trèfle (m)	[trɛfl]
ace	as (m)	[as]
king	roi (m)	[rwa]
queen	dame (f)	[dam]
jack, knave	valet (m)	[valɛ]
playing card	carte (f)	[kart]
cards	jeu (m) de cartes	[ʒø də kart]
trump	atout (m)	[atu]
deck of cards	paquet (m) de cartes	[pakɛ də kart]
point	point (m)	[pwɛ̃]
to deal (vi, vt)	distribuer (vt)	[distribɥe]
to shuffle (cards)	battre les cartes	[batr lekart]
lead, turn (n)	tour (m)	[tur]
cardsharp	tricheur (m)	[triʃœr]

161. Casino. Roulette

casino	**casino** (m)	[kazino]
roulette (game)	**roulette** (f)	[rulɛt]
bet, stake	**mise** (f)	[miz]
to place bets	**miser** (vt)	[mize]
red	**rouge** (m)	[ruʒ]
black	**noir** (m)	[nwar]
to bet on red	**miser sur le rouge**	[mize syr lə ruʒ]
to bet on black	**miser sur le noir**	[mize syr lə nwar]
croupier (dealer)	**croupier** (m)	[krupje]
to turn the wheel	**faire tourner la roue**	[fɛr turne la ru]
rules (of game)	**règles** (f pl) **du jeu**	[rɛgl dy ʒø]
chip	**fiche** (f)	[fiʃ]
to win (vi, vt)	**gagner** (vi, vt)	[gaɲe]
winnings	**gain** (m)	[gɛ̃]
to lose (~ 100 dollars)	**perdre** (vi)	[pɛrdr]
loss	**perte** (f)	[pɛrt]
player	**joueur** (m)	[ʒwœr]
blackjack (card game)	**black-jack** (m)	[blakʒak]
craps (dice game)	**jeu** (m) **de dés**	[ʒø də de]
dice	**dés** (m pl)	[de]
slot machine	**machine** (f) **à sous**	[maʃin a su]

162. Rest. Games. Miscellaneous

to walk, to stroll (vi)	**se promener** (vp)	[sə prɔmne]
walk, stroll	**promenade** (f)	[prɔmnad]
road trip	**tour** (m), **promenade** (f)	[tur], [prɔmnad]
adventure	**aventure** (f)	[avɑ̃tyr]
picnic	**pique-nique** (m)	[piknik]
game (chess, etc.)	**jeu** (m)	[ʒø]
player	**joueur** (m)	[ʒwœr]
game (one ~ of chess)	**partie** (f)	[parti]
collector (e.g., philatelist)	**collectionneur** (m)	[kɔlɛksjɔnœr]
to collect (vt)	**collectionner** (vt)	[kɔlɛksjɔne]
collection	**collection** (f)	[kɔlɛksjɔ̃]
crossword puzzle	**mots** (m pl) **croisés**	[mo krwaze]
racetrack (hippodrome)	**hippodrome** (m)	[ipɔdrom]
discotheque	**discothèque** (f)	[diskɔtɛk]
sauna	**sauna** (m)	[sona]

lottery	**loterie** (f)	[lɔtri]
camping trip	**trekking** (m)	[trɛkiŋ]
camp	**camp** (m)	[kɑ̃]
tent (for camping)	**tente** (f)	[tɑ̃t]
compass	**boussole** (f)	[busɔl]
camper	**campeur** (m)	[kɑ̃pœr]
to watch (movie, etc.)	**regarder** (vt)	[rəgarde]
viewer	**téléspectateur** (m)	[telespɛktatœr]
TV show	**émission** (f) **de télé**	[emisjɔ̃ də tele]

163. Photography

camera (photo)	**appareil** (m) **photo**	[aparɛj foto]
photo, picture	**photo** (f)	[foto]
photographer	**photographe** (m)	[fotɔgraf]
photo studio	**studio** (m) **de photo**	[stydjo də foto]
photo album	**album** (m) **de photos**	[albɔm də foto]
camera lens	**objectif** (m)	[ɔbʒɛktif]
telephoto lens	**téléobjectif** (m)	[teleɔbʒɛktif]
filter	**filtre** (m)	[filtr]
lens	**lentille** (f)	[lɑ̃tij]
optics (high-quality ~)	**optique** (f)	[ɔptik]
diaphragm (aperture)	**diaphragme** (m)	[djafragm]
exposure time	**temps** (m) **de pose**	[tɑ̃ də poz]
viewfinder	**viseur** (m)	[vizœr]
digital camera	**appareil** (m) **photo numérique**	[aparɛj foto nymerik]
tripod	**trépied** (m)	[trepje]
flash	**flash** (m)	[flaʃ]
to photograph (vt)	**photographier** (vt)	[fotɔgrafje]
to take pictures	**prendre en photo**	[prɑ̃dr ɑ̃ foto]
to be photographed	**se faire prendre en photo**	[sə fɛr prɑ̃dr ɑ̃ foto]
focus	**mise** (f) **au point**	[miz o pwɛ̃]
to adjust the focus	**mettre au point**	[mɛtr o pwɛ̃]
sharp, in focus (adj)	**net** (adj)	[nɛt]
sharpness	**netteté** (f)	[nɛtte]
contrast	**contraste** (m)	[kɔ̃trast]
contrasty (adj)	**contrasté** (adj)	[kɔ̃traste]
picture (photo)	**épreuve** (f)	[eprœv]
negative (n)	**négatif** (m)	[negatif]

film (a roll of ~)	pellicule (f)	[pelikyl]
frame (still)	image (f)	[imaʒ]
to print (photos)	tirer (vt)	[tire]

164. Beach. Swimming

beach	plage (f)	[plaʒ]
sand	sable (m)	[sabl]
deserted (beach)	désert (adj)	[dezɛr]

suntan	bronzage (m)	[brɔ̃zaʒ]
to get a tan	se bronzer (vp)	[sə brɔ̃ze]
tan (adj)	bronzé (adj)	[brɔ̃ze]
sunscreen	crème (f) solaire	[krɛm sɔlɛr]

bikini	bikini (m)	[bikini]
bathing suit	maillot (m) de bain	[majo də bɛ̃]
swim briefs	slip (m) de bain	[slip də bɛ̃]

swimming pool	piscine (f)	[pisin]
to swim (vi)	nager (vi)	[naʒe]
shower	douche (f)	[duʃ]
to change (one's clothes)	se changer (vp)	[sə ʃɔ̃ʒe]
towel	serviette (f)	[sɛrvjɛt]

| boat | barque (f) | [bark] |
| motorboat | canot (m) à moteur | [kano ɑ mɔtœr] |

water ski	ski (m) nautique	[ski notik]
paddle boat	pédalo (m)	[pedalo]
surfing	surf (m)	[sœrf]
surfer	surfeur (m)	[sœrfœr]

scuba set	scaphandre (m) autonome	[skafɑ̃dr ɔtɔnɔm]
flippers (swimfins)	palmes (f pl)	[palm]
mask	masque (m)	[mask]
diver	plongeur (m)	[plɔ̃ʒœr]
to dive (vi)	plonger (vi)	[plɔ̃ʒe]
underwater (adv)	sous l'eau	[su lo]

beach umbrella	parasol (m)	[parasɔl]
beach chair	chaise (f) longue	[ʃɛz lɔ̃g]
sunglasses	lunettes (f pl) de soleil	[lynɛt də sɔlɛj]
air mattress	matelas (m) pneumatique	[matla pnømatik]

to play (amuse oneself)	jouer (vi)	[ʒwe]
to go for a swim	se baigner (vp)	[sə beɲe]
beach ball	ballon (m) de plage	[balɔ̃ də plaʒ]
to inflate (vt)	gonfler (vt)	[gɔ̃fle]

inflatable, air- (adj)	**gonflable** (adj)	[gɔ̃flabl]
wave	**vague** (f)	[vag]
buoy	**bouée** (f)	[bwe]
to drown (ab. person)	**se noyer** (vp)	[sə nwaje]
to save, to rescue	**sauver** (vt)	[sove]
life vest	**gilet** (m) **de sauvetage**	[ʒilɛ də sovtaʒ]
to observe, to watch	**observer** (vt)	[ɔpsɛrve]
lifeguard	**maître nageur** (m)	[mɛtr naʒœr]

TECHNICAL EQUIPMENT. TRANSPORTATION

Technical equipment

165. Computer

computer	**ordinateur** (m)	[ɔrdinatœr]
notebook, laptop	**PC** (m) **portable**	[pese pɔrtabl]
to turn on	**allumer** (vt)	[alyme]
to turn off	**éteindre** (vt)	[etɛ̃dr]
keyboard	**clavier** (m)	[klavje]
key	**touche** (f)	[tuʃ]
mouse	**souris** (f)	[suri]
mouse pad	**tapis** (m) **de souris**	[tapi də suri]
button	**bouton** (m)	[butɔ̃]
cursor	**curseur** (m)	[kyrsœr]
monitor	**moniteur** (m)	[mɔnitœr]
screen	**écran** (m)	[ekrɑ̃]
hard disk	**disque** (m) **dur**	[disk dyr]
hard disk volume	**capacité** (f) **du disque dur**	[kapasite dy disk dyr]
memory	**mémoire** (f)	[memwar]
random access memory	**mémoire** (f) **vive**	[memwar viv]
file	**fichier** (m)	[fiʃje]
folder	**dossier** (m)	[dosje]
to open (vt)	**ouvrir** (vt)	[uvrir]
to close (vt)	**fermer** (vt)	[fɛrme]
to save (vt)	**sauvegarder** (vt)	[sovgarde]
to delete (vt)	**supprimer** (vt)	[syprime]
to copy (vt)	**copier** (vt)	[kɔpje]
to sort (vt)	**trier** (vt)	[trije]
to transfer (copy)	**copier** (vt)	[kɔpje]
program	**programme** (m)	[prɔgram]
software	**logiciel** (m)	[lɔʒisjɛl]
programmer	**programmeur** (m)	[prɔgramœr]
to program (vt)	**programmer** (vt)	[prɔgrame]
hacker	**hacker** (m)	[akeːr]
password	**mot** (m) **de passe**	[mo də pɑs]

virus	**virus** (m)	[virys]
to find, to detect	**découvrir** (vt)	[dekuvrir]
byte	**bit** (m)	[bit]
megabyte	**mégabit** (m)	[megabit]
data	**données** (f pl)	[dɔne]
database	**base** (f) **de données**	[baz də dɔne]
cable (USB, etc.)	**câble** (m)	[kabl]
to disconnect (vt)	**déconnecter** (vt)	[dekɔnɛkte]
to connect (sth to sth)	**connecter** (vt)	[kɔnɛkte]

166. Internet. E-mail

Internet	**Internet** (m)	[ɛ̃tɛrnɛt]
browser	**navigateur** (m)	[navigatœr]
search engine	**moteur** (m) **de recherche**	[mɔtœr də rəʃɛrʃ]
provider	**fournisseur** (m) **d'accès**	[furnisœr daksɛ]
web master	**administrateur** (m) **de site**	[administratœr də sit]
website	**site** (m) **web**	[sit wɛb]
web page	**page** (f) **web**	[paʒ wɛb]
address	**adresse** (f)	[adrɛs]
address book	**carnet** (m) **d'adresses**	[karnɛ dadrɛs]
mailbox	**boîte** (f) **de réception**	[bwat də resɛpsjɔ̃]
mail	**courrier** (m)	[kurje]
message	**message** (m)	[mesaʒ]
incoming messages	**messages** (pl) **entrants**	[mesaʒ ɑ̃trɑ̃]
outgoing messages	**messages** (pl) **sortants**	[mesaʒ sɔrtɑ̃]
sender	**expéditeur** (m)	[ɛkspeditœr]
to send (vt)	**envoyer** (vt)	[ɑ̃vwaje]
sending (of mail)	**envoi** (m)	[ɑ̃vwa]
receiver	**destinataire** (m)	[dɛstinatɛr]
to receive (vt)	**recevoir** (vt)	[rəsəvwar]
correspondence	**correspondance** (f)	[kɔrɛspɔ̃dɑ̃s]
to correspond (vi)	**être en correspondance**	[ɛtr ɑ̃ kɔrɛspɔ̃dɑ̃s]
file	**fichier** (m)	[fiʃje]
to download (vt)	**télécharger** (vt)	[teleʃarʒe]
to create (vt)	**créer** (vt)	[kree]
to delete (vt)	**supprimer** (vt)	[syprime]
deleted (adj)	**supprimé** (adj)	[syprime]
connection (ADSL, etc.)	**connexion** (f)	[kɔnɛksjɔ̃]

speed	**vitesse** (f)	[vitɛs]
modem	**modem** (m)	[mɔdɛm]
access	**accès** (m)	[aksɛ]
port (e.g., input ~)	**port** (m)	[pɔr]

| connection (make a ~) | **connexion** (f) | [kɔnɛksjõ] |
| to connect to … (vi) | **se connecter à …** | [sə kɔnɛkte a] |

| to select (vt) | **sélectionner** (vt) | [selɛksjɔne] |
| to search (for …) | **rechercher** (vt) | [rəʃɛrʃe] |

167. Electricity

electricity	**électricité** (f)	[elɛktrisite]
electrical (adj)	**électrique** (adj)	[elɛktrik]
electric power station	**centrale** (f) **électrique**	[sãtral elɛktrik]
energy	**énergie** (f)	[enɛrʒi]
electric power	**énergie** (f) **électrique**	[enɛrʒi elɛktrik]

light bulb	**ampoule** (f)	[ãpul]
flashlight	**torche** (f)	[tɔrʃ]
street light	**réverbère** (m)	[revɛrbɛr]

light	**lumière** (f)	[lymjɛr]
to turn on	**allumer** (vt)	[alyme]
to turn off	**éteindre** (vt)	[etɛ̃dr]
to turn off the light	**éteindre la lumière**	[etɛ̃dr la lymjɛr]

to burn out (vi)	**être grillé**	[ɛtr grije]
short circuit	**court-circuit** (m)	[kursirkɥi]
broken wire	**rupture** (f)	[ryptyr]
contact	**contact** (m)	[kõtakt]

light switch	**interrupteur** (m)	[ɛ̃teryptœr]
wall socket	**prise** (f)	[priz]
plug	**fiche** (f)	[fiʃ]
extension cord	**rallonge** (f)	[ralõʒ]

fuse	**fusible** (m)	[fyzibl]
cable, wire	**fil** (m)	[fil]
wiring	**installation** (f) **électrique**	[ɛ̃stalasjõ elɛktrik]

ampere	**ampère** (m)	[ãpɛr]
amperage	**intensité** (f) **du courant**	[ɛ̃tãsite dy kurã]
volt	**volt** (m)	[vɔlt]
voltage	**tension** (f)	[tãsjõ]

electrical device	**appareil** (m) **électrique**	[aparɛj elɛktrik]
indicator	**indicateur** (m)	[ɛ̃dikatœr]
electrician	**électricien** (m)	[elɛktrisjɛ̃]

to solder (vt)	**souder** (vt)	[sude]
soldering iron	**fer** (m) **à souder**	[fɛr asude]
electric current	**courant** (m)	[kurɑ̃]

168. Tools

tool, instrument	**outil** (m)	[uti]
tools	**outils** (m pl)	[uti]
equipment (factory ~)	**équipement** (m)	[ekipmɑ̃]
hammer	**marteau** (m)	[marto]
screwdriver	**tournevis** (m)	[turnəvis]
ax	**hache** (f)	[aʃ]
saw	**scie** (f)	[si]
to saw (vt)	**scier** (vt)	[sje]
plane (tool)	**rabot** (m)	[rabo]
to plane (vt)	**raboter** (vt)	[rabɔte]
soldering iron	**fer** (m) **à souder**	[fɛr asude]
to solder (vt)	**souder** (vt)	[sude]
file (for metal)	**lime** (f)	[lim]
carpenter pincers	**tenailles** (f pl)	[tənɑj]
lineman's pliers	**pince** (f) **plate**	[pɛ̃s plat]
chisel	**ciseau** (m)	[sizo]
drill bit	**foret** (m)	[fɔrɛ]
electric drill	**perceuse** (f)	[pɛrsøz]
to drill (vi, vt)	**percer** (vt)	[pɛrse]
knife	**couteau** (m)	[kuto]
pocket knife	**canif** (m)	[kanif]
folding (~ knife)	**pliant** (adj)	[plijɑ̃]
blade	**lame** (f)	[lam]
sharp (blade, etc.)	**bien affilé** (adj)	[bjɛn afile]
blunt (adj)	**émoussé** (adj)	[emuse]
to become blunt	**s'émousser** (vp)	[semuse]
to sharpen (vt)	**affiler** (vt)	[afile]
bolt	**boulon** (m)	[bulɔ̃]
nut	**écrou** (m)	[ekru]
thread (of a screw)	**filetage** (m)	[filtaʒ]
wood screw	**vis** (f) **à bois**	[vi za bwa]
nail	**clou** (m)	[klu]
nailhead	**tête** (f) **de clou**	[tɛt də klu]
ruler (for measuring)	**règle** (f)	[rɛgl]
tape measure	**mètre** (m) **à ruban**	[mɛtr a rybɑ̃]
spirit level	**niveau** (m) **à bulle**	[nivo a byl]

magnifying glass	**loupe** (f)	[lup]
measuring instrument	**appareil** (m) **de mesure**	[aparɛj də məzyr]
to measure (vt)	**mesurer** (vt)	[məzyre]
scale (of thermometer, etc.)	**échelle** (f)	[eʃɛl]
readings	**relevé** (m)	[rəlve]
compressor	**compresseur** (m)	[kɔ̃presœr]
microscope	**microscope** (m)	[mikrɔskɔp]
pump (e.g., water ~)	**pompe** (f)	[pɔ̃p]
robot	**robot** (m)	[rɔbo]
laser	**laser** (m)	[lazɛr]
wrench	**clé** (f) **de serrage**	[kle də seraʒ]
adhesive tape	**ruban** (m) **adhésif**	[rybɑ̃ adezif]
glue	**colle** (f)	[kɔl]
emery paper	**papier** (m) **d'émeri**	[papje dɛmri]
spring	**ressort** (m)	[rəsɔr]
magnet	**aimant** (m)	[ɛmɑ̃]
gloves	**gants** (m pl)	[gɑ̃]
rope	**corde** (f)	[kɔrd]
cord	**cordon** (m)	[kɔrdɔ̃]
wire (e.g., telephone ~)	**fil** (m)	[fil]
cable	**câble** (m)	[kabl]
sledgehammer	**masse** (f)	[mas]
crowbar	**pic** (m)	[pik]
ladder	**escabeau** (m)	[ɛskabo]
stepladder	**échelle** (f) **double**	[eʃɛl dubl]
to screw (tighten)	**visser** (vt)	[vise]
to unscrew, untwist (vt)	**dévisser** (vt)	[devise]
to tighten (vt)	**serrer** (vt)	[sere]
to glue, to stick	**coller** (vt)	[kɔle]
to cut (vt)	**couper** (vt)	[kupe]
malfunction (fault)	**défaut** (m)	[defo]
repair (mending)	**réparation** (f)	[reparasjɔ̃]
to repair, to mend (vt)	**réparer** (vt)	[repare]
to adjust (machine, etc.)	**régler** (vt)	[regle]
to check (to examine)	**vérifier** (vt)	[verifje]
checking	**vérification** (f)	[verifikasjɔ̃]
readings	**relevé** (m)	[rəlve]
reliable (machine)	**fiable** (adj)	[fjabl]
complicated (adj)	**complexe** (adj)	[kɔ̃plɛks]
to rust (get rusted)	**rouiller** (vi)	[ruje]
rusty, rusted (adj)	**rouillé** (adj)	[ruje]
rust	**rouille** (f)	[ruj]

Transportation

169. Airplane

airplane	avion (m)	[avjɔ̃]
air ticket	billet (m) d'avion	[bijɛ davjɔ̃]
airline	compagnie (f) aérienne	[kɔ̃paɲi aerjɛn]
airport	aéroport (m)	[aeropɔr]
supersonic (adj)	supersonique (adj)	[sypɛrsɔnik]
captain	commandant (m) de bord	[kɔmɑ̃dɑ̃ də bɔr]
crew	équipage (m)	[ekipaʒ]
pilot	pilote (m)	[pilɔt]
flight attendant	hôtesse (f) de l'air	[otɛs də lɛr]
navigator	navigateur (m)	[navigatœr]
wings	ailes (f pl)	[ɛl]
tail	queue (f)	[kø]
cockpit	cabine (f)	[kabin]
engine	moteur (m)	[mɔtœr]
undercarriage	train (m) d'atterrissage	[trɛ̃ daterisaʒ]
turbine	turbine (f)	[tyrbin]
propeller	hélice (f)	[elis]
black box	boîte (f) noire	[bwat nwar]
control column	gouvernail (m)	[guvɛrnaj]
fuel	carburant (m)	[karbyrɑ̃]
safety card	consigne (f) de sécurité	[kɔ̃siɲ də sekyrite]
oxygen mask	masque (m) à oxygène	[mask ɔ ɔksiʒɛn]
uniform	uniforme (m)	[ynifɔrm]
life vest	gilet (m) de sauvetage	[ʒilɛ də sovtaʒ]
parachute	parachute (m)	[paraʃyt]
takeoff	décollage (m)	[dekɔlaʒ]
to take off (vi)	décoller (vi)	[dekɔle]
runway	piste (f) de décollage	[pist dekɔlaʒ]
visibility	visibilité (f)	[vizibilite]
flight (act of flying)	vol (m)	[vɔl]
altitude	altitude (f)	[altityd]
air pocket	trou (m) d'air	[tru dɛr]
seat	place (f)	[plas]
headphones	écouteurs (m pl)	[ekutœr]
folding tray	tablette (f)	[tablɛt]

| airplane window | **hublot** (m) | [yblo] |
| aisle | **couloir** (m) | [kulwar] |

170. Train

train	**train** (m)	[trɛ̃]
suburban train	**train** (m) **de banlieue**	[trɛ̃ də bɑ̃ljø]
express train	**TGV** (m)	[teʒeve]
diesel locomotive	**locomotive** (f) **diesel**	[lɔkɔmɔtiv djezɛl]
steam engine	**locomotive** (f) **à vapeur**	[lɔkɔmɔtiv ɑ vapœr]
passenger car	**wagon** (m)	[vagɔ̃]
dining car	**wagon-restaurant** (m)	[vagɔ̃rɛstɔrɑ̃]
rails	**rails** (m pl)	[raj]
railroad	**chemin** (m) **de fer**	[ʃəmɛ̃ də fɛr]
railway tie	**traverse** (f)	[travɛrs]
platform (railway ~)	**quai** (m)	[kɛ]
track (~ 1, 2, etc.)	**voie** (f)	[vwa]
semaphore	**sémaphore** (m)	[semafɔr]
station	**station** (f)	[stasjɔ̃]
engineer	**conducteur** (m) **de train**	[kɔ̃dyktœr də trɛ̃]
porter (of luggage)	**porteur** (m)	[pɔrtœr]
train steward	**steward** (m)	[stiwart]
passenger	**passager** (m)	[pɑsaʒe]
conductor	**contrôleur** (m)	[kɔ̃trolœr]
corridor (in train)	**couloir** (m)	[kulwar]
emergency break	**frein** (m) **d'urgence**	[frɛ̃ dyrʒɑ̃s]
compartment	**compartiment** (m)	[kɔ̃partimɑ̃]
berth	**couchette** (f)	[kuʃɛt]
upper berth	**couchette** (f) **d'en haut**	[kuʃɛt dɛ̃ o]
lower berth	**couchette** (f) **d'en bas**	[kuʃɛt dɛ̃ba]
bed linen	**linge** (m) **de lit**	[lɛ̃ʒ də li]
ticket	**ticket** (m)	[tikɛ]
schedule	**horaire** (m)	[ɔrɛr]
information display	**tableau** (m) **d'informations**	[tablo dɛ̃fɔrmasjɔ̃]
to leave, to depart	**partir** (vi)	[partir]
departure (of train)	**départ** (m)	[depar]
to arrive (ab. train)	**arriver** (vi)	[arive]
arrival	**arrivée** (f)	[arive]
to arrive by train	**arriver en train**	[arive ɑ̃ trɛ̃]
to get on the train	**prendre le train**	[prɑ̃dr lə trɛ̃]

to get off the train	descendre du train	[desɑ̃dr dy trɛ̃]
train wreck	accident (m) ferroviaire	[aksidɑ̃ ferɔvjɛr]
to be derailed	dérailler (vi)	[deraje]

steam engine	locomotive (f) à vapeur	[lɔkɔmɔtiv a vapœr]
stoker, fireman	chauffeur (m)	[ʃofœr]
firebox	chauffe (f)	[ʃof]
coal	charbon (m)	[ʃarbɔ̃]

171. Ship

| ship | bateau (m) | [bato] |
| vessel | navire (m) | [navir] |

steamship	bateau (m) à vapeur	[bato a vapœr]
riverboat	paquebot (m)	[pakbo]
ocean liner	bateau (m) de croisière	[bato də krwazjɛr]
cruiser	croiseur (m)	[krwazœr]

yacht	yacht (m)	[jot]
tugboat	remorqueur (m)	[rəmɔrkœr]
barge	péniche (f)	[peniʃ]
ferry	ferry (m)	[feri]

sailing ship	voilier (m)	[vwalje]
brigantine	brigantin (m)	[brigɑ̃tɛ̃]
ice breaker	brise-glace (m)	[brizglas]
submarine	sous-marin (m)	[sumarɛ̃]

boat (flat-bottomed ~)	canot (m) à rames	[kano a ram]
dinghy	dinghy (m)	[diŋgi]
lifeboat	canot (m) de sauvetage	[kano də sovtaʒ]
motorboat	canot (m) à moteur	[kano a mɔtœr]

captain	capitaine (m)	[kapitɛn]
seaman	matelot (m)	[matlo]
sailor	marin (m)	[marɛ̃]
crew	équipage (m)	[ekipaʒ]

boatswain	maître (m) d'équipage	[mɛtr dekipaʒ]
ship's boy	mousse (m)	[mus]
cook	cuisinier (m) du bord	[kɥizinje dy bɔr]
ship's doctor	médecin (m) de bord	[medsɛ̃ də bɔr]

deck	pont (m)	[pɔ̃]
mast	mât (m)	[ma]
sail	voile (f)	[vwal]
hold	cale (f)	[kal]
bow (prow)	proue (f)	[pru]
stern	poupe (f)	[pup]

| oar | **rame** (f) | [ram] |
| screw propeller | **hélice** (f) | [elis] |

cabin	**cabine** (f)	[kabin]
wardroom	**carré** (m) **des officiers**	[kare dezɔfisje]
engine room	**salle** (f) **des machines**	[sal de maʃin]
bridge	**passerelle** (f)	[pɑsrɛl]
radio room	**cabine** (f) **de T.S.F.**	[kabin də teɛsɛf]
wave (radio)	**onde** (f)	[ɔ̃d]
logbook	**journal** (m) **de bord**	[ʒurnal də bɔr]

spyglass	**longue-vue** (f)	[lɔ̃gvy]
bell	**cloche** (f)	[klɔʃ]
flag	**pavillon** (m)	[pavijɔ̃]
rope (mooring ~)	**grosse corde** (f) **tressée**	[gros kɔrd trese]
knot (bowline, etc.)	**nœud** (m) **marin**	[nø marɛ̃]

| deckrail | **rampe** (f) | [rɑ̃p] |
| gangway | **passerelle** (f) | [pɑsrɛl] |

anchor	**ancre** (f)	[ɑ̃kr]
to weigh anchor	**lever l'ancre**	[ləve lɑ̃kr]
to drop anchor	**jeter l'ancre**	[ʒəte lɑ̃kr]
anchor chain	**chaîne** (f) **d'ancrage**	[ʃɛn dɑ̃kraʒ]

port (harbor)	**port** (m)	[pɔr]
berth, wharf	**embarcadère** (m)	[ɑ̃barkadɛr]
to berth (moor)	**accoster** (vi)	[akɔste]
to cast off	**larguer les amarres**	[large lezamar]

trip, voyage	**voyage** (m)	[vwajaʒ]
cruise (sea trip)	**croisière** (f)	[krwazjɛr]
course (route)	**cap** (m)	[kap]
route (itinerary)	**itinéraire** (m)	[itinerɛr]

fairway	**chenal** (m)	[ʃənal]
shallows (shoal)	**bas-fond** (m)	[bafɔ̃]
to run aground	**échouer sur un bas-fond**	[eʃwe syr œ̃ bafɔ̃]

storm	**tempête** (f)	[tɑ̃pɛt]
signal	**signal** (m)	[siɲal]
to sink (vi)	**sombrer** (vi)	[sɔ̃bre]
Man overboard!	**Un homme à la mer!**	[ynɔm alamɛr]
SOS	**SOS** (m)	[ɛsoɛs]
ring buoy	**bouée** (f) **de sauvetage**	[bwe də sovtaʒ]

172. Airport

| airport | **aéroport** (m) | [aeropɔr] |
| airplane | **avion** (m) | [avjɔ̃] |

airline	**compagnie** (f) **aérienne**	[kɔ̃paɲi aerjɛn]
air-traffic controller	**contrôleur** (m) **aérien**	[kɔ̃trolœr aerjɛ̃]
departure	**départ** (m)	[depar]
arrival	**arrivée** (f)	[arive]
to arrive (by plane)	**arriver** (vi)	[arive]
departure time	**temps** (m) **de départ**	[tɑ̃ də depar]
arrival time	**temps** (m) **d'arrivée**	[tɑ̃ darive]
to be delayed	**être retardé**	[ɛtr rətarde]
flight delay	**retard** (m) **de l'avion**	[rətar də lavjɔ̃]
information board	**tableau** (m) **d'informations**	[tablo dɛ̃formasjɔ̃]
information	**information** (f)	[ɛ̃formasjɔ̃]
to announce (vt)	**annoncer** (vt)	[anɔ̃se]
flight (e.g., next ~)	**vol** (m)	[vɔl]
customs	**douane** (f)	[dwan]
customs officer	**douanier** (m)	[dwanje]
customs declaration	**déclaration** (f) **de douane**	[deklarasjɔ̃ də dwan]
to fill out (vt)	**remplir** (vt)	[rɑ̃plir]
to fill out the declaration	**remplir la déclaration**	[rɑ̃plir la deklarasjɔ̃]
passport control	**contrôle** (m) **de passeport**	[kɔ̃trol də paspɔr]
luggage	**bagage** (m)	[bagaʒ]
hand luggage	**bagage** (m) **à main**	[bagaʒ a mɛ̃]
Lost Luggage Desk	**service des objets trouvés**	[sɛrvis de ɔbʒɛ truve]
luggage cart	**chariot** (m)	[ʃarjo]
landing	**atterrissage** (m)	[aterisaʒ]
landing strip	**piste** (f) **d'atterrissage**	[pist daterisaʒ]
to land (vi)	**atterrir** (vi)	[aterir]
airstairs	**escalier** (m) **d'avion**	[ɛskalje davjɔ̃]
check-in	**enregistrement** (m)	[ɑ̃rəʒistrəmɑ̃]
check-in desk	**comptoir** (m) **d'enregistrement**	[kɔ̃twar dɑ̃rəʒistrəmɑ̃]
to check-in (vi)	**s'enregistrer** (vp)	[sɑ̃rəʒistre]
boarding pass	**carte** (f) **d'embarquement**	[kart dɑ̃barkəmɑ̃]
departure gate	**porte** (f) **d'embarquement**	[pɔrt dɑ̃barkəmɑ̃]
transit	**transit** (m)	[trɑ̃zit]
to wait (vt)	**attendre** (vt)	[atɑ̃dr]
departure lounge	**salle** (f) **d'attente**	[sal datɑ̃t]
to see off	**raccompagner** (vt)	[rakɔ̃paɲe]
to say goodbye	**dire au revoir**	[dir ərəvwar]

173. Bicycle. Motorcycle

bicycle	**vélo** (m)	[velo]
scooter	**scooter** (m)	[skutœr]
motorcycle, bike	**moto** (f)	[mɔto]
to go by bicycle	**faire du vélo**	[fɛr dy velo]
handlebars	**guidon** (m)	[gidɔ̃]
pedal	**pédale** (f)	[pedal]
brakes	**freins** (m pl)	[frɛ̃]
bicycle seat	**selle** (f)	[sɛl]
pump	**pompe** (f)	[pɔ̃p]
luggage rack	**porte-bagages** (m)	[pɔrtbagaʒ]
front lamp	**phare** (m)	[far]
helmet	**casque** (m)	[kask]
wheel	**roue** (f)	[ru]
fender	**garde-boue** (m)	[gardəbu]
rim	**jante** (f)	[ʒɑ̃t]
spoke	**rayon** (m)	[rɛjɔ̃]

Cars

174. Types of cars

automobile, car	**automobile** (f)	[otomɔbil]
sports car	**voiture** (f) **de sport**	[vwatyr də spɔr]
limousine	**limousine** (f)	[limuzin]
off-road vehicle	**tout-terrain** (m)	[tutɛrɛ̃]
convertible	**cabriolet** (m)	[kabrijɔlɛ]
minibus	**minibus** (m)	[minibys]
ambulance	**ambulance** (f)	[ɑ̃bylɑ̃s]
snowplow	**chasse-neige** (m)	[ʃasnɛʒ]
truck	**camion** (m)	[kamjɔ̃]
tank truck	**camion-citerne** (m)	[kamjɔ̃ sitɛrn]
van (small truck)	**fourgon** (m)	[furgɔ̃]
tractor (big rig)	**tracteur** (m) **routier**	[traktœr rutje]
trailer	**remorque** (f)	[rəmɔrk]
comfortable (adj)	**confortable** (adj)	[kɔ̃fɔrtabl]
second hand (adj)	**d'occasion** (adj)	[dɔkazjɔ̃]

175. Cars. Bodywork

hood	**capot** (m)	[kapo]
fender	**aile** (f)	[ɛl]
roof	**toit** (m)	[twa]
windshield	**pare-brise** (m)	[parbriz]
rear-view mirror	**rétroviseur** (m)	[retrɔvizœr]
windshield washer	**lave-glace** (m)	[lavglas]
windshield wipers	**essuie-glace** (m)	[esɥiglas]
side window	**fenêtre** (f) **latéral**	[fənɛtr lateral]
window lift	**lève-glace** (m)	[lɛvglas]
antenna	**antenne** (f)	[ɑ̃tɛn]
sun roof	**toit** (m) **ouvrant**	[twa uvrɑ̃]
bumper	**pare-chocs** (m)	[parʃɔk]
trunk	**coffre** (m)	[kɔfr]
roof luggage rack	**galerie** (f) **de toit**	[galri də twa]
door	**portière** (f)	[pɔrtjɛr]

door handle	**poignée** (f)	[pwaɲe]
door lock	**serrure** (f)	[seryr]
license plate	**plaque** (f) **d'immatriculation**	[plak dimatrikylasjɔ̃]
muffler	**silencieux** (m)	[silɑ̃sjø]
gas tank	**réservoir** (m) **d'essence**	[rezɛrvwar desɑ̃s]
tail pipe	**pot** (m) **d'échappement**	[po deʃapmɑ̃]
gas, accelerator	**accélérateur** (m)	[akseleratœr]
pedal	**pédale** (f)	[pedal]
gas pedal	**pédale** (f) **d'accélérateur**	[pedal dakseleratœr]
brake	**frein** (m)	[frɛ̃]
brake pedal	**pédale** (f) **de frein**	[pedal də frɛ̃]
to slow down (to brake)	**freiner** (vi)	[frene]
parking brake	**frein** (m) **à main**	[frɛ̃ ɑ mɛ̃]
clutch	**embrayage** (m)	[ɑ̃brɛjaʒ]
clutch pedal	**pédale** (f) **d'embrayage**	[pedal dɑ̃brɛjaʒ]
clutch plate	**disque** (m) **d'embrayage**	[disk sede]
shock absorber	**amortisseur** (m)	[amɔrtisœr]
wheel	**roue** (f)	[ru]
spare tire	**roue** (f) **de rechange**	[ru də rəʃɑ̃ʒ]
tire	**pneu** (m)	[pnø]
hubcap	**enjoliveur** (m)	[ɑ̃ʒɔlivœr]
driving wheels	**roues** (f pl) **motrices**	[ru mɔtris]
front-wheel drive (as adj)	**à traction avant**	[a traksjɔn avɑ̃]
rear-wheel drive (as adj)	**à traction arrière**	[a traksjɔn arjɛr]
all-wheel drive (as adj)	**à traction intégrale**	[a traksjɔn ɛ̃tegral]
gearbox	**boîte** (f) **de vitesses**	[bwat də vitɛs]
automatic (adj)	**automatique** (adj)	[ɔtɔmatik]
mechanical (adj)	**mécanique** (adj)	[mekanik]
gear shift	**levier** (m) **de vitesse**	[ləvje də vitɛs]
headlight	**phare** (m)	[far]
headlights	**feux** (m pl)	[fø]
low beam	**feux** (m pl) **de croisement**	[fø də krwazmɑ̃]
high beam	**feux** (m pl) **de route**	[fø də rut]
brake light	**feux** (m pl) **stop**	[fø stɔp]
parking lights	**feux** (m pl) **de position**	[fø də pozisjɔ̃]
hazard lights	**feux** (m pl) **de détresse**	[fø də detrɛs]
fog lights	**feux** (m pl) **de brouillard**	[fø də brujar]
turn signal	**clignotant** (m)	[kliɲɔtɑ̃]
back-up light	**feux** (m pl) **de recul**	[fø də rəkyl]

176. Cars. Passenger compartment

car inside	habitacle (m)	[abitakl]
leather (as adj)	en cuir (adj)	[ã kɥir]
velour (as adj)	en velours (adj)	[ã vəlur]
upholstery	revêtement (m)	[rəvɛtmã]
instrument (gage)	instrument (m)	[ɛ̃strymã]
dashboard	tableau (m) de bord	[tablo də bɔr]
speedometer	indicateur (m) de vitesse	[ɛ̃dikatœr də vitɛs]
needle (pointer)	aiguille (f)	[egɥij]
odometer	compteur (m) de kilomètres	[kɔ̃tœr də kilomɛtr]
indicator (sensor)	indicateur (m)	[ɛ̃dikatœr]
level	niveau (m)	[nivo]
warning light	témoin (m)	[temwɛ̃]
steering wheel	volant (m)	[vɔlã]
horn	klaxon (m)	[klaksɔn]
button	bouton (m)	[butɔ̃]
switch	interrupteur (m)	[ɛ̃teryptœr]
seat	siège (m)	[sjɛʒ]
backrest	dossier (m)	[dosje]
headrest	appui-tête (m)	[apɥitɛt]
seat belt	ceinture (f) de sécurité	[sɛ̃tyr də sekyrite]
to fasten the belt	mettre la ceinture	[mɛtr la sɛ̃tyr]
adjustment (of seats)	réglage (m)	[reglaʒ]
airbag	airbag (m)	[ɛrbag]
air-conditioner	climatiseur (m)	[klimatizœr]
radio	radio (f)	[radjo]
CD player	lecteur (m) de CD	[lɛktœr də sede]
to turn on	allumer (vt)	[alyme]
antenna	antenne (f)	[ãtɛn]
glove box	boîte (f) à gants	[bwat ɑ gã]
ashtray	cendrier (m)	[sãdrije]

177. Cars. Engine

engine, motor	moteur (m)	[mɔtœr]
diesel (as adj)	diesel (adj)	[djezɛl]
gasoline (as adj)	à essence (adj)	[ɑ esãs]
engine volume	capacité (f) du moteur	[kapasite dy mɔtœr]
power	puissance (f)	[pɥisãs]
horsepower	cheval-vapeur (m)	[ʃəvalvapœr]

piston	**piston** (m)	[pistõ]
cylinder	**cylindre** (m)	[silɛ̃dr]
valve	**soupape** (f)	[supap]

injector	**injecteur** (m)	[ɛ̃ʒɛktœr]
generator	**générateur** (m)	[ʒeneratœr]
carburetor	**carburateur** (m)	[karbyratœr]
engine oil	**huile** (f) **moteur**	[ɥil mɔtœr]

radiator	**radiateur** (m)	[radjatœr]
coolant	**liquide** (m) **de refroidissement**	[likid də rəfrwadismɑ̃]
cooling fan	**ventilateur** (m)	[vɑ̃tilatœr]

battery (accumulator)	**batterie** (f)	[batri]
starter	**starter** (m)	[stɑ̃dar]
ignition	**allumage** (m)	[alymaʒ]
spark plug	**bougie** (f) **d'allumage**	[buʒi dalymaʒ]

terminal (of battery)	**borne** (f)	[bɔrn]
positive terminal	**borne** (f) **positive**	[bɔrn pozitiv]
negative terminal	**borne** (f) **négative**	[bɔrn negativ]
fuse	**fusible** (m)	[fyzibl]

air filter	**filtre** (m) **à air**	[filtr ɑ ɛr]
oil filter	**filtre** (m) **à huile**	[filtr ɑ ɥil]
fuel filter	**filtre** (m) **à essence**	[filtr ɑ esɑ̃s]

178. Cars. Crash. Repair

car accident	**accident** (m)	[aksidɑ̃]
road accident	**accident** (m) **de route**	[aksidɑ̃ də rut]
to run into ...	**percuter contre ...**	[pɛrkyte kõtr]
to have an accident	**s'écraser** (vp)	[sekraze]
damage	**dégât** (m)	[dega]
intact (adj)	**intact** (adj)	[ɛ̃takt]

breakdown	**panne** (f)	[pan]
to break down (vi)	**tomber en panne**	[tõbe ɑ̃ pan]
towrope	**corde** (f) **de remorquage**	[kɔrd də rəmɔrkaʒ]

puncture	**crevaison** (f)	[krəvɛzõ]
to be flat	**crever** (vi)	[krəve]
to pump up	**gonfler** (vt)	[gõfle]
pressure	**pression** (f)	[prɛsjõ]
to check (to examine)	**vérifier** (vt)	[verifje]

repair	**réparation** (f)	[reparasjõ]
auto repair shop	**garage** (m)	[garaʒ]
spare part	**pièce** (f) **détachée**	[pjɛs detaʃe]

part	**pièce** (f)	[pjɛs]
bolt (with nut)	**boulon** (m)	[bulɔ̃]
screw bolt (without nut)	**vis** (f)	[vis]
nut	**écrou** (m)	[ekru]
washer	**rondelle** (f)	[rɔ̃dɛl]
bearing	**palier** (m)	[palje]
tube	**tuyau** (m)	[tɥijo]
gasket (head ~)	**joint** (m)	[ʒwɛ̃]
cable, wire	**fil** (m)	[fil]
jack	**cric** (m)	[krik]
wrench	**clé** (f) **de serrage**	[kle də seraʒ]
hammer	**marteau** (m)	[marto]
pump	**pompe** (f)	[pɔ̃p]
screwdriver	**tournevis** (m)	[turnəvis]
fire extinguisher	**extincteur** (m)	[ɛkstɛ̃ktœr]
warning triangle	**triangle** (m) **de signalisation**	[trijɑ̃gl də siɲalizasjɔ̃]
to stall (vi)	**caler** (vi)	[kale]
to be broken	**être en panne**	[ɛtr ɑ̃ pan]
to overheat (vi)	**surchauffer** (vi)	[syrʃofe]
to be clogged up	**se boucher** (vp)	[sə buʃe]
to freeze up (pipes, etc.)	**geler** (vi)	[ʒəle]
to burst (vi, ab. tube)	**éclater** (vi) **(tuyau, etc.)**	[eklate]
pressure	**pression** (f)	[prɛsjɔ̃]
level	**niveau** (m)	[nivo]
slack (~ belt)	**lâche** (adj)	[laʃ]
dent	**fosse** (f)	[fos]
abnormal noise (motor)	**bruit** (m)	[brɥi]
crack	**fissure** (f)	[fisyr]
scratch	**égratignure** (f)	[egratiɲyr]

179. Cars. Road

road	**route** (f)	[rut]
highway	**grande route** (f)	[grɑ̃d rut]
freeway	**autoroute** (f)	[otorut]
direction (way)	**direction** (f)	[dirɛksjɔ̃]
distance	**distance** (f)	[distɑ̃s]
bridge	**pont** (m)	[pɔ̃]
parking lot	**parking** (m)	[parkiɲ]
square	**place** (f)	[plas]
interchange	**échangeur** (m)	[eʃɑ̃ʒœr]

tunnel	**tunnel** (m)	[tynɛl]
gas station	**station-service** (f)	[stasjõsɛrvis]
parking lot	**parking** (m)	[parkiŋ]
gas pump	**poste** (m) **d'essence**	[pɔst desãs]
auto repair shop	**garage** (m)	[garaʒ]
to get gas	**se ravitailler** (vp)	[sə ravitaje]
fuel	**carburant** (m)	[karbyrã]
jerrycan	**jerrycan** (m)	[ʒerikan]
asphalt	**asphalte** (m)	[asfalt]
road markings	**marquage** (m)	[markaʒ]
curb	**bordure** (f)	[bɔrdyr]
guardrail	**barrière** (f) **de sécurité**	[barjɛr də sekyrite]
ditch	**fossé** (m)	[fose]
roadside (shoulder)	**bas-côté** (m)	[bakote]
lamppost	**réverbère** (m)	[revɛrbɛr]
to drive (a car)	**conduire** (vt)	[kõdɥir]
to turn (~ to the left)	**tourner** (vi)	[turne]
to make a U-turn	**faire un demi-tour**	[fɛr œ̃ dəmitur]
reverse (~ gear)	**marche** (f) **arrière**	[marʃ arjɛr]
to honk (vi)	**klaxonner** (vi)	[klaksɔne]
honk (sound)	**coup** (m) **de klaxon**	[ku də klaksɔn]
to get stuck	**s'embourber** (vp)	[sãburbe]
to spin (in mud)	**déraper** (vi)	[derape]
to cut, to turn off	**couper** (vt)	[kupe]
speed	**vitesse** (f)	[vitɛs]
to exceed the speed limit	**dépasser la vitesse**	[depase la vitɛs]
to give a ticket	**mettre une amende à qn**	[mɛtr yn amãd]
traffic lights	**feux** (m pl) **de circulation**	[fø də sirkylasjõ]
driver's license	**permis** (m) **de conduire**	[pɛrmi də kõdɥir]
grade crossing	**passage** (m) **à niveau**	[pɑsaʒ ɑ nivo]
intersection	**carrefour** (m)	[karfur]
crosswalk	**passage** (m) **piéton**	[pɑsaʒ pjetõ]
bend, curve	**virage** (m)	[viraʒ]
pedestrian zone	**zone** (f) **piétonne**	[zon pjetɔn]

180. Traffic signs

rules of the road	**code** (m) **de la route**	[kɔd də la rut]
traffic sign	**signe** (m)	[siɲ]
passing (overtaking)	**dépassement** (m)	[depasmã]
curve	**virage** (m)	[viraʒ]
U-turn	**demi-tour** (m)	[dəmitur]
traffic circle	**sens** (m) **giratoire**	[sãs ʒiratwar]
No entry	**sens interdit**	[sãs ɛ̃tɛrdi]
No vehicles allowed	**circulation interdite**	[sirkylasjõ ɛ̃tɛrdi]

No passing	**interdiction**	[ɛ̃tɛrdiksjɔ̃
	de dépasser	də depase]
No parking	**stationnement interdit**	[stasjɔnmɑn ɛ̃tɛrdi]
No stopping	**arrêt interdit**	[arɛt ɛ̃tɛrdi]
dangerous turn	**virage dangereux**	[viraʒ dɑ̃ʒrø]
steep descent	**descente dangereuse**	[desɑ̃t dɑ̃ʒrøz]
one-way traffic	**sens unique**	[sɑ̃s ynik]
crosswalk	**passage** (m) **piéton**	[pɑsaʒ pjetɔ̃]
slippery road	**chaussée glissante**	[ʃose glisɑ̃t]
YIELD	**cédez le passage**	[sede lə pɑsaʒ]

PEOPLE. LIFE EVENTS

Life events

181. Holidays. Event

celebration, holiday	**fête** (f)	[fɛt]
national day	**fête** (f) **nationale**	[fɛt nasjɔnal]
public holiday	**jour** (m) **férié**	[ʒur ferje]
to commemorate (vt)	**célébrer** (vt)	[selebre]

event (happening)	**événement** (m)	[evɛnmɑ̃]
event (organized activity)	**événement** (m)	[evɛnmɑ̃]
banquet (party)	**banquet** (m)	[bɑ̃kɛ]
reception (formal party)	**réception** (f)	[resɛpsjɔ̃]
feast	**festin** (m)	[fɛstɛ̃]

anniversary	**anniversaire** (m)	[anivɛrsɛr]
jubilee	**jubilé** (m)	[ʒybile]
to celebrate (vt)	**fêter, célébrer**	[fete], [selebre]

New Year	**Nouvel An** (m)	[nuvɛl ɑ̃]
Happy New Year!	**Bonne année!**	[bɔn ane]
Santa Claus	**Père Noël** (m)	[pɛr nɔɛl]

Christmas	**Noël** (m)	[nɔɛl]
Merry Christmas!	**Joyeux Noël!**	[ʒwajø nɔɛl]
Christmas tree	**arbre** (m) **de Noël**	[arbr də nɔɛl]
fireworks	**feux** (m pl) **d'artifice**	[fø dartifis]

wedding	**mariage** (m)	[marjaʒ]
groom	**fiancé** (m)	[fijɑ̃se]
bride	**fiancée** (f)	[fijɑ̃se]

to invite (vt)	**inviter** (vt)	[ɛ̃vite]
invitation card	**lettre** (f) **d'invitation**	[lɛtr dɛ̃vitasjɔ̃]

guest	**invité** (m)	[ɛ̃vite]
to visit (~ your parents, etc.)	**visiter** (vt)	[vizite]
to greet the guests	**accueillir les invités**	[akœjir lezɛ̃vite]

gift, present	**cadeau** (m)	[kado]
to give (sth as present)	**offrir** (vt)	[ɔfrir]
to receive gifts	**recevoir des cadeaux**	[rəsəvwar de kado]

bouquet (of flowers)	bouquet (m)	[bukɛ]
congratulations	félicitations (f pl)	[felisitasjɔ̃]
to congratulate (vt)	féliciter (vt)	[felisite]

greeting card	carte (f) de veux	[kart də vœ]
to send a postcard	envoyer une carte	[ɑ̃vwaje yn kart]
to get a postcard	recevoir une carte	[rəsəvwar yn kart]

toast	toast (m)	[tost]
to offer (a drink, etc.)	offrir (vt)	[ɔfrir]
champagne	champagne (m)	[ʃɑ̃paɲ]

to have fun	s'amuser (vp)	[samyze]
fun, merriment	gaieté (f)	[gete]
joy (emotion)	joie (f)	[ʒwa]

| dance | danse (f) | [dɑ̃s] |
| to dance (vi, vt) | danser (vi, vt) | [dɑ̃se] |

| waltz | valse (f) | [vals] |
| tango | tango (m) | [tɑ̃go] |

182. Funerals. Burial

cemetery	cimetière (m)	[simɑ̃tje]
grave, tomb	tombe (f)	[tɔ̃b]
cross	croix (f)	[krwa]
gravestone	pierre (f) tombale	[pjɛr tɔ̃bal]
fence	clôture (f)	[klotyr]
chapel	chapelle (f)	[ʃapɛl]

death	mort (f)	[mɔr]
to die (vi)	mourir (vi)	[murir]
the deceased	défunt (m)	[defœ̃]
mourning	deuil (m)	[dœj]
to bury (vt)	enterrer (vt)	[ɑ̃tere]
funeral home	maison (f) funéraire	[mɛzɔ̃ fynerɛr]
funeral	enterrement (m)	[ɑ̃tɛrmɑ̃]

wreath	couronne (f)	[kurɔn]
casket	cercueil (m)	[sɛrkœj]
hearse	corbillard (m)	[kɔrbijar]
shroud	linceul (m)	[lɛ̃sœl]

funeral procession	cortège (m) funèbre	[kɔrtɛʒ fynɛbr]
cremation urn	urne (f) funéraire	[yrn fynerɛr]
crematory	crématoire (m)	[krematwar]
obituary	nécrologue (m)	[nekrɔlɔg]
to cry (weep)	pleurer (vi)	[plœre]
to sob (vi)	sangloter (vi)	[sɑ̃glɔte]

183. War. Soldiers

platoon	section (f)	[sɛksjõ]
company	compagnie (f)	[kõpaɲi]
regiment	régiment (m)	[reʒimɑ̃]
army	armée (f)	[arme]
division	division (f)	[divizjõ]

| section, squad | détachement (m) | [detaʃmɑ̃] |
| host (army) | armée (f) | [arme] |

| soldier | soldat (m) | [sɔlda] |
| officer | officier (m) | [ɔfisje] |

private	soldat (m)	[sɔlda]
sergeant	sergent (m)	[sɛrʒɑ̃]
lieutenant	lieutenant (m)	[ljøtnɑ̃]
captain	capitaine (m)	[kapitɛn]
major	commandant (m)	[kɔmɑ̃dɑ̃]
colonel	colonel (m)	[kɔlɔnɛl]
general	général (m)	[ʒeneral]

sailor	marin (m)	[marɛ̃]
captain	capitaine (m)	[kapitɛn]
boatswain	maître (m) d'équipage	[mɛtr dekipaʒ]

artilleryman	artilleur (m)	[artijœr]
paratrooper	parachutiste (m)	[paraʃytist]
pilot	pilote (m)	[pilɔt]
navigator	navigateur (m)	[navigatœr]
mechanic	mécanicien (m)	[mekanisjɛ̃]

pioneer (sapper)	démineur (m)	[deminœr]
parachutist	parachutiste (m)	[paraʃytist]
reconnaissance scout	éclaireur (m)	[eklɛrœr]
sniper	tireur (m) d'élite	[tirœr delit]

patrol (group)	patrouille (f)	[patruj]
to patrol (vt)	patrouiller (vi)	[patruje]
sentry, guard	sentinelle (f)	[sɑ̃tinɛl]

warrior	guerrier (m)	[gɛrje]
hero	héros (m)	[ero]
heroine	héroïne (f)	[erɔin]
patriot	patriote (m)	[patrijɔt]

| traitor | traître (m) | [trɛtr] |
| to betray (vt) | trahir (vt) | [trair] |

| deserter | déserteur (m) | [dezɛrtœr] |
| to desert (vi) | déserter (vt) | [dezɛrte] |

mercenary	mercenaire (m)	[mɛrsənɛr]
recruit	recrue (f)	[rəkry]
volunteer	volontaire (m)	[vɔlɔ̃tɛr]

dead (n)	mort (m)	[mɔr]
wounded (n)	blessé (m)	[blese]
prisoner of war	prisonnier (m) de guerre	[prizɔnje də gɛr]

184. War. Military actions. Part 1

war	guerre (f)	[gɛr]
to be at war	faire la guerre	[fɛr la gɛr]
civil war	guerre (f) civile	[gɛr sivil]

treacherously (adv)	perfidement (adv)	[pɛrfidmɑ̃]
declaration of war	déclaration (f) de guerre	[deklarasjɔ̃ də gɛr]
to declare (~ war)	déclarer (vt)	[deklare]
aggression	agression (f)	[agrɛsjɔ̃]
to attack (invade)	attaquer (vt)	[atake]

to invade (vt)	envahir (vt)	[ɑ̃vair]
invader	envahisseur (m)	[ɑ̃vaisœr]
conqueror	conquérant (m)	[kɔ̃kerɑ̃]

defense	défense (f)	[defɑ̃s]
to defend (a country, etc.)	défendre (vt)	[defɑ̃dr]
to defend oneself	se défendre (vp)	[sə defɑ̃dr]

enemy	ennemi (m)	[ɛnmi]
foe, adversary	adversaire (m)	[advɛrsɛr]
enemy (as adj)	ennemi (adj)	[ɛnmi]

| strategy | stratégie (f) | [strateʒi] |
| tactics | tactique (f) | [taktik] |

order	ordre (m)	[ɔrdr]
command (order)	commande (f)	[kɔmɑ̃d]
to order (vt)	ordonner (vt)	[ɔrdɔne]
mission	mission (f)	[misjɔ̃]
secret (adj)	secret (adj)	[səkrɛ]

| battle | bataille (f) | [bataj] |
| combat | combat (m) | [kɔ̃ba] |

attack	attaque (f)	[atak]
storming (assault)	assaut (m)	[aso]
to storm (vt)	prendre d'assaut	[prɑ̃dr daso]
siege (to be under ~)	siège (m)	[sjɛʒ]
offensive (n)	offensive (f)	[ɔfɑ̃siv]
to go on the offensive	passer à l'offensive	[pɑse ɑ lɔfɑ̃siv]

| retreat | retraite (f) | [rətrɛt] |
| to retreat (vi) | faire retraite | [fɛr rətrɛt] |

| encirclement | encerclement (m) | [ɑ̃sɛrkləmɑ̃] |
| to encircle (vt) | encercler (vt) | [ɑ̃sɛrkle] |

bombing (by aircraft)	bombardement (m)	[bɔ̃bardəmɑ̃]
to drop a bomb	lancer une bombe	[lɑ̃se yn bɔ̃b]
to bomb (vt)	bombarder (vt)	[bɔ̃barde]
explosion	explosion (f)	[ɛksplozjɔ̃]

shot	coup (m) de feu	[ku də fø]
to fire a shot	tirer un coup de feu	[tire œ̃ ku də fø]
firing (burst of ~)	fusillade (f)	[fyzijad]

to take aim (at …)	viser (vt)	[vize]
to point (a gun)	pointer (sur …)	[pwɛ̃te syr]
to hit (the target)	atteindre (vt)	[atɛ̃dr]

to sink (~ a ship)	faire sombrer	[fɛr sɔ̃bre]
hole (in a ship)	trou (m)	[tru]
to founder, to sink (vi)	sombrer (vi)	[sɔ̃bre]

front (war ~)	front (m)	[frɔ̃]
rear (homefront)	arrière front (m)	[arjɛr frɔ̃]
evacuation	évacuation (f)	[evakɥasjɔ̃]
to evacuate (vt)	évacuer (vt)	[evakɥe]

trench	tranchée (f)	[trɑ̃ʃe]
barbwire	barbelés (m pl)	[barbəle]
barrier (anti tank ~)	barrage (m)	[baraʒ]
watchtower	tour (f) de guet	[tur də gɛ]

hospital	hôpital (m)	[ɔpital]
to wound (vt)	blesser (vt)	[blese]
wound	blessure (f)	[blesyr]
wounded (n)	blessé (m)	[blese]
to be wounded	être blessé	[ɛtr blese]
serious (wound)	grave (adj)	[grav]

185. War. Military actions. Part 2

captivity	captivité (f)	[kaptivite]
to take captive	captiver (vt)	[kaptive]
to be in captivity	être prisonnier	[ɛtr prizɔnje]
to be taken prisoner	être fait prisonnier	[ɛtr fɛ prizɔnje]

| concentration camp | camp (m) de concentration | [kɑ̃ də kɔ̃sɑ̃trasjɔ̃] |
| prisoner of war | prisonnier (m) de guerre | [prizɔnje də gɛr] |

to escape (vi)	**s'enfuir** (vp)	[sɑ̃fɥir]
to betray (vt)	**trahir** (vt)	[trair]
betrayer	**traître** (m)	[trɛtr]
betrayal	**trahison** (f)	[traizɔ̃]
to execute (shoot)	**fusiller** (vt)	[fyzije]
execution (by firing squad)	**fusillade** (f)	[fyzijad]
equipment (military gear)	**équipement** (m)	[ekipmɑ̃]
shoulder board	**épaulette** (f)	[epolɛt]
gas mask	**masque** (m) **à gaz**	[mask ɑ gaz]
radio transmitter	**émetteur** (m) **radio**	[emetœr radjo]
cipher, code	**chiffre** (m)	[ʃifr]
secrecy	**conspiration** (f)	[kɔ̃spirasjɔ̃]
password	**mot** (m) **de passe**	[mo də pɑs]
land mine	**mine** (f) **terrestre**	[min tɛrɛstr]
to mine (road, etc.)	**miner** (vt)	[mine]
minefield	**champ** (m) **de mines**	[ʃɑ̃ də min]
air-raid warning	**alerte** (f) **aérienne**	[alɛrt aerjɛ̃]
alarm (warning)	**signal** (m) **d'alarme**	[siɲal dalarm]
signal	**signal** (m)	[siɲal]
signal flare	**fusée signal** (f)	[fyze siɲal]
headquarters	**état-major** (m)	[eta maʒɔr]
reconnaissance	**reconnaissance** (f)	[rəkɔnɛsɑ̃s]
situation	**situation** (f)	[sitɥasjɔ̃]
report	**rapport** (m)	[rapɔr]
ambush	**embuscade** (f)	[ɑ̃byskad]
reinforcement (of army)	**renfort** (m)	[rɑ̃fɔr]
target	**cible** (f)	[sibl]
proving ground	**polygone** (m)	[pɔligɔn]
military exercise	**manœuvres** (f pl)	[manœvr]
panic	**panique** (f)	[panik]
devastation	**dévastation** (f)	[devastasjɔ̃]
destruction, ruins	**destructions** (f pl)	[dɛstryksjɔ̃]
to destroy (vt)	**détruire** (vt)	[detrɥir]
to survive (vi, vt)	**survivre** (vi)	[syrvivr]
to disarm (vt)	**désarmer** (vt)	[dezarme]
to handle (~ a gun)	**manier** (vt)	[manje]
Attention!	**Garde-à-vous! Fixe!**	[gardavu], [fiks]
At ease!	**Repos!**	[rəpo]
feat (of courage)	**exploit** (m)	[ɛksplwa]
oath (vow)	**serment** (m)	[sɛrmɑ̃]
to swear (an oath)	**jurer** (vi)	[ʒyre]

decoration (medal, etc.)	**décoration** (f)	[dekɔrasjɔ̃]
to award (give medal to)	**décorer** (vt)	[dekɔre]
medal	**médaille** (f)	[medaj]
order (e.g., ~ of Merit)	**ordre** (m)	[ɔrdr]

victory	**victoire** (f)	[viktwar]
defeat	**défaite** (f)	[defɛt]
armistice	**armistice** (m)	[armistis]

banner (standard)	**drapeau** (m)	[drapo]
glory (honor, fame)	**gloire** (f)	[glwar]
parade	**défilé** (m)	[defile]
to march (on parade)	**marcher** (vi)	[marʃe]

186. Weapons

weapons	**arme** (f)	[arm]
firearm	**armes** (f pl) **à feu**	[arm ɑ fø]
cold weapons (knives, etc.)	**armes** (f pl) **blanches**	[arm blɑ̃ʃ]

chemical weapons	**arme** (f) **chimique**	[arm ʃimik]
nuclear (adj)	**nucléaire** (adj)	[nykleɛr]
nuclear weapons	**arme** (f) **nucléaire**	[arm nykleɛr]

| bomb | **bombe** (f) | [bɔ̃b] |
| atomic bomb | **bombe** (f) **atomique** | [bɔ̃b atɔmik] |

pistol (gun)	**pistolet** (m)	[pistɔlɛ]
rifle	**fusil** (m)	[fyzi]
submachine gun	**mitraillette** (f)	[mitrɑjɛt]
machine gun	**mitrailleuse** (f)	[mitrɑjøz]

muzzle	**bouche** (f)	[buʃ]
barrel	**canon** (m)	[kanɔ̃]
caliber	**calibre** (m)	[kalibr]

trigger	**gâchette** (f)	[gaʃɛt]
sight (aiming device)	**mire** (f)	[mir]
magazine	**magasin** (m)	[magazɛ̃]
butt (of rifle)	**crosse** (f)	[krɔs]

| hand grenade | **grenade** (f) | [grənad] |
| explosive | **explosif** (m) | [ɛksplozif] |

bullet	**balle** (f)	[bal]
cartridge	**cartouche** (f)	[kartuʃ]
charge	**charge** (f)	[ʃarʒ]
ammunition	**munitions** (f pl)	[mynisjɔ̃]
bomber (aircraft)	**bombardier** (m)	[bɔ̃bardje]

fighter	**avion** (m) **de chasse**	[avjɔ̃ də ʃas]
helicopter	**hélicoptère** (m)	[elikɔptɛr]
anti-aircraft gun	**pièce** (f) **de D.C.A.**	[pjɛs də desea]
tank	**char** (m)	[ʃar]
tank gun	**canon** (m)	[kanɔ̃]
artillery	**artillerie** (f)	[artijri]
cannon	**canon** (m)	[kanɔ̃]
to lay (a gun)	**pointer sur ...**	[pwɛ̃te syr]
shell (projectile)	**obus** (m)	[ɔby]
mortar bomb	**obus** (m) **de mortier**	[ɔby də mɔrtje]
mortar	**mortier** (m)	[mɔrtje]
splinter (shell fragment)	**éclat** (m) **d'obus**	[ekla dɔby]
submarine	**sous-marin** (m)	[sumarɛ̃]
torpedo	**torpille** (f)	[tɔrpij]
missile	**missile** (m)	[misil]
to load (gun)	**charger** (vt)	[ʃarʒe]
to shoot (vi)	**tirer** (vi)	[tire]
to point at (the cannon)	**viser** (vt)	[vize]
bayonet	**baïonnette** (f)	[bajɔnɛt]
epee	**épée** (f)	[epe]
saber (e.g., cavalry ~)	**sabre** (m)	[sabr]
spear (weapon)	**lance** (f)	[lɑ̃s]
bow	**arc** (m)	[ark]
arrow	**flèche** (f)	[flɛʃ]
musket	**mousquet** (m)	[muskɛ]
crossbow	**arbalète** (f)	[arbalɛt]

187. Ancient people

primitive (prehistoric)	**primitif** (adj)	[primitif]
prehistoric (adj)	**préhistorique** (adj)	[preistɔrik]
ancient (~ civilization)	**ancien** (adj)	[ɑ̃sjɛ̃]
Stone Age	**Âge** (m) **de Pierre**	[ɑʒ də pjɛr]
Bronze Age	**Âge** (m) **de Bronze**	[ɑʒ də brɔ̃z]
Ice Age	**période** (f) **glaciaire**	[perjɔd glasjɛr]
tribe	**tribu** (f)	[triby]
cannibal	**cannibale** (m)	[kanibal]
hunter	**chasseur** (m)	[ʃasœr]
to hunt (vi, vt)	**chasser** (vi, vt)	[ʃase]
mammoth	**mammouth** (m)	[mamut]
cave	**caverne** (f)	[kavɛrn]
fire	**feu** (m)	[fø]

| campfire | feu (m) de bois | [fø də bwa] |
| rock painting | dessin (m) rupestre | [desɛ̃ rypɛstr] |

tool (e.g., stone ax)	outil (m)	[uti]
spear	lance (f)	[lɑ̃s]
stone ax	hache (f) en pierre	[aʃɑ̃ pjɛr]
to be at war	faire la guerre	[fɛr la gɛr]
to domesticate (vt)	domestiquer (vt)	[dɔmɛstike]

idol	idole (f)	[idɔl]
to worship (vt)	adorer, vénérer (vt)	[adɔre], [venere]
superstition	superstition (f)	[sypɛrstisjɔ̃]
rite	rite (m)	[rit]

evolution	évolution (f)	[evɔlysjɔ̃]
development	développement (m)	[devlɔpmɑ̃]
disappearance (extinction)	disparition (f)	[disparisjɔ̃]
to adapt oneself	s'adapter (vp)	[sadapte]

archeology	archéologie (f)	[arkeɔlɔʒi]
archeologist	archéologue (m)	[arkeɔlɔg]
archeological (adj)	archéologique (adj)	[arkeɔlɔʒik]

excavation site	site (m) d'excavation	[sit dɛkskavasjɔ̃]
excavations	fouilles (f pl)	[fuj]
find (object)	trouvaille (f)	[truvaj]
fragment	fragment (m)	[fragmɑ̃]

188. Middle Ages

people (ethnic group)	peuple (m)	[pœpl]
peoples	peuples (m pl)	[pœpl]
tribe	tribu (f)	[triby]
tribes	tribus (f pl)	[triby]

barbarians	Barbares (m pl)	[barbar]
Gauls	Gaulois (m pl)	[golwa]
Goths	Goths (m pl)	[go]
Slavs	Slaves (m pl)	[slav]
Vikings	Vikings (m pl)	[vikiŋ]

| Romans | Romains (m pl) | [rɔmɛ̃] |
| Roman (adj) | romain (adj) | [rɔmɛ̃] |

Byzantines	byzantins (m pl)	[bizɑ̃tɛ̃]
Byzantium	Byzance (f)	[bizɑ̃s]
Byzantine (adj)	byzantin (adj)	[bizɑ̃tɛ̃]

| emperor | empereur (m) | [ɑ̃prœr] |
| leader, chief | chef (m) | [ʃɛf] |

powerful (~ king)	**puissant** (adj)	[pɥisɑ̃]
king	**roi** (m)	[rwa]
ruler (sovereign)	**gouverneur** (m)	[guvɛrnœr]
knight	**chevalier** (m)	[ʃəvalje]
feudal lord	**féodal** (m)	[feɔdal]
feudal (adj)	**féodal** (adj)	[feɔdal]
vassal	**vassal** (m)	[vasal]
duke	**duc** (m)	[dyk]
earl	**comte** (m)	[kɔ̃t]
baron	**baron** (m)	[barɔ̃]
bishop	**évêque** (m)	[evɛk]
armor	**armure** (f)	[armyr]
shield	**bouclier** (m)	[buklije]
sword	**épée** (f), **glaive** (m)	[epe], [glɛv]
visor	**visière** (f)	[vizjɛr]
chainmail	**cotte** (f) **de mailles**	[kɔt də maj]
crusade	**croisade** (f)	[krwazad]
crusader	**croisé** (m)	[krwaze]
territory	**territoire** (m)	[tɛritwar]
to attack (invade)	**attaquer** (vt)	[atake]
to conquer (vt)	**conquérir** (vt)	[kɔ̃kerir]
to occupy (invade)	**occuper** (vt)	[ɔkype]
siege (to be under ~)	**siège** (m)	[sjɛʒ]
besieged (adj)	**assiégé** (adj)	[asjeʒe]
to besiege (vt)	**assiéger** (vt)	[asjeʒe]
inquisition	**inquisition** (f)	[ɛ̃kizisjɔ̃]
inquisitor	**inquisiteur** (m)	[ɛ̃kizitœr]
torture	**torture** (f)	[tɔrtyr]
cruel (adj)	**cruel** (adj)	[kryɛl]
heretic	**hérétique** (m)	[eretik]
heresy	**hérésie** (f)	[erezi]
seafaring	**navigation** (f) **en mer**	[navigasjɔn ɑ̃ mɛr]
pirate	**pirate** (m)	[pirat]
piracy	**piraterie** (f)	[piratri]
boarding (attack)	**abordage** (m)	[abɔrdaʒ]
loot, booty	**butin** (m)	[bytɛ̃]
treasures	**trésor** (m)	[trezɔr]
discovery	**découverte** (f)	[dekuvɛrt]
to discover (new land, etc.)	**découvrir** (vt)	[dekuvrir]
expedition	**expédition** (f)	[ɛkspedisjɔ̃]
musketeer	**mousquetaire** (m)	[muskətɛr]
cardinal	**cardinal** (m)	[kardinal]

| heraldry | **héraldique** (f) | [eraldik] |
| heraldic (adj) | **héraldique** (adj) | [eraldik] |

189. Leader. Chief. Authorities

king	**roi** (m)	[rwa]
queen	**reine** (f)	[rɛn]
royal (adj)	**royal** (adj)	[rwajal]
kingdom	**royaume** (m)	[rwajom]
prince	**prince** (m)	[prɛ̃s]
princess	**princesse** (f)	[prɛ̃sɛs]

president	**président** (m)	[prezidɑ̃]
vice-president	**vice-président** (m)	[visprezidɑ̃]
senator	**sénateur** (m)	[senatœr]

monarch	**monarque** (m)	[mɔnark]
ruler (sovereign)	**gouverneur** (m)	[guvɛrnœr]
dictator	**dictateur** (m)	[diktatœr]
tyrant	**tyran** (m)	[tirɑ̃]
magnate	**magnat** (m)	[maɲa]

director	**directeur** (m)	[dirɛktœr]
chief	**chef** (m)	[ʃɛf]
manager (director)	**gérant** (m)	[ʒerɑ̃]
boss	**boss** (m)	[bɔs]
owner	**patron** (m)	[patrɔ̃]

leader	**leader** (m)	[lidœr]
head (~ of delegation)	**chef** (m)	[ʃɛf]
authorities	**autorités** (f pl)	[ɔtɔrite]
superiors	**supérieurs** (m pl)	[syperjœr]

governor	**gouverneur** (m)	[guvɛrnœr]
consul	**consul** (m)	[kɔ̃syl]
diplomat	**diplomate** (m)	[diplɔmat]
mayor	**maire** (m)	[mɛr]
sheriff	**shérif** (m)	[ʃerif]

emperor	**empereur** (m)	[ɑ̃prœr]
tsar, czar	**tsar** (m)	[tsar]
pharaoh	**pharaon** (m)	[faraɔ̃]
khan	**khan** (m)	[kɑ̃]

190. Road. Way. Directions

| road | **route** (f) | [rut] |
| way (direction) | **voie** (f) | [vwa] |

freeway	**autoroute** (f)	[otorut]
highway	**grande route** (f)	[grɑ̃d rut]
interstate	**route** (f) **nationale**	[rut nasjɔnal]
main road	**route** (f) **principale**	[rut prɛ̃sipal]
dirt road	**route** (f) **de campagne**	[rut də kɑ̃paɲ]
pathway	**chemin** (m)	[ʃəmɛ̃]
footpath (troddenpath)	**sentier** (m)	[sɑ̃tje]
Where?	**Où?**	[u]
Where (to)?	**Où?**	[u]
Where ... from?	**D'où?**	[du]
direction (way)	**direction** (f)	[dirɛksjɔ̃]
to point (~ the way)	**indiquer** (vt)	[ɛ̃dike]
to the left	**à gauche** (adv)	[agoʃ]
to the right	**à droite** (adv)	[adrwat]
straight ahead (adv)	**tout droit** (adv)	[tu drwa]
back (e.g., to turn ~)	**en arrière** (adv)	[ɑn arjɛr]
bend, curve	**virage** (m)	[viraʒ]
to turn (~ to the left)	**tourner** (vi)	[turne]
to make a U-turn	**faire un demi-tour**	[fɛr œ̃ dəmitur]
to be visible	**se dessiner** (vp)	[sə desine]
to appear (come into view)	**apparaître** (vi)	[aparɛtr]
stop, halt (in journey)	**halte** (f)	[alt]
to rest, to halt (vi)	**se reposer** (vp)	[sə rəpoze]
rest (pause)	**repos** (m)	[rəpo]
to lose one's way	**s'égarer** (vp)	[segare]
to lead to ... (ab. road)	**mener à ...**	[məne a]
to arrive at ...	**arriver à ...**	[arive a]
stretch (of road)	**tronçon** (m)	[trɔ̃sɔ̃]
asphalt	**asphalte** (m)	[asfalt]
curb	**bordure** (f)	[bɔrdyr]
ditch	**fossé** (m)	[fose]
manhole	**bouche** (f) **d'égout**	[buʃ degu]
roadside (shoulder)	**bas-côté** (m)	[bakote]
pit, pothole	**nid-de-poule** (m)	[nidpul]
to go (on foot)	**aller** (vi)	[ale]
to pass (overtake)	**dépasser** (vt)	[depase]
step (footstep)	**pas** (m)	[pɑ]
on foot (adv)	**à pied** (adv)	[a pje]
to block (road)	**barrer** (vt)	[bare]
boom barrier	**barrière** (f)	[barjɛr]
dead end	**impasse** (f)	[ɛ̃pas]

191. Breaking the law. Criminals. Part 1

bandit	**bandit** (m)	[bãdi]
crime	**crime** (m)	[krim]
criminal (person)	**criminel** (m)	[kriminɛl]
thief	**voleur** (m)	[vɔlœr]
to steal (vi, vt)	**voler** (vt)	[vɔle]
stealing, theft	**vol** (m)	[vɔl]
to kidnap (vt)	**kidnapper** (vt)	[kidnape]
kidnapping	**kidnapping** (m)	[kidnapiŋ]
kidnapper	**kidnappeur** (m)	[kidnapœr]
ransom	**rançon** (f)	[rãsõ]
to demand ransom	**exiger une rançon**	[ɛgziʒe yn rãsõ]
to rob (vt)	**cambrioler** (vt)	[kãbrijɔle]
robbery	**cambriolage** (m)	[kãbrijɔlaʒ]
robber	**cambrioleur** (m)	[kãbrijɔlœr]
to extort (vt)	**extorquer** (vt)	[ɛkstɔrke]
extortionist	**extorqueur** (m)	[ɛkstɔrkœr]
extortion	**extorsion** (f)	[ɛkstɔrsjõ]
to murder, to kill	**tuer** (vt)	[tɥe]
murder	**meurtre** (m)	[mœrtr]
murderer	**meurtrier** (m)	[mœrtrije]
gunshot	**coup** (m) **de feu**	[ku də fø]
to fire a shot	**tirer un coup de feu**	[tire œ̃ ku də fø]
to shoot to death	**abattre** (vt)	[abatr]
to shoot (vi)	**tirer** (vi)	[tire]
shooting	**coups** (m pl) **de feu**	[ku də fø]
incident (fight, etc.)	**incident** (m)	[ɛ̃sidã]
fight, brawl	**bagarre** (f)	[bagar]
Help!	**Au secours!**	[osəkur]
victim	**victime** (f)	[viktim]
to damage (vt)	**endommager** (vt)	[ãdɔmaʒe]
damage	**dommage** (m)	[dɔmaʒ]
dead body	**cadavre** (m)	[kadavr]
grave (~ crime)	**grave** (adj)	[grav]
to attack (vt)	**attaquer** (vt)	[atake]
to beat (dog, person)	**battre** (vt)	[batr]
to beat up	**passer à tabac**	[pɑse ɑ taba]
to take (rob of sth)	**prendre** (vt)	[prãdr]
to stab to death	**poignarder** (vt)	[pwaɲarde]
to maim (vt)	**mutiler** (vt)	[mytile]

to wound (vt)	blesser (vt)	[blese]
blackmail	chantage (m)	[ʃɑ̃taʒ]
to blackmail (vt)	faire chanter	[fɛr ʃɑ̃te]
blackmailer	maître (m) chanteur	[mɛtr ʃɑ̃tœr]
protection racket	racket (m) de protection	[rakɛt də prɔtɛksjɔ̃]
racketeer	racketteur (m)	[rakɛtœr]
gangster	gangster (m)	[gɑ̃gstɛr]
mafia, Mob	mafia (f)	[mafja]
pickpocket	pickpocket (m)	[pikpɔkɛt]
burglar	cambrioleur (m)	[kɑ̃brijɔlœr]
smuggling	contrebande (f)	[kɔ̃trəbɑ̃d]
smuggler	contrebandier (m)	[kɔ̃trebɑ̃dje]
forgery	contrefaçon (f)	[kɔ̃trəfasɔ̃]
to forge (counterfeit)	falsifier (vt)	[falsifje]
fake (forged)	faux (adj)	[fo]

192. Breaking the law. Criminals. Part 2

rape	viol (m)	[vjɔl]
to rape (vt)	violer (vt)	[vjɔle]
rapist	violeur (m)	[vjɔlœr]
maniac	maniaque (m)	[manjak]
prostitute (fem.)	prostituée (f)	[prɔstitɥe]
prostitution	prostitution (f)	[prɔstitysjɔ̃]
pimp	souteneur (m)	[sutnœr]
drug addict	drogué (m)	[drɔge]
drug dealer	trafiquant (m) de drogue	[trafikɑ̃ də drɔg]
to blow up (bomb)	faire exploser	[fɛr ɛksploze]
explosion	explosion (f)	[ɛksplozjɔ̃]
to set fire	mettre feu	[mɛtr fø]
incendiary (arsonist)	incendiaire (m)	[ɛ̃sɑ̃djɛr]
terrorism	terrorisme (m)	[tɛrɔrism]
terrorist	terroriste (m)	[tɛrɔrist]
hostage	otage (m)	[ɔtaʒ]
to swindle (vt)	escroquer (vt)	[ɛskrɔke]
swindle	escroquerie (f)	[ɛskrɔkri]
swindler	escroc (m)	[ɛskro]
to bribe (vt)	soudoyer (vt)	[sudwaje]
bribery	corruption (f)	[kɔrypsjɔ̃]
bribe	pot-de-vin (m)	[podvɛ̃]
poison	poison (m)	[pwazɔ̃]

to poison (vt)	empoisonner (vt)	[ɑ̃pwazɔne]
to poison oneself	s'empoisonner (vp)	[sɑ̃pwazɔne]
suicide (act)	suicide (m)	[sɥisid]
suicide (person)	suicidé (m)	[sɥiside]
to threaten (vt)	menacer (vt)	[mənase]
threat	menace (f)	[mənas]
to make an attempt	attenter (vt)	[atɑ̃te]
attempt (attack)	attentat (m)	[atɑ̃ta]
to steal (a car)	voler (vt)	[vɔle]
to hijack (a plane)	détourner (vt)	[deturne]
revenge	vengeance (f)	[vɑ̃ʒɑ̃s]
to revenge (vt)	se venger (vp)	[sə vɑ̃ʒe]
to torture (vt)	torturer (vt)	[tɔrtyre]
torture	torture (f)	[tɔrtyr]
to torment (vt)	tourmenter (vt)	[turmɑ̃te]
pirate	pirate (m)	[pirat]
hooligan	voyou (m)	[vwaju]
armed (adj)	armé (adj)	[arme]
violence	violence (f)	[vjɔlɑ̃s]
illegal (unlawful)	illégal (adj)	[ilegal]
spying (n)	espionnage (m)	[ɛspjɔnaʒ]
to spy (vi)	espionner (vt)	[ɛspjɔne]

193. Police. Law. Part 1

justice	justice (f)	[ʒystis]
court (court room)	tribunal (m)	[tribynal]
judge	juge (m)	[ʒyʒ]
jurors	jury (m)	[ʒyri]
jury trial	cour (f) d'assises	[kur dasiz]
to judge (vt)	juger (vt)	[ʒyʒe]
lawyer, attorney	avocat (m)	[avɔka]
accused	accusé (m)	[akyze]
dock	banc (m) des accusés	[bɑ̃ dezakyze]
charge	inculpation (f)	[ɛ̃kylpasjɔ̃]
accused	inculpé (m)	[ɛ̃kylpe]
sentence	condamnation (f)	[kɔ̃danasjɔ̃]
to sentence (vt)	condamner (vt)	[kɔ̃dane]
guilty (culprit)	coupable (m)	[kupabl]

to punish (vt)	**punir** (vt)	[pynir]
punishment	**punition** (f)	[pynisjɔ̃]
fine (penalty)	**amende** (f)	[amɑ̃d]
life imprisonment	**détention** (f) **à vie**	[detɑ̃sjɔ̃ ɑ vi]
death penalty	**peine** (f) **de mort**	[pɛn də mɔr]
electric chair	**chaise** (f) **électrique**	[ʃɛz elɛktrik]
gallows	**potence** (f)	[pɔtɑ̃s]

| to execute (vt) | **exécuter** (vt) | [ɛgzekyte] |
| execution | **exécution** (f) | [ɛgzekysjɔ̃] |

| prison, jail | **prison** (f) | [prizɔ̃] |
| cell | **cellule** (f) | [selyl] |

escort	**escorte** (f)	[ɛskɔrt]
prison guard	**gardien** (m) **de prison**	[gardjɛ̃ də prizɔ̃]
prisoner	**prisonnier** (m)	[prizɔnje]
handcuffs	**menottes** (f pl)	[mənɔt]
to handcuff (vt)	**mettre les menottes**	[mɛtr le mənɔt]

prison break	**évasion** (f)	[evazjɔ̃]
to break out (vi)	**s'évader** (vp)	[sevade]
to disappear (vi)	**disparaître** (vi)	[disparɛtr]
to release (from prison)	**libérer** (vt)	[libere]
amnesty	**amnistie** (f)	[amnisti]

police	**police** (f)	[pɔlis]
police officer	**policier** (m)	[pɔlisje]
police station	**commissariat** (m) **de police**	[kɔmisarja də pɔlis]

| billy club | **matraque** (f) | [matrak] |
| bullhorn | **haut parleur** (m) | [o parlœr] |

patrol car	**voiture** (f) **de patrouille**	[vwatyr də patruj]
siren	**sirène** (f)	[sirɛn]
to turn on the siren	**enclencher la sirène**	[ɑ̃klɑ̃ʃe la sirɛn]
siren call	**hurlement** (m) **de la sirène**	[yrləmɑ̃ dəla sirɛn]

crime scene	**lieu** (m) **du crime**	[ljø dy krim]
witness	**témoin** (m)	[temwɛ̃]
freedom	**liberté** (f)	[libɛrte]
accomplice	**complice** (m)	[kɔ̃plis]
to flee (vi)	**s'enfuir** (vp)	[sɑ̃fɥir]
trace (to leave a ~)	**trace** (f)	[tras]

194. Police. Law. Part 2

| search (investigation) | **recherche** (f) | [rəʃɛrʃ] |
| to look for ... | **rechercher** (vt) | [rəʃɛrʃe] |

suspicion	**suspicion** (f)	[syspisjɔ̃]
suspicious (suspect)	**suspect** (adj)	[syspɛ]
to stop (cause to halt)	**arrêter** (vt)	[arete]
to detain (keep in custody)	**détenir** (vt)	[detnir]

case (lawsuit)	**affaire** (f)	[afɛr]
investigation	**enquête** (f)	[ɑ̃kɛt]
detective	**détective** (m)	[detɛktiv]
investigator	**enquêteur** (m)	[ɑ̃kɛtœr]
hypothesis	**hypothèse** (f)	[ipotɛz]

motive	**motif** (m)	[mɔtif]
interrogation	**interrogatoire** (m)	[ɛ̃terɔgatwar]
to interrogate (vt)	**interroger** (vt)	[ɛ̃terɔʒe]
to question (vt)	**interroger** (vt)	[ɛ̃terɔʒe]
check (identity ~)	**inspection** (f)	[ɛ̃spɛksjɔ̃]

round-up	**rafle** (f)	[rafl]
search (~ warrant)	**perquisition** (f)	[pɛrkizisjɔ̃]
chase (pursuit)	**poursuite** (f)	[pursɥit]
to pursue, to chase	**poursuivre** (vt)	[pursɥivr]
to track (a criminal)	**dépister** (vt)	[depiste]
arrest	**arrestation** (f)	[arɛstasjɔ̃]
to arrest (sb)	**arrêter** (vt)	[arete]
to catch (thief, etc.)	**attraper** (vt)	[atrape]
capture	**capture** (f)	[kaptyr]

document	**document** (m)	[dɔkymɑ̃]
proof (evidence)	**preuve** (f)	[prœv]
to prove (vt)	**prouver** (vt)	[pruve]
footprint	**empreinte** (f) **de pied**	[ɑ̃prɛ̃t də pje]
fingerprints	**empreintes** (f pl) **digitales**	[ɑ̃prɛ̃t diʒital]
piece of evidence	**élément** (m) **de preuve**	[elemɑ̃ də prœv]

alibi	**alibi** (m)	[alibi]
innocent (not guilty)	**innocent** (adj)	[inɔsɑ̃]
injustice	**injustice** (f)	[ɛ̃ʒystis]
unjust, unfair (adj)	**injuste** (adj)	[ɛ̃ʒyst]

criminal (adj)	**criminel** (adj)	[kriminɛl]
to confiscate (vt)	**confisquer** (vt)	[kɔ̃fiske]
drug (illegal substance)	**drogue** (f)	[drɔg]
weapon, gun	**arme** (f)	[arm]
to disarm (vt)	**désarmer** (vt)	[dezarme]
to order (command)	**ordonner** (vt)	[ɔrdɔne]
to disappear (vi)	**disparaître** (vi)	[disparɛtr]

law	**loi** (f)	[lwa]
legal, lawful (adj)	**légal** (adj)	[legal]
illegal, illicit (adj)	**illégal** (adj)	[ilegal]
responsibility (blame)	**responsabilité** (f)	[rɛspɔ̃sabilite]
responsible (adj)	**responsable** (adj)	[rɛspɔ̃sabl]

NATURE

The Earth. Part 1

195. Outer space

cosmos	**cosmos** (m)	[kɔsmos]
space (as adj)	**cosmique** (adj)	[kɔsmik]
outer space	**espace** (m) **cosmique**	[ɛspas kɔsmik]
world	**monde** (m)	[mɔ̃d]
universe	**univers** (m)	[ynivɛr]
galaxy	**galaxie** (f)	[galaksi]
star	**étoile** (f)	[etwal]
constellation	**constellation** (f)	[kɔ̃stelasjɔ̃]
planet	**planète** (f)	[planɛt]
satellite	**satellite** (m)	[satelit]
meteorite	**météorite** (m)	[meteɔrit]
comet	**comète** (f)	[kɔmɛt]
asteroid	**astéroïde** (m)	[asterɔid]
orbit	**orbite** (f)	[ɔrbit]
to revolve	**tourner** (vi)	[turne]
(~ around the Earth)		
atmosphere	**atmosphère** (f)	[atmɔsfɛr]
the Sun	**Soleil** (m)	[sɔlɛj]
solar system	**système** (m) **solaire**	[sistɛm sɔlɛr]
solar eclipse	**éclipse** (f) **de soleil**	[leklips də sɔlɛj]
the Earth	**Terre** (f)	[tɛr]
the Moon	**Lune** (f)	[lyn]
Mars	**Mars** (m)	[mars]
Venus	**Vénus** (f)	[venys]
Jupiter	**Jupiter** (m)	[ʒypitɛr]
Saturn	**Saturne** (m)	[satyrn]
Mercury	**Mercure** (m)	[mɛrkyr]
Uranus	**Uranus** (m)	[yranys]
Neptune	**Neptune**	[nɛptyn]
Pluto	**Pluton** (m)	[plytɔ̃]
Milky Way	**la Voie Lactée**	[la vwa lakte]
Great Bear	**la Grande Ours**	[la grɑ̃d urs]

North Star	la Polaire	[la polɛr]
Martian	martien (m)	[marsjɛ̃]
extraterrestrial (n)	extraterrestre (m)	[ɛkstratɛrɛstr]
alien	alien (m)	[aljen]
flying saucer	soucoupe (f) volante	[sukup vɔlɑ̃t]

spaceship	vaisseau (m) spatial	[vɛso spasjal]
space station	station (f) orbitale	[stasjɔ̃ ɔrbital]
blast-off	lancement (m)	[lɑ̃smɑ̃]

engine	moteur (m)	[mɔtœr]
nozzle	tuyère (f)	[tyjɛr]
fuel	carburant (m)	[karbyrɑ̃]

cockpit, flight deck	cabine (f)	[kabin]
antenna	antenne (f)	[ɑ̃tɛn]
porthole	hublot (m)	[yblo]
solar battery	batterie (f) solaire	[batri sɔlɛr]
spacesuit	scaphandre (m)	[skafɑ̃dr]

| weightlessness | apesanteur (f) | [apezɑ̃tœr] |
| oxygen | oxygène (m) | [ɔksiʒɛn] |

| docking (in space) | arrimage (m) | [arimaʒ] |
| to dock (vi, vt) | s'arrimer à ... | [sarime a] |

observatory	observatoire (m)	[ɔpsɛrvatwar]
telescope	télescope (m)	[teleskɔp]
to observe (vt)	observer (vt)	[ɔpsɛrve]
to explore (vt)	explorer (vt)	[ɛksplɔre]

196. The Earth

the Earth	Terre (f)	[tɛr]
globe (the Earth)	globe (m) terrestre	[glob tɛrɛstr]
planet	planète (f)	[planɛt]

atmosphere	atmosphère (f)	[atmɔsfɛr]
geography	géographie (f)	[ʒeografi]
nature	nature (f)	[natyr]

globe (table ~)	globe (m) de table	[glob də tabl]
map	carte (f)	[kart]
atlas	atlas (m)	[atlas]

Europe	Europe (f)	[ørɔp]
Asia	Asie (f)	[azi]
Africa	Afrique (f)	[afrik]
Australia	Australie (f)	[ostrali]
America	Amérique (f)	[amerik]

North America	**Amérique** (f) **du Nord**	[amerik dy nɔr]
South America	**Amérique** (f) **du Sud**	[amerik dy syd]
Antarctica	**l'Antarctique** (m)	[lɑ̃tarktik]
the Arctic	**l'Arctique** (m)	[larktik]

197. Cardinal directions

north	**nord** (m)	[nɔr]
to the north	**vers le nord**	[vɛr lə nɔr]
in the north	**au nord**	[onɔr]
northern (adj)	**du nord** (adj)	[dy nɔr]
south	**sud** (m)	[syd]
to the south	**vers le sud**	[vɛr lə syd]
in the south	**au sud**	[osyd]
southern (adj)	**du sud** (adj)	[dy syd]
west	**ouest** (m)	[wɛst]
to the west	**vers l'occident**	[vɛr lɔksidɑ̃]
in the west	**à l'occident**	[alɔksidɑ̃]
western (adj)	**occidental** (adj)	[ɔksidɑ̃tal]
east	**est** (m)	[ɛst]
to the east	**vers l'orient**	[vɛr lɔrjɑ̃]
in the east	**à l'orient**	[alɔrjɑ̃]
eastern (adj)	**oriental** (adj)	[ɔrjɑ̃tal]

198. Sea. Ocean

sea	**mer** (f)	[mɛr]
ocean	**océan** (m)	[ɔseɑ̃]
gulf (bay)	**golfe** (m)	[gɔlf]
straits	**détroit** (m)	[detrwa]
solid ground	**terre** (f) **ferme**	[tɛr fɛrm]
continent (mainland)	**continent** (m)	[kɔ̃tinɑ̃]
island	**île** (f)	[il]
peninsula	**presqu'île** (f)	[prɛskil]
archipelago	**archipel** (m)	[arʃipɛl]
bay, cove	**baie** (f)	[bɛ]
harbor	**port** (m)	[pɔr]
lagoon	**lagune** (f)	[lagyn]
cape	**cap** (m)	[kap]
atoll	**atoll** (m)	[atɔl]
reef	**récif** (m)	[resif]

coral	**corail** (m)	[kɔraj]
coral reef	**récif** (m) **de corail**	[resif də kɔraj]
deep (adj)	**profond** (adj)	[prɔfɔ̃]
depth (deep water)	**profondeur** (f)	[prɔfɔ̃dœr]
abyss	**abîme** (m)	[abim]
trench (e.g., Mariana ~)	**fosse** (f) **océanique**	[fos ɔseanik]
current, stream	**courant** (m)	[kurɑ̃]
to surround (bathe)	**baigner** (vt)	[beɲe]
shore	**littoral** (m)	[litɔral]
coast	**côte** (f)	[kot]
high tide	**marée** (f) **haute**	[mare ot]
low tide	**marée** (f) **basse**	[mare bas]
sandbank	**banc** (m) **de sable**	[bɑ̃ də sabl]
bottom	**fond** (m)	[fɔ̃]
wave	**vague** (f)	[vag]
crest (~ of a wave)	**crête** (f) **de la vague**	[krɛt də la vag]
froth (foam)	**mousse** (f)	[mus]
storm	**tempête** (f) **en mer**	[tɑ̃pɛt ɑ̃mɛr]
hurricane	**ouragan** (m)	[uragɑ̃]
tsunami	**tsunami** (m)	[tsynami]
calm (dead ~)	**calme** (m)	[kalm]
quiet, calm (adj)	**calme** (adj)	[kalm]
pole	**pôle** (m)	[pol]
polar (adj)	**polaire** (adj)	[pɔlɛr]
latitude	**latitude** (f)	[latityd]
longitude	**longitude** (f)	[lɔ̃ʒityd]
parallel	**parallèle** (f)	[paralɛl]
equator	**équateur** (m)	[ekwatœr]
sky	**ciel** (m)	[sjɛl]
horizon	**horizon** (m)	[ɔrizɔ̃]
air	**air** (m)	[ɛr]
lighthouse	**phare** (m)	[far]
to dive (vi)	**plonger** (vi)	[plɔ̃ʒe]
to sink (ab. boat)	**sombrer** (vi)	[sɔ̃bre]
treasures	**trésor** (m)	[trezɔr]

199. Seas' and Oceans' names

Atlantic Ocean	**océan** (m) **Atlantique**	[ɔseɑn atlɑ̃tik]
Indian Ocean	**océan** (m) **Indien**	[ɔseɑn ɛ̃djɛ̃]

| Pacific Ocean | océan (m) Pacifique | [ɔseã pasifik] |
| Arctic Ocean | océan (m) Glacial | [ɔseã glasjal] |

Black Sea	mer (f) Noire	[mɛr nwar]
Red Sea	mer (f) Rouge	[mɛr ruʒ]
Yellow Sea	mer (f) Jaune	[mɛr ʒon]
White Sea	mer (f) Blanche	[mɛr blãʃ]

Caspian Sea	mer (f) Caspienne	[mɛr kaspjɛn]
Dead Sea	mer (f) Morte	[mɛr mort]
Mediterranean Sea	mer (f) Méditerranée	[mɛr meditɛrane]

| Aegean Sea | mer (f) Égée | [mɛr eʒe] |
| Adriatic Sea | mer (f) Adriatique | [mɛr adrijatik] |

Arabian Sea	mer (f) Arabique	[mɛr arabik]
Sea of Japan	mer (f) du Japon	[mɛr dy ʒapõ]
Bering Sea	mer (f) de Béring	[mɛr də beriŋ]
South China Sea	mer (f) de Chine Méridionale	[mɛr də ʃin meridjonal]

Coral Sea	mer (f) de Corail	[mɛr də kɔraj]
Tasman Sea	mer (f) de Tasman	[mɛr də tasman]
Caribbean Sea	mer (f) Caraïbe	[mɛr karaib]

| Barents Sea | mer (f) de Barents | [mɛr də barɛ̃s] |
| Kara Sea | mer (f) de Kara | [mɛr də kara] |

North Sea	mer (f) du Nord	[mɛr dy nor]
Baltic Sea	mer (f) Baltique	[mɛr baltik]
Norwegian Sea	mer (f) de Norvège	[mɛr də norvɛʒ]

200. Mountains

mountain	montagne (f)	[mõtaɲ]
mountain range	chaîne (f) de montagnes	[ʃɛn də mõtaɲ]
mountain ridge	crête (f)	[krɛt]

| summit, top | sommet (m) | [sɔmɛ] |
| peak | pic (m) | [pik] |

| foot (of mountain) | pied (m) | [pje] |
| slope (mountainside) | pente (f) | [pãt] |

volcano	volcan (m)	[vɔlkã]
active volcano	volcan (m) actif	[vɔlkɑn aktif]
dormant volcano	volcan (m) éteint	[vɔlkɑn etɛ̃]

| eruption | éruption (f) | [erypsjõ] |
| crater | cratère (m) | [kratɛr] |

magma	**magma** (m)	[magma]
lava	**lave** (f)	[lav]
molten (~ lava)	**en fusion**	[ɑ̃ fyzjɔ̃]

canyon	**canyon** (m)	[kanjɔ̃]
gorge	**défilé** (m)	[defile]
crevice	**crevasse** (f)	[krəvas]
abyss (chasm)	**précipice** (m)	[presipis]

pass, col	**col** (m)	[kɔl]
plateau	**plateau** (m)	[plato]
cliff	**rocher** (m)	[rɔʃe]
hill	**colline** (f)	[kɔlin]

glacier	**glacier** (m)	[glasje]
waterfall	**chute** (f) **d'eau**	[ʃyt do]
geyser	**geyser** (m)	[ʒɛzɛr]
lake	**lac** (m)	[lak]

plain	**plaine** (f)	[plɛn]
landscape	**paysage** (m)	[peizaʒ]
echo	**écho** (m)	[eko]

alpinist	**alpiniste** (m)	[alpinist]
rock climber	**varappeur** (m)	[varapœr]

to conquer (in climbing)	**conquérir** (vt)	[kɔ̃kerir]
climb (an easy ~)	**ascension** (f)	[asɑ̃sjɔ̃]

201. Mountains names

Alps	**Alpes** (f pl)	[alp]
Mont Blanc	**Mont Blanc** (m)	[mɔ̃blɑ̃]
Pyrenees	**Pyrénées** (f pl)	[pirene]

Carpathians	**Carpates** (f pl)	[karpat]
Ural Mountains	**Monts Oural** (m pl)	[mɔ̃ ural]

Caucasus	**Caucase** (m)	[kokaz]
Elbrus	**Elbrous** (m)	[ɛlbrys]

Altai	**Altaï** (m)	[altaj]
Tien Shan	**Tian Chan** (m)	[tjɑ̃ ʃɑ̃]
Pamir Mountains	**Pamir** (m)	[pamir]

Himalayas	**Himalaya** (m)	[imalaja]
Everest	**Everest** (m)	[evrɛst]

Andes	**Andes** (f pl)	[ɑ̃d]
Kilimanjaro	**Kilimandjaro** (m)	[kilimɑ̃dʒaro]

202. Rivers

river	**rivière** (f), **fleuve** (m)	[rivjɛr], [flœv]
spring (natural source)	**source** (f)	[surs]
riverbed	**lit** (m)	[li]
basin	**bassin** (m)	[basɛ̃]
to flow into ...	**se jeter dans ...**	[sə ʒəte dɑ̃]
tributary	**affluent** (m)	[aflyɑ̃]
bank (of river)	**rive** (f)	[riv]
current, stream	**courant** (m)	[kurɑ̃]
downstream (adv)	**en aval**	[ɑn aval]
upstream (adv)	**en amont**	[ɑn amɔ̃]
inundation	**inondation** (f)	[inɔ̃dasjɔ̃]
flooding	**les grandes crues**	[le grɑ̃d kry]
to overflow (vi)	**déborder** (vt)	[debɔrde]
to flood (vt)	**inonder** (vt)	[inɔ̃de]
shallows (shoal)	**bas-fond** (m)	[bafɔ̃]
rapids	**rapide** (m)	[rapid]
dam	**barrage** (m)	[baraʒ]
canal	**canal** (m)	[kanal]
artificial lake	**lac** (m) **de barrage**	[lak də baraʒ]
sluice, lock	**écluse** (f)	[eklyz]
water body (pond, etc.)	**plan** (m) **d'eau**	[plɑ̃ do]
swamp, bog	**marais** (m)	[marɛ]
marsh	**fondrière** (f)	[fɔ̃drijɛr]
whirlpool	**tourbillon** (m)	[turbijɔ̃]
stream (brook)	**ruisseau** (m)	[rɥiso]
drinking (ab. water)	**potable** (adj)	[pɔtabl]
fresh (~ water)	**douce** (adj)	[dus]
ice	**glace** (f)	[glas]
to freeze (ab. river, etc.)	**être gelé**	[ɛtr ʒəle]

203. Rivers' names

Seine	**Seine** (f)	[sɛn]
Loire	**Loire** (f)	[lwar]
Thames	**Tamise** (f)	[tamiz]
Rhine	**Rhin** (m)	[rɛ̃]
Danube	**Danube** (m)	[danyb]
Volga	**Volga** (f)	[vɔlga]

| Don | **Don** (m) | [dɔ̃] |
| Lena | **Lena** (f) | [lena] |

Yellow River	**Huang He** (m)	[waŋ e]
Yangtze	**Yangzi Jiang** (m)	[jãgzijãg]
Mekong	**Mékong** (m)	[mekɔ̃g]
Ganges	**Gange** (m)	[gãʒ]

Nile River	**Nil** (m)	[nil]
Congo	**Congo** (m)	[kɔ̃go]
Okavango	**Okavango** (m)	[ɔkavangɔ]
Zambezi	**Zambèze** (m)	[zãbɛz]
Limpopo	**Limpopo** (m)	[limpɔpo]
Mississippi River	**Mississippi** (m)	[misisipi]

204. Forest

| forest | **forêt** (f) | [fɔrɛ] |
| forest (as adj) | **forestier** (adj) | [fɔrɛstje] |

thick forest	**fourré** (m)	[fure]
grove	**bosquet** (m)	[bɔskɛ]
forest clearing	**clairière** (f)	[klɛrjɛr]

| thicket | **broussailles** (f pl) | [brusaj] |
| scrubland | **taillis** (m) | [taji] |

| footpath (troddenpath) | **sentier** (m) | [sãtje] |
| gully | **ravin** (m) | [ravɛ̃] |

tree	**arbre** (m)	[arbr]
leaf	**feuille** (f)	[fœj]
leaves	**feuillage** (m)	[fœjaʒ]

fall of leaves	**chute** (f) **de feuilles**	[ʃyt də fœj]
to fall (ab. leaves)	**tomber** (vi)	[tɔ̃be]
top (of the tree)	**sommet** (m)	[sɔmɛ]

branch	**rameau** (m)	[ramo]
bough	**branche** (f)	[brãʃ]
bud (on shrub, tree)	**bourgeon** (m)	[burʒɔ̃]
needle (of pine tree)	**aiguille** (f)	[egɥij]
pine cone	**pomme** (f) **de pin**	[pɔm də pɛ̃]

hollow (in a tree)	**creux** (m)	[krø]
nest	**nid** (m)	[ni]
burrow (animal hole)	**terrier** (m)	[tɛrje]

| trunk | **tronc** (m) | [trɔ̃] |
| root | **racine** (f) | [rasin] |

| bark | **écorce** (f) | [ekɔrs] |
| moss | **mousse** (f) | [mus] |

to uproot (vt)	**déraciner** (vt)	[derasine]
to chop down	**abattre** (vt)	[abatr]
to deforest (vt)	**déboiser** (vt)	[debwaze]
tree stump	**souche** (f)	[suʃ]

campfire	**feu** (m) **de bois**	[fø də bwa]
forest fire	**incendie** (m)	[ɛ̃sɑ̃di]
to extinguish (vt)	**éteindre** (vt)	[etɛ̃dr]

forest ranger	**garde** (m) **forestier**	[gard fɔrɛstje]
protection	**protection** (f)	[prɔtɛksjɔ̃]
to protect (~ nature)	**protéger** (vt)	[prɔteʒe]
poacher	**braconnier** (m)	[brakɔnje]
trap (e.g., bear ~)	**piège** (m) **à mâchoires**	[pjɛʒ ɑ maʃwar]

| to gather, to pick (vt) | **cueillir** (vt) | [kœjir] |
| to lose one's way | **s'égarer** (vp) | [segare] |

205. Natural resources

natural resources	**ressources** (f pl) **naturelles**	[rəsurs natyrɛl]
minerals	**minéraux** (m pl)	[minero]
deposits	**gisement** (m)	[ʒizmɑ̃]
field (e.g., oilfield)	**champ** (m)	[ʃɑ̃]

to mine (extract)	**extraire** (vt)	[ɛkstrɛr]
mining (extraction)	**extraction** (f)	[ɛkstraksjɔ̃]
ore	**minerai** (m)	[minrɛ]
mine (e.g., for coal)	**mine** (f)	[min]
mine shaft, pit	**puits** (m) **de mine**	[pɥi də min]
miner	**mineur** (m)	[minœr]

| gas | **gaz** (m) | [gaz] |
| gas pipeline | **gazoduc** (m) | [gazɔdyk] |

oil (petroleum)	**pétrole** (m)	[petrɔl]
oil pipeline	**pipeline** (m)	[piplin]
oil well	**tour** (f) **de forage**	[tur də fɔraʒ]
derrick	**derrick** (m)	[derik]
tanker	**pétrolier** (m)	[petrɔlje]

sand	**sable** (m)	[sabl]
limestone	**calcaire** (m)	[kalkɛr]
gravel	**gravier** (m)	[gravje]
peat	**tourbe** (f)	[turb]
clay	**argile** (f)	[arʒil]

coal	**charbon** (m)	[ʃarbɔ̃]
iron	**fer** (m)	[fɛr]
gold	**or** (m)	[ɔr]
silver	**argent** (m)	[arʒɑ̃]
nickel	**nickel** (m)	[nikɛl]
copper	**cuivre** (m)	[kɥivr]
zinc	**zinc** (m)	[zɛ̃g]
manganese	**manganèse** (m)	[mɑ̃ganɛz]
mercury	**mercure** (m)	[mɛrkyr]
lead	**plomb** (m)	[plɔ̃]
mineral	**minéral** (m)	[mineral]
crystal	**cristal** (m)	[kristal]
marble	**marbre** (m)	[marbr]
uranium	**uranium** (m)	[yranjɔm]

The Earth. Part 2

206. Weather

weather	**temps** (m)	[tɑ̃]
weather forecast	**météo** (f)	[meteo]
temperature	**température** (f)	[tɑ̃peratyr]
thermometer	**thermomètre** (m)	[tɛrmɔmɛtr]
barometer	**baromètre** (m)	[barɔmɛtr]
humid (adj)	**humide** (adj)	[ymid]
humidity	**humidité** (f)	[ymidite]
heat (extreme ~)	**chaleur** (f)	[ʃalœr]
hot (torrid)	**torride** (adj)	[tɔrid]
it's hot	**il fait très chaud**	[il fɛ trɛ ʃo]
it's warm	**il fait chaud**	[il fɛʃo]
warm (moderately hot)	**chaud** (adj)	[ʃo]
it's cold	**il fait froid**	[il fɛ frwa]
cold (adj)	**froid** (adj)	[frwa]
sun	**soleil** (m)	[sɔlɛj]
to shine (vi)	**briller** (vi)	[brije]
sunny (day)	**ensoleillé** (adj)	[ɑ̃sɔleje]
to come up (vi)	**se lever** (vp)	[sə ləve]
to set (vi)	**se coucher** (vp)	[sə kuʃe]
cloud	**nuage** (m)	[nɥaʒ]
cloudy (adj)	**nuageux** (adj)	[nɥaʒø]
rain cloud	**nuée** (f)	[nɥe]
somber (gloomy)	**sombre** (adj)	[sɔ̃br]
rain	**pluie** (f)	[plɥi]
it's raining	**il pleut**	[il plø]
rainy (day)	**pluvieux** (adj)	[plyvjø]
to drizzle (vi)	**bruiner** (v imp)	[brɥine]
pouring rain	**pluie** (f) **torrentielle**	[plɥi tɔrɑ̃sjɛl]
downpour	**averse** (f)	[avɛrs]
heavy (e.g., ~ rain)	**forte** (adj)	[fɔrt]
puddle	**flaque** (f)	[flak]
to get wet (in rain)	**se faire mouiller**	[sə fɛr muje]
fog (mist)	**brouillard** (m)	[brujar]
foggy	**brumeux** (adj)	[brymø]

snow	neige (f)	[nɛʒ]
it's snowing	il neige	[il nɛʒ]

207. Severe weather. Natural disasters

thunderstorm	orage (m)	[ɔraʒ]
lightning (~ strike)	éclair (m)	[eklɛr]
to flash (vi)	éclater (vi)	[eklate]

thunder	tonnerre (m)	[tɔnɛr]
to thunder (vi)	gronder (vi)	[grõde]
it's thundering	le tonnerre gronde	[lə tɔnɛr grõd]

hail	grêle (f)	[grɛl]
it's hailing	il grêle	[il grɛl]

to flood (vt)	inonder (vt)	[inõde]
flood, inundation	inondation (f)	[inõdasjõ]

earthquake	tremblement (m) de terre	[trãbləmã də tɛr]
tremor, quake	secousse (f)	[səkus]
epicenter	épicentre (m)	[episãtr]
eruption	éruption (f)	[erypsjõ]
lava	lave (f)	[lav]

twister	tourbillon (m)	[turbijõ]
tornado	tornade (f)	[tɔrnad]
typhoon	typhon (m)	[tifõ]

hurricane	ouragan (m)	[uragã]
storm	tempête (f)	[tãpɛt]
tsunami	tsunami (m)	[tsynami]

cyclone	cyclone (m)	[siklon]
bad weather	intempéries (f pl)	[ɛ̃tãperi]
fire (accident)	incendie (m)	[ɛ̃sãdi]
disaster	catastrophe (f)	[katastrɔf]
meteorite	météorite (m)	[meteorit]

avalanche	avalanche (f)	[avalãʃ]
snowslide	éboulement (m)	[ebulmã]
blizzard	blizzard (m)	[blizar]
snowstorm	tempête (f) de neige	[tãpɛt də nɛʒ]

208. Noises. Sounds

silence (quiet)	silence (m)	[silãs]
sound	son (m)	[sõ]

noise	**bruit** (m)	[brɥi]
to make noise	**faire du bruit**	[fɛr dy brɥi]
noisy (adj)	**bruyant** (adj)	[brɥijɑ̃]
loudly (to speak, etc.)	**fort** (adv)	[fɔr]
loud (voice, etc.)	**fort** (adj)	[fɔr]
constant (continuous)	**constant** (adj)	[kɔ̃stɑ̃]
shout (n)	**cri** (m)	[kri]
to shout (vi)	**crier** (vi)	[krije]
whisper	**chuchotement** (m)	[ʃyʃɔtmɑ̃]
to whisper (vi, vt)	**chuchoter** (vi, vt)	[ʃyʃɔte]
barking (of dog)	**aboiement** (m)	[abwamɑ̃]
to bark (vi)	**aboyer** (vi)	[abwaje]
groan (of pain)	**gémissement** (m)	[ʒemismɑ̃]
to groan (vi)	**gémir** (vi)	[ʒemir]
cough	**toux** (f)	[tu]
to cough (vi)	**tousser** (vi)	[tuse]
whistle	**sifflement** (m)	[sifləmɑ̃]
to whistle (vi)	**siffler** (vi)	[sifle]
knock (at the door)	**coups** (m pl) **à la porte**	[ku ɑla pɔrt]
to knock (at the door)	**frapper** (vi)	[frape]
to crack (vi)	**craquer** (vi)	[krake]
crack (plank, etc.)	**craquement** (m)	[krakmɑ̃]
siren	**sirène** (f)	[sirɛn]
whistle (factory ~)	**sifflement** (m)	[sifləmɑ̃]
to whistle (ship, train)	**siffler** (vi)	[sifle]
honk (signal)	**coup** (m) **de klaxon**	[ku də klaksɔn]
to honk (vi)	**klaxonner** (vi)	[klaksɔne]

209. Winter

winter (n)	**hiver** (m)	[ivɛr]
winter (as adj)	**d'hiver** (adj)	[divɛr]
in winter	**en hiver**	[ɑn ivɛr]
snow	**neige** (f)	[nɛʒ]
it's snowing	**il neige**	[il nɛʒ]
snowfall	**chute** (f) **de neige**	[ʃyt də nɛʒ]
snowdrift	**congère** (f)	[kɔ̃ʒɛr]
snowflake	**flocon** (m) **de neige**	[flɔkɔ̃ də nɛʒ]
snowball	**boule** (f) **de neige**	[bul də nɛʒ]
snowman	**bonhomme** (m) **de neige**	[bɔnɔm də nɛʒ]
icicle	**glaçon** (m)	[glasɔ̃]

December	**décembre** (m)	[desɑ̃br]
January	**janvier** (m)	[ʒɑ̃vje]
February	**février** (m)	[fevrije]
severe frost	**gel** (m)	[ʒɛl]
frosty (weather, air)	**glacial** (adj)	[glasjal]
below zero (adv)	**au-dessous de zéro**	[odsu də zero]
first frost	**premières gelées** (f pl)	[prəmjɛr ʒəle]
hoarfrost	**givre** (m)	[ʒivr]
cold (cold weather)	**froid** (m)	[frwa]
it's cold	**il fait froid**	[il fɛ frwa]
fur coat	**manteau** (m) **de fourrure**	[mɑ̃to də furyr]
mittens	**moufles** (f pl)	[mufl]
to get sick	**tomber malade**	[tɔ̃be malad]
cold (illness)	**refroidissement** (m)	[rəfrwadismɑ̃]
to catch a cold	**prendre froid**	[prɑ̃dr frwa]
ice	**glace** (f)	[glas]
black ice	**verglas** (m)	[vɛrgla]
to freeze (ab. river, etc.)	**être gelé**	[ɛtr ʒəle]
ice floe	**bloc** (m) **de glace**	[blɔk də glas]
skis	**skis** (m pl)	[ski]
skier	**skieur** (m)	[skjœr]
to ski (vi)	**faire du ski**	[fɛr dy ski]
to skate (vi)	**patiner** (vi)	[patine]

Fauna

210. Mammals. Predators

predator	**prédateur** (m)	[predatœr]
tiger	**tigre** (m)	[tigr]
lion	**lion** (m)	[ljɔ̃]
wolf	**loup** (m)	[lu]
fox	**renard** (m)	[rənar]
jaguar	**jaguar** (m)	[ʒagwar]
leopard	**léopard** (m)	[leɔpar]
cheetah	**guépard** (m)	[gepar]
black panther	**panthère** (f)	[pɑ̃tɛr]
puma	**puma** (m)	[pyma]
snow leopard	**léopard** (m) **de neiges**	[leɔpar də nɛʒ]
lynx	**lynx** (m)	[lɛ̃ks]
coyote	**coyote** (m)	[kɔjɔt]
jackal	**chacal** (m)	[ʃakal]
hyena	**hyène** (f)	[jɛn]

211. Wild animals

animal	**animal** (m)	[animal]
beast (animal)	**bête** (f)	[bɛt]
squirrel	**écureuil** (m)	[ekyrœj]
hedgehog	**hérisson** (m)	[erisɔ̃]
hare	**lièvre** (m)	[ljɛvr]
rabbit	**lapin** (m)	[lapɛ̃]
badger	**blaireau** (m)	[blɛro]
raccoon	**raton** (m)	[ratɔ̃]
hamster	**hamster** (m)	[amstɛr]
marmot	**marmotte** (f)	[marmɔt]
mole	**taupe** (f)	[top]
mouse	**souris** (f)	[suri]
rat	**rat** (m)	[ra]
bat	**chauve-souris** (f)	[ʃovsuri]
ermine	**hermine** (f)	[ɛrmin]
sable	**zibeline** (f)	[ziblin]

marten	**martre** (f)	[martr]
weasel	**belette** (f)	[bəlɛt]
mink	**vison** (m)	[vizɔ̃]

| beaver | **castor** (m) | [kastɔr] |
| otter | **loutre** (f) | [lutr] |

horse	**cheval** (m)	[ʃəval]
moose	**élan** (m)	[elɑ̃]
deer	**cerf** (m)	[sɛr]
camel	**chameau** (m)	[ʃamo]

bison	**bison** (m)	[bizɔ̃]
aurochs	**aurochs** (m)	[orɔk]
buffalo	**buffle** (m)	[byfl]

zebra	**zèbre** (m)	[zɛbr]
antelope	**antilope** (f)	[ɑ̃tilɔp]
roe deer	**chevreuil** (m)	[ʃəvrœj]
fallow deer	**biche** (f)	[biʃ]
chamois	**chamois** (m)	[ʃamwa]
wild boar	**sanglier** (m)	[sɑ̃glije]

whale	**baleine** (f)	[balɛn]
seal	**phoque** (m)	[fɔk]
walrus	**morse** (m)	[mɔrs]
fur seal	**ours** (m) **de mer**	[urs də mɛr]
dolphin	**dauphin** (m)	[dofɛ̃]

bear	**ours** (m)	[urs]
polar bear	**ours** (m) **blanc**	[urs blɑ̃]
panda	**panda** (m)	[pɑ̃da]

monkey	**singe** (m)	[sɛ̃ʒ]
chimpanzee	**chimpanzé** (m)	[ʃɛ̃pɑ̃ze]
orangutan	**orang-outang** (m)	[ɔrɑ̃utɑ̃]
gorilla	**gorille** (m)	[gɔrij]
macaque	**macaque** (m)	[makak]
gibbon	**gibbon** (m)	[ʒibɔ̃]

elephant	**éléphant** (m)	[elefɑ̃]
rhinoceros	**rhinocéros** (m)	[rinɔserɔs]
giraffe	**girafe** (f)	[ʒiraf]
hippopotamus	**hippopotame** (m)	[ipopotam]

| kangaroo | **kangourou** (m) | [kɑ̃guru] |
| koala (bear) | **koala** (m) | [kɔala] |

mongoose	**mangouste** (f)	[mɑ̃gust]
chinchilla	**chinchilla** (m)	[ʃɛ̃ʃila]
skunk	**mouffette** (f)	[mufɛt]
porcupine	**porc-épic** (m)	[pɔrkepik]

212. Domestic animals

cat	**chat** (m)	[ʃa]
tomcat	**chat** (m)	[ʃa]
dog	**chien** (m)	[ʃjɛ̃]
horse	**cheval** (m)	[ʃəval]
stallion	**étalon** (m)	[etalɔ̃]
mare	**jument** (f)	[ʒymɑ̃]
cow	**vache** (f)	[vaʃ]
bull	**taureau** (m)	[tɔro]
ox	**bœuf** (m)	[bœf]
sheep	**brebis** (f)	[brəbi]
ram	**mouton** (m)	[mutɔ̃]
goat	**chèvre** (f)	[ʃɛvr]
billy goat, he-goat	**bouc** (m)	[buk]
donkey	**âne** (m)	[ɑn]
mule	**mulet** (m)	[mylɛ]
pig	**cochon** (m)	[kɔʃɔ̃]
piglet	**pourceau** (m)	[purso]
rabbit	**lapin** (m)	[lapɛ̃]
hen (chicken)	**poule** (f)	[pul]
rooster	**coq** (m)	[kɔk]
duck	**canard** (m)	[kanar]
drake	**canard** (m) **mâle**	[kanar mal]
goose	**oie** (f)	[wa]
tom turkey	**dindon** (m)	[dɛ̃dɔ̃]
turkey (hen)	**dinde** (f)	[dɛ̃d]
domestic animals	**animaux** (m pl) **domestiques**	[animo dɔmɛstik]
tame (e.g., ~ hamster)	**apprivoisé** (adj)	[aprivwaze]
to tame (vt)	**apprivoiser** (vt)	[aprivwaze]
to breed (vt)	**élever** (vt)	[elve]
farm	**ferme** (f)	[fɛrm]
poultry	**volaille** (f)	[vɔlaj]
cattle	**bétail** (m)	[betaj]
herd (cattle)	**troupeau** (m)	[trupo]
stable	**écurie** (f)	[ekyri]
pigsty	**porcherie** (f)	[pɔrʃəri]
cowshed	**vacherie** (f)	[vaʃri]
rabbit hutch	**cabane** (f) **à lapins**	[kaban ɑ lapɛ̃]
hen house	**poulailler** (m)	[pulaje]

213. Dogs. Dog breeds

dog	**chien** (m)	[ʃjɛ̃]
sheepdog	**berger** (m)	[bɛrʒe]
German shepherd dog	**berger** (m) **allemand**	[bɛrʒe almɑ̃]
poodle	**caniche** (f)	[kaniʃ]
dachshund	**teckel** (m)	[tekɛl]
bulldog	**bouledogue** (m)	[buldɔg]
boxer	**boxer** (m)	[bɔksɛr]
mastiff	**mastiff** (m)	[mastif]
rottweiler	**rottweiler** (m)	[rɔtvajlœr]
Doberman	**doberman** (m)	[dɔbɛrman]
basset	**basset** (m)	[basɛ]
bobtail	**bobtail** (m)	[bɔbtɛjl]
Dalmatian	**dalmatien** (m)	[dalmasjɛ̃]
cocker spaniel	**cocker** (m)	[kɔkɛr]
Newfoundland	**terre-neuve** (m)	[tɛrnœv]
Saint Bernard	**saint-bernard** (m)	[sɛ̃bɛrnar]
husky	**husky** (m)	[œski]
Chow Chow	**chow-chow** (m)	[ʃoʃo]
spitz	**spitz** (m)	[spitz]
pug	**carlin** (m)	[karlɛ̃]

214. Sounds made by animals

barking (n)	**aboiement** (m)	[abwamɑ̃]
to bark (vi)	**aboyer** (vi)	[abwaje]
to meow (vi)	**miauler** (vi)	[mjole]
to purr (vi)	**ronronner** (vi)	[rɔ̃rɔne]
to moo (vi)	**meugler** (vi)	[møgle]
to bellow (bull)	**beugler** (vi)	[bøgle]
to growl (vi)	**rugir** (vi)	[ryʒir]
howl (n)	**hurlement** (m)	[yrləmɑ̃]
to howl (vi)	**hurler** (vi)	[yrle]
to whine (vi)	**geindre** (vi)	[ʒɛ̃dr]
to bleat (sheep)	**bêler** (vi)	[bele]
to oink, to grunt (pig)	**grogner** (vi)	[grɔɲe]
to squeal (vi)	**glapir** (vi)	[glapir]
to croak (vi)	**coasser** (vi)	[kɔase]
to buzz (insect)	**bourdonner** (vi)	[burdɔne]
to stridulate (vi)	**striduler** (vi)	[stridyle]

215. Young animals

cub	**bébé** (m)	[bebe]
kitten	**chaton** (m)	[ʃatɔ̃]
baby mouse	**souriceau** (m)	[suriso]
pup, puppy	**chiot** (m)	[ʃjo]
leveret	**levraut** (m)	[ləvro]
baby rabbit	**lapereau** (m)	[lapro]
wolf cub	**louveteau** (m)	[luvto]
fox cub	**renardeau** (m)	[rənardo]
bear cub	**ourson** (m)	[ursɔ̃]
lion cub	**lionceau** (m)	[ljɔ̃so]
tiger cub	**bébé** (m) **tigre**	[bebe tigr]
elephant calf	**éléphanteau** (m)	[elefɑ̃to]
piglet	**pourceau** (m)	[purso]
calf (young cow, bull)	**veau** (m)	[vo]
kid (young goat)	**chevreau** (m)	[ʃəvro]
lamb	**agneau** (m)	[aɲo]
fawn (young deer)	**faon** (m)	[fɑ̃]
young camel	**bébé** (m) **chameau**	[bebe ʃamo]
baby snake	**serpenteau** (m)	[sɛrpɑ̃to]
baby frog	**bébé** (m) **grenouille**	[bebe grənuj]
nestling	**oisillon** (m)	[wazijɔ̃]
chick (of chicken)	**poussin** (m)	[pusɛ̃]
duckling	**canardeau** (m)	[kanardo]

216. Birds

bird	**oiseau** (m)	[wazo]
pigeon	**pigeon** (m)	[piʒɔ̃]
sparrow	**moineau** (m)	[mwano]
tit	**mésange** (f)	[mezɑ̃ʒ]
magpie	**pie** (f)	[pi]
raven	**corbeau** (m)	[kɔrbo]
crow	**corneille** (f)	[kɔrnɛj]
jackdaw	**choucas** (m)	[ʃuka]
rook	**freux** (m)	[frø]
duck	**canard** (m)	[kanar]
goose	**oie** (f)	[wa]
pheasant	**faisan** (m)	[fəzɑ̃]
eagle	**aigle** (m)	[ɛgl]
hawk	**épervier** (m)	[epɛrvje]

falcon	**faucon** (m)	[fokɔ̃]
vulture	**vautour** (m)	[votur]
condor (Andean ~)	**condor** (m)	[kɔ̃dɔr]
swan	**cygne** (m)	[siɲ]
crane	**grue** (f)	[gry]
stork	**cigogne** (f)	[sigɔɲ]
parrot	**perroquet** (m)	[perɔkɛ]
hummingbird	**colibri** (m)	[kɔlibri]
peacock	**paon** (m)	[pɑ̃]
ostrich	**autruche** (f)	[otryʃ]
heron	**héron** (m)	[erɔ̃]
flamingo	**flamant** (m)	[flamɑ̃]
pelican	**pélican** (m)	[pelikɑ̃]
nightingale	**rossignol** (m)	[rɔsiɲɔl]
swallow	**hirondelle** (f)	[irɔ̃dɛl]
thrush	**merle** (m)	[mɛrl]
song thrush	**grive** (f)	[griv]
blackbird	**merle** (m) **noir**	[mɛrl nwar]
swift	**martinet** (m)	[martinɛ]
lark	**alouette** (f) **des champs**	[alwɛt de ʃɑ̃]
quail	**caille** (f)	[kaj]
woodpecker	**pivert** (m)	[pivɛr]
cuckoo	**coucou** (m)	[kuku]
owl	**chouette** (f)	[ʃwɛt]
eagle owl	**hibou** (m)	[ibu]
wood grouse	**tétras** (m)	[tetra]
black grouse	**tétras-lyre** (m)	[tetralir]
partridge	**perdrix** (f)	[pɛrdri]
starling	**étourneau** (m)	[eturno]
canary	**canari** (m)	[kanari]
hazel grouse	**gélinotte** (f) **des bois**	[ʒelinɔt də bwa]
chaffinch	**pinson** (m)	[pɛ̃sɔ̃]
bullfinch	**bouvreuil** (m)	[buvrœj]
seagull	**mouette** (f)	[mwɛt]
albatross	**albatros** (m)	[albatros]
penguin	**pingouin** (m)	[pɛ̃gwɛ̃]

217. Birds. Singing and sounds

to sing (vi)	**chanter** (vi)	[ʃɑ̃te]
to call (animal, bird)	**crier** (vi)	[krije]

to crow (rooster)	chanter (vi)	[ʃɑ̃te]
cock-a-doodle-doo	cocorico (m)	[kɔkɔriko]
to cluck (hen)	glousser (vi)	[gluse]
to caw (vi)	croasser (vi)	[krɔase]
to quack (duck)	cancaner (vi)	[kɑ̃kane]
to cheep (vi)	piauler (vi)	[pjole]
to chirp, to twitter	pépier (vi)	[pepje]

218. Fish. Marine animals

bream	brème (f)	[brɛm]
carp	carpe (f)	[karp]
perch	perche (f)	[pɛrʃ]
catfish	silure (m)	[silyr]
pike	brochet (m)	[brɔʃɛ]
salmon	saumon (m)	[somɔ̃]
sturgeon	esturgeon (m)	[ɛstyrʒɔ̃]
herring	hareng (m)	[arɑ̃]
Atlantic salmon	saumon (m) atlantique	[somɔ̃ atlɑ̃tik]
mackerel	maquereau (m)	[makro]
flatfish	flet (m)	[flɛ]
zander, pike perch	sandre (f)	[sɑ̃dr]
cod	morue (f)	[mɔry]
tuna	thon (m)	[tɔ̃]
trout	truite (f)	[trɥit]
eel	anguille (f)	[ɑ̃gij]
electric ray	torpille (f)	[tɔrpij]
moray eel	murène (f)	[myrɛn]
piranha	piranha (m)	[piraɲa]
shark	requin (m)	[rəkɛ̃]
dolphin	dauphin (m)	[dofɛ̃]
whale	baleine (f)	[balɛn]
crab	crabe (m)	[krab]
jellyfish	méduse (f)	[medyz]
octopus	pieuvre (f), poulpe (m)	[pjœvr], [pulp]
starfish	étoile (f) de mer	[etwal də mɛr]
sea urchin	oursin (m)	[ursɛ̃]
seahorse	hippocampe (m)	[ipɔkɑ̃p]
oyster	huître (f)	[ɥitr]
shrimp	crevette (f)	[krəvɛt]
lobster	homard (m)	[ɔmar]
spiny lobster	langoustine (f)	[lɑ̃gustin]

219. Amphibians. Reptiles

snake	**serpent** (m)	[sɛrpɑ̃]
venomous (snake)	**venimeux** (adj)	[vənimø]
viper	**vipère** (f)	[vipɛr]
cobra	**cobra** (m)	[kɔbra]
python	**python** (m)	[pitɔ̃]
boa	**boa** (m)	[bɔa]
grass snake	**couleuvre** (f)	[kulœvr]
rattle snake	**serpent** (m) **à sonnettes**	[sɛrpɑ̃ a sɔnɛt]
anaconda	**anaconda** (m)	[anakɔ̃da]
lizard	**lézard** (m)	[lezar]
iguana	**iguane** (m)	[igwan]
monitor lizard	**varan** (m)	[varɑ̃]
salamander	**salamandre** (f)	[salamɑ̃dr]
chameleon	**caméléon** (m)	[kameleɔ̃]
scorpion	**scorpion** (m)	[skɔrpjɔ̃]
turtle	**tortue** (f)	[tɔrty]
frog	**grenouille** (f)	[grənuj]
toad	**crapaud** (m)	[krapo]
crocodile	**crocodile** (m)	[krɔkɔdil]

220. Insects

insect, bug	**insecte** (m)	[ɛ̃sɛkt]
butterfly	**papillon** (m)	[papijɔ̃]
ant	**fourmi** (f)	[furmi]
fly	**mouche** (f)	[muʃ]
mosquito	**moustique** (m)	[mustik]
beetle	**scarabée** (m)	[skarabe]
wasp	**guêpe** (f)	[gɛp]
bee	**abeille** (f)	[abɛj]
bumblebee	**bourdon** (m)	[burdɔ̃]
gadfly	**œstre** (m)	[ɛstr]
spider	**araignée** (f)	[arɛɲe]
spider's web	**toile** (f) **d'araignée**	[twal darɛɲe]
dragonfly	**libellule** (f)	[libelyl]
grasshopper	**sauterelle** (f)	[sotrɛl]
moth (night butterfly)	**papillon** (m)	[papijɔ̃]
cockroach	**cafard** (m)	[kafar]
tick	**tique** (f)	[tik]

| flea | puce (f) | [pys] |
| midge | moucheron (m) | [muʃrɔ̃] |

locust	criquet (m)	[krikɛ]
snail	escargot (m)	[ɛskargo]
cricket	grillon (m)	[grijɔ̃]

lightning bug	luciole (f)	[lysjɔl]
ladybug	coccinelle (f)	[kɔksinɛl]
cockchafer	hanneton (m)	[antɔ̃]

leech	sangsue (f)	[sɑ̃sy]
caterpillar	chenille (f)	[ʃənij]
earthworm	ver (m)	[vɛr]
larva	larve (f)	[larv]

221. Animals. Body parts

beak	bec (m)	[bɛk]
wings	ailes (f pl)	[ɛl]
foot (of bird)	patte (f)	[pat]
feathering	plumage (m)	[plymaʒ]

| feather | plume (f) | [plym] |
| crest | houppe (f) | [up] |

gill	ouïes (f pl)	[wi]
spawn	les œufs (m pl)	[lezø]
larva	larve (f)	[larv]

| fin | nageoire (f) | [naʒwar] |
| scales (of fish, reptile) | écaille (f) | [ekaj] |

fang (canine)	croc (m)	[kro]
paw (e.g., cat's ~)	patte (f)	[pat]
muzzle (snout)	museau (m)	[myzo]
mouth (of cat, dog)	gueule (f)	[gœl]

| tail | queue (f) | [kø] |
| whiskers | moustaches (f pl) | [mustaʃ] |

| hoof | sabot (m) | [sabo] |
| horn | corne (f) | [kɔrn] |

carapace	carapace (f)	[karapas]
shell (of mollusk)	coquillage (m)	[kɔkijaʒ]
eggshell	coquille (f) d'œuf	[kɔkij dœf]

| animal's hair (pelage) | poil (m) | [pwal] |
| pelt (hide) | peau (f) | [po] |

222. Actions of animals

to fly (vi)	**voler** (vi)	[vɔle]
to make circles	**faire des cercles**	[fɛr de sɛrkl]
to fly away	**s'envoler** (vp)	[sɑ̃vɔle]
to flap (~ the wings)	**battre des ailes**	[batr dezɛl]
to peck (vi)	**picorer** (vt)	[pikɔre]
to sit on eggs	**couver** (vt)	[kuve]
to hatch out (vi)	**éclore** (vt)	[eklɔr]
to build the nest	**faire un nid**	[fɛr œ̃ ni]
to slither, to crawl	**ramper** (vi)	[rɑ̃pe]
to sting, to bite (insect)	**piquer** (vi)	[pike]
to bite (ab. animal)	**mordre** (vt)	[mɔrdr]
to sniff (vt)	**flairer** (vt)	[flɛre]
to bark (vi)	**aboyer** (vi)	[abwaje]
to hiss (snake)	**siffler** (vi)	[sifle]
to scare (vt)	**effrayer** (vt)	[efreje]
to attack (vt)	**attaquer** (vt)	[atake]
to gnaw (bone, etc.)	**ronger** (vt)	[rɔ̃ʒe]
to scratch (with claws)	**griffer** (vt)	[grife]
to hide (vi)	**se cacher** (vp)	[sə kaʃe]
to play (kittens, etc.)	**jouer** (vt)	[ʒwe]
to hunt (vi, vt)	**chasser** (vi, vt)	[ʃase]
to hibernate (vi)	**être en hibernation**	[ɛtr ɑ̃ ibɛrnasjɔ̃]
to become extinct	**disparaître** (vi)	[disparɛtr]

223. Animals. Habitats

habitat	**habitat** (m) **naturel**	[abita natyrɛl]
migration	**migration** (f)	[migrasjɔ̃]
mountain	**montagne** (f)	[mɔ̃taɲ]
reef	**récif** (m)	[resif]
cliff	**rocher** (m)	[rɔʃe]
forest	**forêt** (f)	[fɔrɛ]
jungle	**jungle** (f)	[ʒœ̃gl]
savanna	**savane** (f)	[savan]
tundra	**toundra** (f)	[tundra]
steppe	**steppe** (f)	[stɛp]
desert	**désert** (m)	[dezɛr]
oasis	**oasis** (f)	[ɔazis]
sea	**mer** (f)	[mɛr]

lake	**lac** (m)	[lak]
ocean	**océan** (m)	[ɔseɑ̃]
swamp	**marais** (m)	[marɛ]
freshwater (adj)	**d'eau douce** (adj)	[do dus]
pond	**étang** (m)	[etɑ̃]
river	**rivière** (f), **fleuve** (m)	[rivjɛr], [flœv]
den	**tanière** (f)	[tanjɛr]
nest	**nid** (m)	[ni]
hollow (in a tree)	**creux** (m)	[krø]
burrow (animal hole)	**terrier** (m)	[tɛrje]
anthill	**fourmilière** (f)	[furmiljɛr]

224. Animal care

zoo	**zoo** (m)	[zoo]
nature preserve	**réserve** (f) **naturelle**	[rezɛrv natyrɛl]
breeder, breed club	**pépinière** (f)	[pepinjɛr]
open-air cage	**volière** (f)	[vɔljɛr]
cage	**cage** (f)	[kaʒ]
kennel	**niche** (f)	[niʃ]
dovecot	**pigeonnier** (m)	[piʒɔnje]
aquarium	**aquarium** (m)	[akwarjɔm]
dolphinarium	**delphinarium** (m)	[dɛlfinarjɔm]
to breed (animals)	**élever** (vt)	[elve]
brood, litter	**nichée** (f), **portée** (f)	[niʃe], [pɔrte]
to tame (vt)	**apprivoiser** (vt)	[aprivwaze]
feed (fodder, etc.)	**aliments** (pl) **pour animaux**	[alimɑ̃ pur animo]
to feed (vt)	**nourrir** (vt)	[nurir]
to train (animals)	**dresser** (vt)	[drese]
pet store	**magasin** (m) **d'animaux**	[magazɛ̃ danimo]
muzzle (for dog)	**muselière** (f)	[myzeljɛr]
collar	**collier** (m)	[kɔlje]
name (of animal)	**nom** (m)	[nɔ̃]
pedigree (of dog)	**pedigree** (m)	[pedigre]

225. Animals. Miscellaneous

pack (wolves)	**meute** (f)	[møt]
flock (birds)	**volée** (f)	[vɔle]
shoal (fish)	**banc** (m)	[bɑ̃]
herd of horses	**troupeau** (m)	[trupo]

| male (n) | mâle (m) | [mal] |
| female | femelle (f) | [fəmɛl] |

hungry (adj)	affamé (adj)	[afame]
wild (adj)	sauvage (adj)	[sovaʒ]
dangerous (adj)	dangereux (adj)	[dɑ̃ʒrø]

226. Horses

| horse | cheval (m) | [ʃəval] |
| breed (race) | race (f) | [ras] |

| foal, colt | poulain (m) | [pulɛ̃] |
| mare | jument (f) | [ʒymɑ̃] |

mustang	mustang (m)	[mystɑ̃g]
pony	poney (m)	[pɔnɛ]
draft horse	cheval (m) de trait	[ʃəval də trɛ]

| mane | crin (m) | [krɛ̃] |
| tail | queue (f) | [kø] |

hoof	sabot (m)	[sabo]
horseshoe	fer (m) à cheval	[fɛr ɑ ʃəval]
to shoe (vt)	ferrer (vt)	[fɛre]
blacksmith	maréchal-ferrant (m)	[mareʃalferɑ̃]

saddle	selle (f)	[sɛl]
stirrup	étrier (m)	[etrije]
bridle	bride (f)	[brid]
reins	rênes (f pl)	[rɛn]
whip (for riding)	fouet (m)	[fwɛ]

rider	cavalier (m)	[kavalje]
to break in (horse)	débourrer (vt)	[debure]
to saddle (vt)	seller (vt)	[sele]
to mount a horse	se mettre en selle	[sə mɛtr ɑ̃ sɛl]

gallop	galop (m)	[galo]
to gallop (vi)	aller au galop	[ale o galo]
trot (n)	trot (m)	[tro]
at a trot (adv)	au trot (adv)	[otro]
to go at a trot	aller au trot	[ale otro]

| racehorse | cheval (m) de course | [ʃəval də kurs] |
| horse racing | courses (f pl) à chevaux | [kurs ɑ ʃəvø] |

stable	écurie (f)	[ekyri]
to feed (vt)	nourrir (vt)	[nurir]
hay	foin (m)	[fwɛ̃]

to water (animals)	**abreuver** (vt)	[abrœve]
to wash (horse)	**laver** (vt)	[lave]
to hobble (tether)	**entraver** (vt)	[ɑ̃trave]
horse-drawn cart	**charrette** (f)	[ʃarɛt]
to graze (vi)	**paître** (vi)	[pɛtr]
to neigh (vi)	**hennir** (vi)	[enir]
to kick (horse)	**ruer** (vi)	[rɥe]

Flora

227. Trees

tree	**arbre** (m)	[arbr]
deciduous (adj)	**à feuilles caduques**	[a fœj kadyk]
coniferous (adj)	**conifère** (adj)	[kɔnifɛr]
evergreen (adj)	**à feuilles persistantes**	[a fœj pɛrsistãt]
apple tree	**pommier** (m)	[pɔmje]
pear tree	**poirier** (m)	[pwarje]
sweet cherry tree	**merisier** (m)	[mərizje]
sour cherry tree	**cerisier** (m)	[sərizje]
plum tree	**prunier** (m)	[prynje]
birch	**bouleau** (m)	[bulo]
oak	**chêne** (m)	[ʃɛn]
linden tree	**tilleul** (m)	[tijœl]
aspen	**tremble** (m)	[trãbl]
maple	**érable** (m)	[erabl]
spruce	**épicéa** (m)	[episea]
pine	**pin** (m)	[pɛ̃]
larch	**mélèze** (m)	[melɛz]
fir tree	**sapin** (m)	[sapɛ̃]
cedar	**cèdre** (m)	[sɛdr]
poplar	**peuplier** (m)	[pøplije]
rowan	**sorbier** (m)	[sɔrbje]
willow	**saule** (m)	[sol]
alder	**aune** (m)	[on]
beech	**hêtre** (m)	[ɛtr]
elm	**orme** (m)	[ɔrm]
ash (tree)	**frêne** (m)	[frɛn]
chestnut	**marronnier** (m)	[marɔnje]
magnolia	**magnolia** (m)	[maɲɔlja]
palm tree	**palmier** (m)	[palmje]
cypress	**cyprès** (m)	[siprɛ]
mangrove	**palétuvier** (m)	[paletyvje]
baobab	**baobab** (m)	[baɔbab]
eucalyptus	**eucalyptus** (m)	[økaliptys]
sequoia	**séquoia** (m)	[sekɔja]

228. Shrubs

bush	**buisson** (m)	[bɥisõ]
shrub	**arbrisseau** (m)	[arbriso]
grapevine	**vigne** (f)	[viɲ]
vineyard	**vigne** (f)	[viɲ]
raspberry bush	**framboise** (f)	[frãbwaz]
blackcurrant bush	**cassis** (m)	[kasis]
redcurrant bush	**groseille** (f) **rouge**	[grozɛj ruʒ]
gooseberry bush	**groseille** (f) **verte**	[grozɛj vɛrt]
acacia	**acacia** (m)	[akasja]
barberry	**berbéris** (m)	[bɛrberis]
jasmine	**jasmin** (m)	[ʒasmɛ̃]
juniper	**genévrier** (m)	[ʒənevrije]
rosebush	**rosier** (m)	[rozje]
dog rose	**églantier** (m)	[eglãtje]

229. Mushrooms

mushroom	**champignon** (m)	[ʃãpiɲõ]
edible mushroom	**champignon** (m) **comestible**	[ʃãpiɲõ kɔmɛstibl]
toadstool	**champignon** (m) **vénéneux**	[ʃãpiɲõ venenø]
cap (of mushroom)	**chapeau** (m)	[ʃapo]
stipe (of mushroom)	**pied** (m)	[pje]
cep (Boletus edulis)	**cèpe** (m)	[sɛp]
orange-cap boletus	**bolet** (m) **orangé**	[bolɛ ɔrãʒe]
birch bolete	**bolet** (m) **bai**	[bolɛ bɛ]
chanterelle	**girolle** (f)	[ʒirɔl]
russula	**russule** (f)	[rysyl]
morel	**morille** (f)	[mɔrij]
fly agaric	**amanite** (f) **tue-mouches**	[amanit tymuʃ]
death cap	**oronge** (f) **verte**	[ɔrõʒ vɛrt]

230. Fruits. Berries

fruit	**fruit** (m)	[frɥi]
fruits	**fruits** (m pl)	[frɥi]
apple	**pomme** (f)	[pɔm]
pear	**poire** (f)	[pwar]

plum	**prune** (f)	[pryn]
strawberry	**fraise** (f)	[frɛz]
sour cherry	**cerise** (f)	[səriz]
sweet cherry	**merise** (f)	[məriz]
grape	**raisin** (m)	[rɛzɛ̃]

raspberry	**framboise** (f)	[frãbwaz]
blackcurrant	**cassis** (m)	[kasis]
redcurrant	**groseille** (f) **rouge**	[grozɛj ruʒ]
gooseberry	**groseille** (f) **verte**	[grozɛj vɛrt]
cranberry	**canneberge** (f)	[kanbɛrʒ]

orange	**orange** (f)	[ɔrãʒ]
mandarin	**mandarine** (f)	[mãdarin]
pineapple	**ananas** (m)	[anana]
banana	**banane** (f)	[banan]
date	**datte** (f)	[dat]

lemon	**citron** (m)	[sitrɔ̃]
apricot	**abricot** (m)	[abriko]
peach	**pêche** (f)	[pɛʃ]
kiwi	**kiwi** (m)	[kiwi]
grapefruit	**pamplemousse** (m)	[pãpləmus]

berry	**baie** (f)	[bɛ]
berries	**baies** (f pl)	[bɛ]
cowberry	**airelle** (f) **rouge**	[ɛrɛl ruʒ]
field strawberry	**fraise** (f) **des bois**	[frɛz de bwa]
bilberry	**myrtille** (f)	[mirtij]

231. Flowers. Plants

| flower | **fleur** (f) | [flœr] |
| bouquet (of flowers) | **bouquet** (m) | [bukɛ] |

rose (flower)	**rose** (f)	[roz]
tulip	**tulipe** (f)	[tylip]
carnation	**oeillet** (m)	[œjɛ]
gladiolus	**glaïeul** (m)	[glajœl]

cornflower	**bleuet** (m)	[bløɛ]
bluebell	**campanule** (f)	[kãpanyl]
dandelion	**dent-de-lion** (f)	[dãdəljɔ̃]
camomile	**marguerite** (f)	[margərit]

aloe	**aloès** (m)	[alɔɛs]
cactus	**cactus** (m)	[kaktys]
rubber plant, ficus	**ficus** (m)	[fikys]
lily	**lis** (m)	[li]
geranium	**géranium** (m)	[ʒeranjɔm]

hyacinth	**jacinthe** (f)	[ʒasɛ̃t]
mimosa	**mimosa** (m)	[mimɔza]
narcissus	**jonquille** (f)	[ʒɔ̃kij]
nasturtium	**capucine** (f)	[kapysin]
orchid	**orchidée** (f)	[ɔrkide]
peony	**pivoine** (f)	[pivwan]
violet	**violette** (f)	[vjɔlɛt]
pansy	**pensée** (f)	[pɑ̃se]
forget-me-not	**myosotis** (m)	[mjɔzɔtis]
daisy	**pâquerette** (f)	[pɑkrɛt]
poppy	**coquelicot** (m)	[kɔkliko]
hemp	**chanvre** (m)	[ʃɑ̃vr]
mint	**menthe** (f)	[mɑ̃t]
lily of the valley	**muguet** (m)	[mygɛ]
snowdrop	**perce-neige** (f)	[pɛrsənɛʒ]
nettle	**ortie** (f)	[ɔrti]
sorrel	**oseille** (f)	[ozɛj]
water lily	**nénuphar** (m)	[nenyfar]
fern	**fougère** (f)	[fuʒɛr]
lichen	**lichen** (m)	[likɛn]
tropical greenhouse	**serre** (f) **tropicale**	[sɛr trɔpikal]
grass lawn	**gazon** (m)	[gazɔ̃]
flowerbed	**parterre** (m) **de fleurs**	[partɛr də flœr]
plant	**plante** (f)	[plɑ̃t]
grass, herb	**herbe** (f)	[ɛrb]
blade of grass	**brin** (m) **d'herbe**	[brɛ̃ dɛrb]
leaf	**feuille** (f)	[fœj]
petal	**pétale** (m)	[petal]
stem	**tige** (f)	[tiʒ]
tuber	**tubercule** (m)	[tybɛrkyl]
young plant (shoot)	**pousse** (f)	[pus]
thorn	**épine** (f)	[epin]
to blossom (vi)	**fleurir** (vi)	[flœrir]
to fade, to wither	**se faner** (vp)	[sə fane]
smell (odor)	**odeur** (f)	[ɔdœr]
to cut (flowers)	**couper** (vt)	[kupe]
to pick (a flower)	**cueillir** (vt)	[kœjir]

232. Cereals, grains

grain	**grains** (m pl)	[grɛ̃]
cereal crops	**céréales** (f pl)	[sereal]

ear (of barley, etc.)	**épi** (m)	[epi]
wheat	**blé** (m)	[ble]
rye	**seigle** (m)	[sɛgl]
oats	**avoine** (f)	[avwan]
millet	**millet** (m)	[mijɛ]
barley	**orge** (f)	[ɔrʒ]
corn	**maïs** (m)	[mais]
rice	**riz** (m)	[ri]
buckwheat	**sarrasin** (m)	[sarazɛ̃]
pea plant	**pois** (m)	[pwa]
kidney bean	**haricot** (m)	[ariko]
soy	**soja** (m)	[sɔʒa]
lentil	**lentille** (f)	[lɑ̃tij]

233. Vegetables. Greens

vegetables	**légumes** (m pl)	[legym]
greens	**verdure** (f)	[vɛrdyr]
tomato	**tomate** (f)	[tɔmat]
cucumber	**concombre** (m)	[kɔ̃kɔ̃br]
carrot	**carotte** (f)	[karɔt]
potato	**pomme** (f) **de terre**	[pɔm də tɛr]
onion	**oignon** (m)	[ɔɲɔ̃]
garlic	**ail** (m)	[aj]
cabbage	**chou** (m)	[ʃu]
cauliflower	**chou-fleur** (m)	[ʃuflœr]
Brussels sprouts	**chou** (m) **de Bruxelles**	[ʃu də brysɛl]
broccoli	**brocoli** (m)	[brɔkɔli]
beetroot	**betterave** (f)	[bɛtrav]
eggplant	**aubergine** (f)	[obɛrʒin]
zucchini	**courgette** (f)	[kurʒɛt]
pumpkin	**potiron** (m)	[pɔtirɔ̃]
turnip	**navet** (m)	[navɛ]
parsley	**persil** (m)	[pɛrsi]
dill	**fenouil** (m)	[fənuj]
lettuce	**laitue** (f)	[lety]
celery	**céleri** (m)	[sɛlri]
asparagus	**asperge** (f)	[aspɛrʒ]
spinach	**épinard** (m)	[epinar]
pea	**pois** (m)	[pwa]
beans	**fèves** (f pl)	[fɛv]
corn (maize)	**maïs** (m)	[mais]
kidney bean	**haricot** (m)	[ariko]

pepper	**poivron** (m)	[pwavrɔ̃]
radish	**radis** (m)	[radi]
artichoke	**artichaut** (m)	[artiʃo]

REGIONAL GEOGRAPHY

Countries. Nationalities

234. Western Europe

Europe	**Europe** (f)	[ørɔp]
European Union	**Union** (f) **européenne**	[ynjɔn ørɔpeɛn]
European (n)	**européen** (m)	[ørɔpeɛ̃]
European (adj)	**européen** (adj)	[ørɔpeɛ̃]
Austria	**Autriche** (f)	[otriʃ]
Austrian (masc.)	**Autrichien** (m)	[otriʃjɛ̃]
Austrian (fem.)	**Autrichienne** (f)	[otriʃjɛn]
Austrian (adj)	**autrichien** (adj)	[otriʃjɛ̃]
Great Britain	**Grande-Bretagne** (f)	[grɑ̃dbrətaɲ]
England	**Angleterre** (f)	[ɑ̃glətɛr]
British (masc.)	**Anglais** (m)	[ɑ̃glɛ]
British (fem.)	**Anglaise** (f)	[ɑ̃glɛz]
English, British (adj)	**anglais** (adj)	[ɑ̃glɛ]
Belgium	**Belgique** (f)	[bɛlʒik]
Belgian (masc.)	**Belge** (m)	[bɛlʒ]
Belgian (fem.)	**Belge** (f)	[bɛlʒ]
Belgian (adj)	**belge** (adj)	[bɛlʒ]
Germany	**Allemagne** (f)	[almaɲ]
German (masc.)	**Allemand** (m)	[almɑ̃]
German (fem.)	**Allemande** (f)	[almɑ̃d]
German (adj)	**allemand** (adj)	[almɑ̃]
Netherlands	**Pays-Bas** (m)	[peiba]
Holland	**Hollande** (f)	[ɔlɑ̃d]
Dutchman	**Hollandais** (m)	[ɔlɑ̃dɛ]
Dutchwoman	**Hollandaise** (f)	[ɔlɑ̃dɛz]
Dutch (adj)	**hollandais** (adj)	[ɔlɑ̃dɛ]
Greece	**Grèce** (f)	[grɛs]
Greek (masc.)	**Grec** (m)	[grɛk]
Greek (fem.)	**Grecque** (f)	[grɛk]
Greek (adj)	**grec** (adj)	[grɛk]
Denmark	**Danemark** (m)	[danmark]
Dane (masc.)	**Danois** (m)	[danwa]

Dane (fem.)	**Danoise** (f)	[danwaz]
Danish (adj)	**danois** (adj)	[danwa]
Ireland	**Irlande** (f)	[irlɑ̃d]
Irishman	**Irlandais** (m)	[irlɑ̃dɛ]
Irishwoman	**Irlandaise** (f)	[irlɑ̃dɛz]
Irish (adj)	**irlandais** (adj)	[irlɑ̃dɛ]
Iceland	**Islande** (f)	[islɑ̃d]
Icelander (masc.)	**Islandais** (m)	[islɑ̃dɛ]
Icelander (fem.)	**Islandaise** (f)	[islɑ̃dɛz]
Icelandic (adj)	**islandais** (adj)	[islɑ̃dɛ]
Spain	**Espagne** (f)	[ɛspaɲ]
Spaniard (masc.)	**Espagnol** (m)	[ɛspaɲɔl]
Spaniard (fem.)	**Espagnole** (f)	[ɛspaɲɔl]
Spanish (adj)	**espagnol** (adj)	[ɛspaɲɔl]
Italy	**Italie** (f)	[itali]
Italian (masc.)	**Italien** (m)	[italjɛ̃]
Italian (fem.)	**Italienne** (f)	[italjɛn]
Italian (adj)	**italien** (adj)	[italjɛ̃]
Cyprus	**Chypre** (m)	[ʃipr]
Cypriot (masc.)	**Chypriote** (m)	[ʃiprijɔt]
Cypriot (fem.)	**Chypriote** (f)	[ʃiprijɔt]
Cypriot (adj)	**chypriote** (adj)	[ʃiprijɔt]
Malta	**Malte** (f)	[malt]
Maltese (masc.)	**Maltais** (m)	[maltɛ]
Maltese (fem.)	**Maltaise** (f)	[maltɛz]
Maltese (adj)	**maltais** (adj)	[maltɛ]
Norway	**Norvège** (f)	[nɔrvɛʒ]
Norwegian (masc.)	**Norvégien** (m)	[nɔrveʒjɛ̃]
Norwegian (fem.)	**Norvégienne** (f)	[nɔrveʒjɛn]
Norwegian (adj)	**norvégien** (adj)	[nɔrveʒjɛ̃]
Portugal	**Portugal** (m)	[pɔrtygal]
Portuguese (masc.)	**Portugais** (m)	[pɔrtygɛ]
Portuguese (fem.)	**Portugaise** (f)	[pɔrtygɛz]
Portuguese (adj)	**portugais** (adj)	[pɔrtygɛ]
Finland	**Finlande** (f)	[fɛ̃lɑ̃d]
Finn (masc.)	**Finlandais** (m)	[fɛ̃lɑ̃dɛ]
Finn (fem.)	**Finlandaise** (f)	[fɛ̃lɑ̃dɛz]
Finnish (adj)	**finlandais** (adj)	[fɛ̃lɑ̃dɛ]
France	**France** (f)	[frɑ̃s]
Frenchman	**Français** (m)	[frɑ̃sɛ]
Frenchwoman	**Française** (f)	[frɑ̃sɛz]
French (adj)	**français** (adj)	[frɑ̃sɛ]

Sweden	Suède (f)	[sɥɛd]
Swede (masc.)	Suédois (m)	[sɥedwa]
Swede (fem.)	Suédoise (f)	[sɥedwaz]
Swedish (adj)	suédois (adj)	[sɥedwa]

Switzerland	Suisse (f)	[sɥis]
Swiss (masc.)	Suisse (m)	[sɥis]
Swiss (fem.)	Suissesse (f)	[sɥisɛs]
Swiss (adj)	suisse (adj)	[sɥis]

Scotland	Écosse (f)	[ekɔs]
Scottish (masc.)	Écossais (m)	[ekɔsɛ]
Scottish (fem.)	Écossaise (f)	[ekɔsɛz]
Scottish (adj)	écossais (adj)	[ekɔsɛ]

Vatican	Vatican (m)	[vatikɑ̃]
Liechtenstein	Liechtenstein (m)	[liʃtɛnʃtajn]
Luxembourg	Luxembourg (m)	[lyksɑ̃bur]
Monaco	Monaco (m)	[mɔnako]

235. Central and Eastern Europe

Albania	Albanie (f)	[albani]
Albanian (masc.)	Albanais (m)	[albanɛ]
Albanian (fem.)	Albanaise (f)	[albanɛz]
Albanian (adj)	albanais (adj)	[albanɛ]

Bulgaria	Bulgarie (f)	[bylgari]
Bulgarian (masc.)	Bulgare (m)	[bylgar]
Bulgarian (fem.)	Bulgare (f)	[bylgar]
Bulgarian (adj)	bulgare (adj)	[bylgar]

Hungary	Hongrie (f)	[ɔ̃gri]
Hungarian (masc.)	Hongrois (m)	[ɔ̃grwa]
Hungarian (fem.)	Hongroise (f)	[ɔ̃grwaz]
Hungarian (adj)	hongrois (adj)	[ɔ̃grwa]

Latvia	Lettonie (f)	[lɛtɔni]
Latvian (masc.)	Letton (m)	[lɛtɔ̃]
Latvian (fem.)	Lettonne (f)	[letɔn]
Latvian (adj)	letton (adj)	[lɛtɔ̃]

Lithuania	Lituanie (f)	[litɥani]
Lithuanian (masc.)	Lituanien (m)	[litɥanjɛ̃]
Lithuanian (fem.)	Lituanienne (f)	[litɥanjɛn]
Lithuanian (adj)	lituanien (adj)	[litɥanjɛ̃]

Poland	Pologne (f)	[pɔlɔɲ]
Pole (masc.)	Polonais (m)	[pɔlɔnɛ]
Pole (fem.)	Polonaise (f)	[pɔlɔnɛz]

Polish (adj)	polonais (adj)	[pɔlɔnɛ]
Romania	Roumanie (f)	[rumani]
Romanian (masc.)	Roumain (m)	[rumɛ̃]
Romanian (fem.)	Roumaine (f)	[rumɛn]
Romanian (adj)	roumain (adj)	[rumɛ̃]

Serbia	Serbie (f)	[sɛrbi]
Serbian (masc.)	Serbe (m)	[sɛrb]
Serbian (fem.)	Serbe (f)	[sɛrb]
Serbian (adj)	serbe (adj)	[sɛrb]

Slovakia	Slovaquie (f)	[slɔvaki]
Slovak (masc.)	Slovaque (m)	[slɔvak]
Slovak (fem.)	Slovaque (f)	[slɔvak]
Slovak (adj)	slovaque (adj)	[slɔvak]

Croatia	Croatie (f)	[krɔasi]
Croatian (masc.)	Croate (m)	[krɔat]
Croatian (fem.)	Croate (f)	[krɔat]
Croatian (adj)	croate (adj)	[krɔat]

Czech Republic	République (f) Tchèque	[repyblik tʃɛk]
Czech (masc.)	Tchèque (m)	[tʃɛk]
Czech (fem.)	Tchèque (f)	[tʃɛk]
Czech (adj)	tchèque (adj)	[tʃɛk]

Estonia	Estonie (f)	[ɛstɔni]
Estonian (masc.)	Estonien (m)	[ɛstɔnjɛ̃]
Estonian (fem.)	Estonienne (f)	[ɛstɔnjɛn]
Estonian (adj)	estonien (adj)	[ɛstɔnjɛ̃]

Bosnia-Herzegovina	Bosnie (f)	[bɔsni]
Macedonia	Macédoine (f)	[masedwan]
Slovenia	Slovénie (f)	[slɔveni]
Montenegro	Monténégro (m)	[mɔ̃tenegro]

236. Former USSR countries

Azerbaijan	Azerbaïdjan (m)	[azɛrbajdʒɑ̃]
Azerbaijani (masc.)	Azerbaïdjanais (m)	[azɛrbaidʒanɛ]
Azerbaijani (fem.)	Azerbaïdjanaise (f)	[azɛrbaidʒanɛz]
Azerbaijani (adj)	azerbaïdjanais (adj)	[azɛrbaidʒanɛ]

Armenia	Arménie (f)	[armeni]
Armenian (masc.)	Arménien (m)	[armenjɛ̃]
Armenian (fem.)	Arménienne (f)	[armenjɛn]
Armenian (adj)	arménien (adj)	[armenjɛ̃]

| Belarus | Biélorussie (f) | [bjelɔrysi] |
| Belarusian (masc.) | Biélorusse (m) | [bjelɔrys] |

| Belarusian (fem.) | Biélorusse (f) | [bjelɔrys] |
| Belarusian (adj) | biélorusse (adj) | [bjelɔrys] |

Georgia	Géorgie (f)	[ʒeɔrʒi]
Georgian (masc.)	Géorgien (m)	[ʒeɔrʒjɛ̃]
Georgian (fem.)	Géorgienne (f)	[ʒeɔrʒjɛn]
Georgian (adj)	géorgien (adj)	[ʒeɔrʒjɛ̃]
Kazakhstan	Kazakhstan (m)	[kazakstɑ̃]
Kazakh (masc.)	Kazakh (m)	[kazak]
Kazakh (fem.)	Kazakhe (f)	[kazak]
Kazakh (adj)	kazakh (adj)	[kazak]

Kirghizia	Kirghizistan (m)	[kirgizistɑ̃]
Kirghiz (masc.)	Kirghiz (m)	[kirgiz]
Kirghiz (fem.)	Kirghize (f)	[kirgiz]
Kirghiz (adj)	kirghiz (adj)	[kirgiz]

Moldavia	Moldavie (f)	[mɔldavi]
Moldavian (masc.)	Moldave (m)	[mɔldav]
Moldavian (fem.)	Moldave (f)	[mɔldav]
Moldavian (adj)	moldave (adj)	[mɔldav]
Russia	Russie (f)	[rysi]
Russian (masc.)	Russe (m)	[rys]
Russian (fem.)	Russe (f)	[rys]
Russian (adj)	russe (adj)	[rys]

Tajikistan	Tadjikistan (m)	[tadʒikistɑ̃]
Tajik (masc.)	Tadjik (m)	[tadʒik]
Tajik (fem.)	Tadjik (f)	[tadʒik]
Tajik (adj)	tadjik (adj)	[tadʒik]

Turkmenistan	Turkménistan (m)	[tyrkmenistɑ̃]
Turkmen (masc.)	Turkmène (m)	[tyrkmɛn]
Turkmen (fem.)	Turkmène (f)	[tyrkmɛn]
Turkmenian (adj)	turkmène (adj)	[tyrkmɛn]

Uzbekistan	Ouzbékistan (m)	[uzbekistɑ̃]
Uzbek (masc.)	Ouzbek (m)	[uzbɛk]
Uzbek (fem.)	Ouzbek (f)	[uzbɛk]
Uzbek (adj)	ouzbek (adj)	[uzbɛk]

Ukraine	Ukraine (f)	[ykrɛn]
Ukrainian (masc.)	Ukrainien (m)	[ykrɛnjɛ̃]
Ukrainian (fem.)	Ukrainienne (f)	[ykrɛnjɛn]
Ukrainian (adj)	ukrainien (adj)	[ykrɛnjɛ̃]

237. Asia

| Asia | Asie (f) | [azi] |
| Asian (adj) | asiatique (adj) | [azjatik] |

Vietnam	**Vietnam** (m)	[vjɛtnam]
Vietnamese (masc.)	**Vietnamien** (m)	[vjɛtnamjɛ̃]
Vietnamese (fem.)	**Vietnamienne** (f)	[vjɛtnamjɛn]
Vietnamese (adj)	**vietnamien** (adj)	[vjɛtnamjɛ̃]
India	**Inde** (f)	[ɛ̃d]
Indian (masc.)	**Indien** (m)	[ɛ̃djɛ̃]
Indian (fem.)	**Indienne** (f)	[ɛ̃djɛn]
Indian (adj)	**indien** (adj)	[ɛ̃djɛ̃]
Israel	**Israël** (m)	[israɛl]
Israeli (masc.)	**Israélien** (m)	[israeljɛ̃]
Israeli (fem.)	**Israélienne** (f)	[israeljɛn]
Israeli (adj)	**israélien** (adj)	[israeljɛ̃]
Jew (n)	**Juif** (m)	[ʒɥif]
Jewess (n)	**Juive** (f)	[ʒɥiv]
Jewish (adj)	**juif** (adj)	[ʒɥif]
China	**Chine** (f)	[ʃin]
Chinese (masc.)	**Chinois** (m)	[ʃinwa]
Chinese (fem.)	**Chinoise** (f)	[ʃinwaz]
Chinese (adj)	**chinois** (adj)	[ʃinwa]
Korean (masc.)	**Coréen** (m)	[kɔreɛ̃]
Korean (fem.)	**Coréenne** (f)	[kɔreɛn]
Korean (adj)	**coréen** (adj)	[kɔreɛ̃]
Lebanon	**Liban** (m)	[libɑ̃]
Lebanese (masc.)	**Libanais** (m)	[libanɛ]
Lebanese (fem.)	**Libanaise** (f)	[libanɛz]
Lebanese (adj)	**libanais** (adj)	[libanɛ]
Mongolia	**Mongolie** (f)	[mɔ̃gɔli]
Mongolian (masc.)	**Mongole** (m)	[mɔ̃gɔl]
Mongolian (fem.)	**Mongole** (f)	[mɔ̃gɔl]
Mongolian (adj)	**mongole** (adj)	[mɔ̃gɔl]
Malaysia	**Malaisie** (f)	[malɛzi]
Malaysian (masc.)	**Malaisien** (m)	[malɛzjɛ̃]
Malaysian (fem.)	**Malaisienne** (f)	[malɛzjɛn]
Malaysian (adj)	**malais** (adj)	[malɛ]
Pakistan	**Pakistan** (m)	[pakistɑ̃]
Pakistani (masc.)	**Pakistanais** (m)	[pakistanɛ]
Pakistani (fem.)	**Pakistanaise** (f)	[pakistanɛz]
Pakistani (adj)	**pakistanais** (adj)	[pakistanɛ]
Saudi Arabia	**Arabie** (f) **Saoudite**	[arabi saudit]
Arab (masc.)	**Arabe** (m)	[arab]
Arab (fem.)	**Arabe** (f)	[arab]
Arabian (adj)	**arabe** (adj)	[arab]

Thailand	**Thaïlande** (f)	[tajlɑ̃d]
Thai (masc.)	**Thaïlandais** (m)	[tajlɑ̃dɛ]
Thai (fem.)	**Thaïlandaise** (f)	[tajlɑ̃dɛz]
Thai (adj)	**thaïlandais** (adj)	[tajlɑ̃dɛ]

Taiwan	**Taïwan** (m)	[tajwan]
Taiwanese (masc.)	**Taïwanais** (m)	[tajwanɛ]
Taiwanese (fem.)	**Taïwanaise** (f)	[tajwanɛz]
Taiwanese (adj)	**taïwanais** (adj)	[tajwanɛ]

Turkey	**Turquie** (f)	[tyrki]
Turk (masc.)	**Turc** (m)	[tyrk]
Turk (fem.)	**Turque** (f)	[tyrk]
Turkish (adj)	**turc** (adj)	[tyrk]

Japan	**Japon** (m)	[ʒapɔ̃]
Japanese (masc.)	**Japonais** (m)	[ʒapɔnɛ]
Japanese (fem.)	**Japonaise** (f)	[ʒapɔnɛz]
Japanese (adj)	**japonais** (adj)	[ʒapɔnɛ]

Afghanistan	**Afghanistan** (m)	[afganistɑ̃]
Bangladesh	**Bangladesh** (m)	[bɑ̃gladɛʃ]
Indonesia	**Indonésie** (f)	[ɛ̃dɔnezi]
Jordan	**Jordanie** (f)	[ʒɔrdani]

Iraq	**Iraq** (m)	[irak]
Iran	**Iran** (m)	[irɑ̃]
Cambodia	**Cambodge** (m)	[kɑ̃bɔdʒ]
Kuwait	**Koweït** (m)	[kɔwɛjt]

Laos	**Laos** (m)	[laos]
Myanmar	**Myanmar** (m)	[mjanmar]
Nepal	**Népal** (m)	[nepal]
United Arab Emirates	**Fédération** (f) **des Émirats Arabes Unis**	[federasjɔ̃ dezemira arabzyni]

Syria	**Syrie** (f)	[siri]
Palestine	**Palestine** (f)	[palɛstin]
South Korea	**Corée** (f) **du Sud**	[kɔre dy syd]
North Korea	**Corée** (f) **du Nord**	[kɔre dy nɔr]

238. North America

United States of America	**les États Unis**	[lezeta zyni]
American (masc.)	**Américain** (m)	[amerikɛ̃]
American (fem.)	**Américaine** (f)	[amerikɛn]
American (adj)	**américain** (adj)	[amerikɛ̃]

| Canada | **Canada** (m) | [kanada] |
| Canadian (masc.) | **Canadien** (m) | [kanadjɛ̃] |

| Canadian (fem.) | Canadienne (f) | [kanadjɛn] |
| Canadian (adj) | canadien (adj) | [kanadjɛ̃] |

Mexico	Mexique (m)	[mɛksik]
Mexican (masc.)	Mexicain (m)	[mɛksikɛ̃]
Mexican (fem.)	Mexicaine (f)	[mɛksikɛn]
Mexican (adj)	mexicain (adj)	[mɛksikɛ̃]

239. Central and South America

Argentina	Argentine (f)	[arʒɑ̃tin]
Argentinian (masc.)	Argentin (m)	[arʒɑ̃tɛ̃]
Argentinian (fem.)	Argentine (f)	[arʒɑ̃tin]
Argentinian (adj)	argentin (adj)	[arʒɑ̃tɛ̃]

Brazil	Brésil (m)	[brezil]
Brazilian (masc.)	Brésilien (m)	[breziljɛ̃]
Brazilian (fem.)	Brésilienne (f)	[breziljɛn]
Brazilian (adj)	brésilien (adj)	[breziljɛ̃]

Colombia	Colombie (f)	[kɔlɔ̃bi]
Colombian (masc.)	Colombien (m)	[kɔlɔ̃bjɛ̃]
Colombian (fem.)	Colombienne (f)	[kɔlɔ̃bjɛn]
Colombian (adj)	colombien (adj)	[kɔlɔ̃bjɛ̃]

Cuba	Cuba (f)	[kyba]
Cuban (masc.)	Cubain (m)	[kybɛ̃]
Cuban (fem.)	Cubaine (f)	[kybɛn]
Cuban (adj)	cubain (adj)	[kybɛ̃]

Chile	Chili (m)	[ʃili]
Chilean (masc.)	Chilien (m)	[ʃiljɛ̃]
Chilean (fem.)	Chilienne (f)	[ʃiljɛn]
Chilean (adj)	chilien (adj)	[ʃiljɛ̃]

Bolivia	Bolivie (f)	[bɔlivi]
Venezuela	Venezuela (f)	[venezɥela]
Paraguay	Paraguay (m)	[paragwɛ]
Peru	Pérou (m)	[peru]

Suriname	Surinam (m)	[syrinam]
Uruguay	Uruguay (m)	[yrygwɛ]
Ecuador	Équateur (m)	[ekwatœr]

The Bahamas	Bahamas (f pl)	[baamas]
Haiti	Haïti (m)	[aiti]
Dominican Republic	République (f) Dominicaine	[repyblik dɔminikɛn]
Panama	Panamá (m)	[panama]
Jamaica	Jamaïque (f)	[ʒamaik]

240. Africa

Egypt	**Égypte** (f)	[eʒipt]
Egyptian (masc.)	**Égyptien** (m)	[eʒipsjɛ̃]
Egyptian (fem.)	**Égyptienne** (f)	[eʒipsjɛn]
Egyptian (adj)	**égyptien** (adj)	[eʒipsjɛ̃]

Morocco	**Maroc** (m)	[marɔk]
Moroccan (masc.)	**Marocain** (m)	[marɔkɛ̃]
Moroccan (fem.)	**Marocaine** (f)	[marɔkɛn]
Moroccan (adj)	**marocain** (adj)	[marɔkɛ̃]

Tunisia	**Tunisie** (f)	[tynizi]
Tunisian (masc.)	**Tunisien** (m)	[tynizjɛ̃]
Tunisian (fem.)	**Tunisienne** (f)	[tynizjɛn]
Tunisian (adj)	**tunisien** (adj)	[tynizjɛ̃]

Ghana	**Ghana** (m)	[gana]
Zanzibar	**Zanzibar** (m)	[zãzibar]
Kenya	**Kenya** (m)	[kenja]
Libya	**Libye** (f)	[libi]
Madagascar	**Madagascar** (f)	[madagaskar]

Namibia	**Namibie** (f)	[namibi]
Senegal	**Sénégal** (m)	[senegal]
Tanzania	**Tanzanie** (f)	[tãzani]
South Africa	**République** (f) **Sud-africaine**	[repyblik sydafrikɛn]

African (masc.)	**Africain** (m)	[afrikɛ̃]
African (fem.)	**Africaine** (f)	[afrikɛn]
African (adj)	**africain** (adj)	[afrikɛ̃]

241. Australia. Oceania

Australia	**Australie** (f)	[ostrali]
Australian (masc.)	**Australien** (m)	[ostraljɛ̃]

Australian (fem.)	**Australienne** (f)	[ostraljɛn]
Australian (adj)	**australien** (adj)	[ostraljɛ̃]

New Zealand	**Nouvelle Zélande** (f)	[nuvɛl zelãd]
New Zealander (masc.)	**Néo-Zélandais** (m)	[neɔzelãdɛ]

New Zealander (fem.)	**Néo-Zélandaise** (f)	[neɔzelãdɛz]
New Zealand (as adj)	**néo-zélandais** (adj)	[neɔzelãdɛ]

Tasmania	**Tasmanie** (f)	[tasmani]
French Polynesia	**Polynésie** (f) **Française**	[pɔlinezi frãsɛz]

242. Cities

Amsterdam	**Amsterdam** (f)	[amstɛrdam]
Ankara	**Ankara** (m)	[ɑ̃kara]
Athens	**Athènes** (m)	[atɛn]
Baghdad	**Bagdad** (m)	[bagdad]
Bangkok	**Bangkok** (m)	[bɑ̃kɔk]
Barcelona	**Barcelone** (f)	[barsəlɔn]
Beijing	**Pékin** (m)	[pekɛ̃]
Beirut	**Beyrouth** (m)	[berut]
Berlin	**Berlin** (m)	[bɛrlɛ̃]
Bombay, Mumbai	**Bombay** (m)	[bɔ̃bɛ]
Bonn	**Bonn** (f)	[bɔn]
Bordeaux	**Bordeaux** (f)	[bɔrdo]
Bratislava	**Bratislava** (m)	[bratislava]
Brussels	**Bruxelles** (m)	[brysɛl]
Bucharest	**Bucarest** (m)	[bykarɛst]
Budapest	**Budapest** (m)	[bydapɛst]
Cairo	**Caire** (m)	[kɛr]
Calcutta	**Calcutta** (f)	[kalkyta]
Chicago	**Chicago** (f)	[ʃikago]
Copenhagen	**Copenhague** (f)	[kɔpənag]
Dar-es-Salaam	**Dar es-Salaam** (f)	[darɛssalam]
Delhi	**Delhi** (f)	[deli]
Dubai	**Dubaï** (f)	[dybaj]
Dublin	**Dublin** (f)	[dyblɛ̃]
Düsseldorf	**Düsseldorf** (f)	[dysɛldɔrf]
Florence	**Florence** (f)	[flɔrɑ̃s]
Frankfurt	**Francfort** (f)	[frɑ̃kfɔr]
Geneva	**Genève** (f)	[ʒənɛv]
The Hague	**Hague** (f)	[ag]
Hamburg	**Hambourg** (f)	[ɑ̃bur]
Hanoi	**Hanoi** (f)	[anɔj]
Havana	**Havane** (f)	[avan]
Helsinki	**Helsinki** (f)	[ɛlsiŋki]
Hiroshima	**Hiroshima** (f)	[irɔʃima]
Hong Kong	**Hong Kong** (m)	[ɔ̃gkɔ̃g]
Istanbul	**Istanbul** (f)	[istɑ̃bul]
Jerusalem	**Jérusalem** (f)	[ʒeryzalɛm]
Kiev	**Kiev** (f)	[kjɛf]
Kuala Lumpur	**Kuala Lumpur** (f)	[kwalalumpur]
Lisbon	**Lisbonne** (f)	[lizbɔn]
London	**Londres** (m)	[lɔ̃dr]
Los Angeles	**Los Angeles** (f)	[lɔsɑ̃dʒəlɛs]

Lyons	**Lyon** (f)	[ljɔ̃]
Madrid	**Madrid** (f)	[madrid]
Marseille	**Marseille** (f)	[marsɛj]
Mexico City	**Mexico** (f)	[mɛksiko]
Miami	**Miami** (f)	[miami]
Montreal	**Montréal** (f)	[mɔ̃real]
Moscow	**Moscou** (f)	[mɔsku]
Munich	**Munich** (f)	[mynik]
Nairobi	**Nairobi** (f)	[nɛrɔbi]
Naples	**Naples** (f)	[napl]
New York	**New York** (f)	[nujɔrk]
Nice	**Nice** (f)	[nis]
Oslo	**Oslo** (m)	[ɔslo]
Ottawa	**Ottawa** (m)	[ɔtawa]
Paris	**Paris** (m)	[pari]
Prague	**Prague** (m)	[prag]
Rio de Janeiro	**Rio de Janeiro** (m)	[rijodədʒanɛro]
Rome	**Rome** (f)	[rɔm]
Saint Petersburg	**Saint-Pétersbourg** (m)	[sɛ̃petɛrsbur]
Seoul	**Séoul** (m)	[seul]
Shanghai	**Shanghai** (m)	[ʃɑ̃gaj]
Singapore	**Singapour** (f)	[sɛ̃gapur]
Stockholm	**Stockholm** (m)	[stɔkɔlm]
Sydney	**Sidney** (m)	[sidnɛ]
Taipei	**Taipei** (m)	[tajbɛj]
Tokyo	**Tokyo** (m)	[tɔkjo]
Toronto	**Toronto** (m)	[tɔrɔ̃to]
Venice	**Venise** (f)	[vəniz]
Vienna	**Vienne** (f)	[vjɛn]
Warsaw	**Varsovie** (f)	[varsɔvi]
Washington	**Washington** (f)	[waʃiŋtɔn]

243. Politics. Government. Part 1

politics	**politique** (f)	[pɔlitik]
political (adj)	**politique** (adj)	[pɔlitik]
politician	**homme** (m) **politique**	[nɔm pɔlitik]
state (country)	**état** (m)	[eta]
citizen	**citoyen** (m)	[sitwajɛ̃]
citizenship	**citoyenneté** (f)	[sitwajɛnte]
national emblem	**armoiries** (f pl) **nationales**	[armwari nasjɔnal]
national anthem	**hymne** (m) **national**	[imn nasjɔnal]

government	**gouvernement** (m)	[guvɛrnəmɑ̃]
head of state	**chef** (m) **d'état**	[ʃɛf deta]
parliament	**parlement** (m)	[parləmɑ̃]
party	**parti** (m)	[parti]

| capitalism | **capitalisme** (m) | [kapitalism] |
| capitalist (adj) | **capitaliste** (adj) | [kapitalist] |

| socialism | **socialisme** (m) | [sɔsjalism] |
| socialist (adj) | **socialiste** (adj) | [sɔsjalist] |

communism	**communisme** (m)	[kɔmynism]
communist (adj)	**communiste** (adj)	[kɔmynist]
communist (n)	**communiste** (m)	[kɔmynist]

democracy	**démocratie** (f)	[demɔkrasi]
democrat	**démocrate** (m)	[demɔkrat]
democratic (adj)	**démocratique** (adj)	[demɔkratik]
Democratic party	**parti** (m) **démocratique**	[parti demɔkratik]

liberal (n)	**libéral** (m)	[liberal]
liberal (adj)	**libéral** (adj)	[liberal]
conservative (n)	**conservateur** (m)	[kɔ̃sɛrvatœr]
conservative (adj)	**conservateur** (adj)	[kɔ̃sɛrvatœr]

republic (n)	**république** (f)	[repyblik]
republican (n)	**républicain** (m)	[repyblikɛ̃]
Republican party	**parti** (m) **républicain**	[parti repyblikɛ̃]

| poll, elections | **élections** (f pl) | [elɛksjɔ̃] |
| to elect (vt) | **élire** (vt) | [elir] |

| elector, voter | **électeur** (m) | [elɛktœr] |
| election campaign | **campagne** (f) **électorale** | [kɑ̃paɲ elɛktɔral] |

voting (n)	**vote** (m)	[vɔt]
to vote (vi)	**voter** (vi)	[vɔte]
suffrage, right to vote	**droit** (m) **de vote**	[drwa də vɔt]

candidate	**candidat** (m)	[kɑ̃dida]
to be a candidate	**poser sa candidature**	[poze sa kɑ̃didatyr]
campaign	**campagne** (f)	[kɑ̃paɲ]

| opposition (as adj) | **d'opposition** (adj) | [dɔpozisjɔ̃] |
| opposition (n) | **opposition** (f) | [ɔpozisjɔ̃] |

visit	**visite** (f)	[vizit]
official visit	**visite** (f) **officielle**	[vizit ɔfisjɛl]
international (adj)	**international** (adj)	[ɛ̃tɛrnasjɔnal]

| negotiations | **négociations** (f pl) | [negɔsjasjɔ̃] |
| to negotiate (vi) | **négocier** (vi) | [negɔsje] |

244. Politics. Government. Part 2

society	société (f)	[sɔsjete]
constitution	constitution (f)	[kɔ̃stitysjɔ̃]
power (political control)	pouvoir (m)	[puvwar]
corruption	corruption (f)	[kɔrypsjɔ̃]

| law (justice) | loi (f) | [lwa] |
| legal (legitimate) | légal (adj) | [legal] |

| justice (fairness) | justice (f) | [ʒystis] |
| just (fair) | juste (adj) | [ʒyst] |

committee	comité (m)	[kɔmite]
bill (draft law)	projet (m) de loi	[prɔʒɛ də lwa]
budget	budget (m)	[bydʒɛ]
policy	politique (f)	[pɔlitik]
reform	réforme (f)	[reflɛʃir]
radical (adj)	radical (adj)	[radikal]

power (strength, force)	puissance (f)	[pɥisɑ̃s]
powerful (adj)	puissant (adj)	[pɥisɑ̃]
supporter	partisan (m)	[partizɑ̃]
influence	influence (f)	[ɛ̃flyɑ̃s]

regime (e.g., military ~)	régime (m)	[reʒim]
conflict	conflit (m)	[kɔ̃fli]
conspiracy (plot)	complot (m)	[kɔ̃plo]
provocation	provocation (f)	[prɔvɔkasjɔ̃]

to overthrow (regime, etc.)	renverser (vt)	[rɑ̃vɛrse]
overthrow (of government)	renversement (m)	[rɑ̃vɛrsəmɑ̃]
revolution	révolution (f)	[revɔlysjɔ̃]

| coup d'état | coup (m) d'État | [ku deta] |
| military coup | coup (m) d'État militaire | [ku deta militɛr] |

crisis	crise (f)	[kriz]
economic recession	baisse (f) économique	[bɛs ekɔnɔmik]
demonstrator (protester)	manifestant (m)	[manifɛstɑ̃]
demonstration	manifestation (f)	[manifɛstasjɔ̃]
martial law	loi (f) martiale	[lwa marsjal]
military base	base (f) militaire	[baz militɛr]

| stability | stabilité (f) | [stabilite] |
| stable (adj) | stable (adj) | [stabl] |

exploitation	exploitation (f)	[ɛksplwatasjɔ̃]
to exploit (workers)	exploiter (vt)	[ɛksplwate]
racism	racisme (m)	[rasism]
racist	raciste (m)	[rasist]

| fascism | **fascisme** (m) | [faʃism] |
| fascist | **fasciste** (m) | [faʃist] |

245. Countries. Miscellaneous

foreigner	**étranger** (m)	[etrɑ̃ʒe]
foreign (adj)	**étranger** (adj)	[etrɑ̃ʒe]
abroad (adv)	**à l'étranger** (adv)	[ɑletrɑ̃ʒe]

emigrant	**émigré** (m)	[emigre]
emigration	**émigration** (f)	[emigrasjɔ̃]
to emigrate (vi)	**émigrer** (vi)	[emigre]

the West	**Ouest** (m)	[wɛst]
the East	**Est** (m)	[ɛst]
the Far East	**Extrême Orient** (m)	[ɛkstrɛm ɔrjɑ̃]

| civilization | **civilisation** (f) | [sivilizasjɔ̃] |
| humanity (mankind) | **humanité** (f) | [ymanite] |

world (earth)	**monde** (m)	[mɔ̃d]
peace	**paix** (f)	[pɛ]
worldwide (adj)	**mondial** (adj)	[mɔ̃djal]

homeland	**patrie** (f)	[patri]
people (population)	**peuple** (m)	[pœpl]
population	**population** (f)	[pɔpylasjɔ̃]
people (a lot of ~)	**gens** (m pl)	[ʒɛ̃s]

| nation (people) | **nation** (f) | [nasjɔ̃] |
| generation | **génération** (f) | [ʒenerasjɔ̃] |

territory (area)	**territoire** (m)	[tɛritwar]
region	**région** (f)	[reʒjɔ̃]
state (part of a country)	**état** (m)	[eta]

tradition	**tradition** (f)	[tradisjɔ̃]
custom (tradition)	**coutume** (f)	[kutym]
ecology	**écologie** (f)	[ekɔlɔʒi]

Indian (Native American)	**indien** (m)	[ɛ̃djɛ̃]
Gipsy (masc.)	**bohémien** (m)	[bɔemjɛ̃]
Gipsy (fem.)	**bohémienne** (f)	[bɔemjɛn]
Gipsy (adj)	**bohémien** (adj)	[bɔemjɛ̃]

empire	**empire** (m)	[ɑ̃pir]
colony	**colonie** (f)	[kɔlɔni]
slavery	**esclavage** (m)	[ɛsklavaʒ]
invasion	**invasion** (f)	[ɛ̃vazjɔ̃]
famine	**famine** (f)	[famin]

246. Major religious groups. Confessions

religion	religion (f)	[rəliʒjɔ̃]
religious (adj)	religieux (adj)	[rəliʒjø]
faith, belief	foi (f)	[fwa]
to believe (in God)	croire (vi)	[krwar]
believer	croyant (m)	[krwajɑ̃]
atheism	athéisme (m)	[ateism]
atheist	athée (m)	[ate]
Christianity	christianisme (m)	[kristjanism]
Christian (n)	chrétien (m)	[kretjɛ̃]
Christian (adj)	chrétien (adj)	[kretjɛ̃]
Catholicism	catholicisme (m)	[katɔlisism]
Catholic (n)	catholique (m)	[katɔlik]
Catholic (adj)	catholique (adj)	[katɔlik]
Protestantism	protestantisme (m)	[prɔtɛstɑ̃tism]
Protestant Church	Église (f) protestante	[egliz prɔtɛstɑ̃t]
Protestant	protestant (m)	[prɔtɛstɑ̃]
Orthodoxy	Orthodoxie (f)	[ɔrtɔdɔksi]
Orthodox Church	Église (f) orthodoxe	[egliz ɔrtɔdɔks]
Orthodox	orthodoxe (m)	[ɔrtɔdɔks]
Presbyterianism	Presbytérianisme (m)	[prɛsbiterjanism]
Presbyterian Church	Église (f) presbytérienne	[egliz prɛsbiterjɛn]
Presbyterian (n)	presbytérien (m)	[prɛsbiterjɛ̃]
Lutheranism	Église (f) luthérienne	[egliz lyterjɛn]
Lutheran (n)	luthérien (m)	[lyterjɛ̃]
Baptist Church	Baptisme (m)	[batism]
Baptist (n)	baptiste (m)	[batist]
Anglican Church	Église (f) anglicane	[egliz ɑ̃glikan]
Anglican (n)	anglican (m)	[ɑ̃glikɑ̃]
Mormonism	Mormonisme (m)	[mɔrmɔnism]
Mormon (n)	mormon (m)	[mɔrmɔ̃]
Judaism	judaïsme (m)	[ʒydaism]
Jew (n)	juif (m)	[ʒɥif]
Buddhism	Bouddhisme (m)	[budism]
Buddhist (n)	bouddhiste (m)	[budist]
Hinduism	hindouisme (m)	[ɛ̃duism]
Hindu (n)	hindouiste (m)	[ɛ̃duist]

Islam	islam (m)	[islam]
Muslim (n)	musulman (m)	[myzylmã]
Muslim (adj)	musulman (adj)	[myzylmã]

Shiah Islam	Chiisme (m)	[ʃiism]
Shiite (n)	chiite (m)	[ʃiit]
Sunni Islam	Sunnisme (m)	[synism]
Sunnite (n)	sunnite (m)	[synit]

247. Religions. Priests

| priest | prêtre (m) | [prɛtr] |
| the Pope | Pape (m) | [pap] |

monk, friar	moine (m)	[mwan]
nun	bonne sœur (f)	[bɔn sœr]
pastor	pasteur (m)	[pastœr]

abbot	abbé (m)	[abe]
vicar (parish priest)	vicaire (m)	[vikɛr]
bishop	évêque (m)	[evɛk]
cardinal	cardinal (m)	[kardinal]

preacher	prédicateur (m)	[predikatœr]
preaching	sermon (m)	[sɛrmɔ̃]
parishioners	paroissiens (m pl)	[parwasjɛ̃]

| believer | croyant (m) | [krwajã] |
| atheist | athée (m) | [ate] |

248. Faith. Christianity. Islam

| Adam | Adam | [adã] |
| Eve | Ève | [ɛv] |

God	Dieu (m)	[djø]
the Lord	le Seigneur	[lə sɛɲœr]
the Almighty	le Tout-Puissant	[lə tupɥisã]

sin	péché (m)	[peʃe]
to sin (vi)	pécher (vi)	[peʃe]
sinner (masc.)	pécheur (m)	[peʃœr]
sinner (fem.)	pécheresse (f)	[peʃrɛs]

hell	enfer (m)	[ãfɛr]
paradise	paradis (m)	[paradi]
Jesus	Jésus	[ʒezy]
Jesus Christ	Jésus Christ	[ʒezykri]

the Holy Spirit	le Saint Esprit	[lə sɛ̃tɛspri]
the Savior	le Sauveur	[lə sovœr]
the Virgin Mary	la Sainte Vierge	[la sɛt vjɛrʒ]

the Devil	le Diable	[djabl]
devil's (adj)	diabolique (adj)	[djabɔlik]
Satan	Satan	[satɑ̃]
satanic (adj)	satanique (adj)	[satanik]

angel	ange (m)	[ɑ̃ʒ]
guardian angel	ange (m) gardien	[ɑ̃ʒ gardjɛ̃]
angelic (adj)	angélique (adj)	[ɑ̃ʒelik]

apostle	apôtre (m)	[apotr]
archangel	archange (m)	[arkɑ̃ʒ]
the Antichrist	Antéchrist (m)	[ɑ̃tekrist]

Church	Église (f)	[egliz]
Bible	Bible (f)	[bibl]
biblical (adj)	biblique (adj)	[biblik]

Old Testament	Ancien Testament (m)	[ɑ̃sjɛ̃ tɛstamɑ̃]
New Testament	Nouveau Testament (m)	[nuvo tɛstamɑ̃]
Gospel	Évangile (m)	[evɑ̃ʒil]
Holy Scripture	Sainte Écriture (f)	[sɛt ekrityr]
heaven	Cieux (m pl)	[sjø]

Commandment	commandement (m)	[kɔmɑ̃dmɑ̃]
prophet	prophète (m)	[prɔfɛt]
prophecy	prophétie (f)	[prɔfesi]

Allah	Allah	[ala]
Mohammed	Mahomet	[maɔmɛ]
the Koran	le Coran	[kɔrɑ̃]

mosque	mosquée (f)	[mɔske]
mullah	mulla (m)	[mula]
prayer	prière (f)	[prijɛr]
to pray (vi, vt)	prier (vt)	[prije]

pilgrimage	pèlerinage (m)	[pɛlrinaʒ]
pilgrim	pèlerin (m)	[pɛlrɛ̃]
Mecca	La Mecque	[la mɛk]

church	église (f)	[egliz]
temple	temple (m)	[tɑ̃pl]
cathedral	cathédrale (f)	[katedral]
Gothic (adj)	gothique (adj)	[gɔtik]
synagogue	synagogue (f)	[sinagɔg]
mosque	mosquée (f)	[mɔske]
chapel	chapelle (f)	[ʃapɛl]
abbey	abbaye (f)	[abei]

convent	**couvent** (m)	[kuvã]
monastery	**monastère** (m)	[mɔnastɛr]
bell (in church)	**cloche** (f)	[klɔʃ]
bell tower	**clocher** (m)	[klɔʃe]
to ring (ab. bells)	**sonner** (vi)	[sõ]
cross	**croix** (f)	[krwa]
cupola (roof)	**coupole** (f)	[kupɔl]
icon	**icône** (f)	[ikon]
soul	**âme** (f)	[ɑm]
fate (destiny)	**sort** (m)	[sɔr]
evil (n)	**mal** (m)	[mal]
good (n)	**bien** (m)	[bjɛ̃]
vampire	**vampire** (m)	[vãpir]
witch (sorceress)	**sorcière** (f)	[sɔrsjɛr]
demon	**démon** (m)	[demõ]
devil	**diable** (m)	[djabl]
spirit	**esprit** (m)	[ɛspri]
redemption (giving us ~)	**rachat** (m)	[raʃa]
to redeem (vt)	**racheter** (vt)	[raʃte]
church service, mass	**messe** (f)	[mɛs]
to say mass	**dire la messe**	[dir la mɛs]
confession	**confession** (f)	[kõfesjõ]
to confess (vi)	**se confesser** (vp)	[sə kõfese]
saint (n)	**saint** (m)	[sɛ̃]
sacred (holy)	**sacré** (adj)	[sakre]
holy water	**l'eau bénite**	[lo benit]
ritual (n)	**rite** (m)	[rit]
ritual (adj)	**rituel** (adj)	[rityɛl]
sacrifice	**sacrifice** (m)	[sakrifis]
superstition	**superstition** (f)	[sypɛrstisjõ]
superstitious (adj)	**superstitieux** (adj)	[sypɛrstisjø]
afterlife	**vie** (f) **après la mort**	[vi aprɛ la mɔr]
eternal life	**vie** (f) **éternelle**	[vi etɛrnɛl]

MISCELLANEOUS

249. Various useful words

background (green ~)	**fond** (m)	[fɔ̃]
balance (of situation)	**balance** (f)	[balɑ̃s]
barrier (obstacle)	**barrière** (f)	[barjɛr]
base (basis)	**base** (f)	[baz]
beginning	**début** (m)	[dəbu]
category	**catégorie** (f)	[kategɔri]
cause (reason)	**cause** (f)	[koz]
choice	**choix** (m)	[ʃwa]
coincidence	**coïncidence** (f)	[kɔɛ̃sidɑ̃s]
comfortable (~ chair)	**confortable** (adj)	[kɔ̃fɔrtabl]
comparison	**comparaison** (f)	[kɔ̃parɛzɔ̃]
compensation	**compensation** (f)	[kɔ̃pɑ̃sasjɔ̃]
degree (extent, amount)	**degré** (m)	[dəgre]
development	**développement** (m)	[devlɔpmɑ̃]
difference	**différence** (f)	[diferɑ̃s]
effect (e.g., of drugs)	**effet** (m)	[efɛ]
effort (exertion)	**effort** (m)	[efɔr]
element	**élément** (m)	[elemɑ̃]
end (finish)	**fin** (f)	[fɛ̃]
example (illustration)	**exemple** (m)	[ɛgzɑ̃p]
fact	**fait** (m)	[fɛ]
frequent (adj)	**fréquent** (adj)	[frekɑ̃]
growth (development)	**croissance** (f)	[krwasɑ̃s]
help	**aide** (f)	[ɛd]
ideal	**idéal** (m)	[ideal]
kind (sort, type)	**type** (m)	[tip]
labyrinth	**labyrinthe** (m)	[labirɛ̃t]
mistake, error	**faute** (f)	[fot]
moment	**moment** (m)	[mɔmɑ̃]
object (thing)	**objet** (m)	[ɔbʒɛ]
obstacle	**obstacle** (m)	[ɔpstakl]
original (original copy)	**original** (m)	[ɔriʒinal]
part (~ of sth)	**part** (f)	[par]
particle, small part	**particule** (f)	[partikyl]
pause (break)	**pause** (f)	[poz]

position	**position** (f)	[pozisjõ]
principle	**principe** (m)	[prɛ̃sip]
problem	**problème** (m)	[prɔblɛm]

process	**processus** (m)	[prɔsesys]
progress	**progrès** (m)	[prɔgrɛ]
property (quality)	**propriété** (f)	[prɔprijete]
reaction	**réaction** (f)	[reaksjõ]
risk	**risque** (m)	[risk]

secret	**secret** (m)	[səkrɛ]
section (sector)	**section** (f)	[sɛksjõ]
series	**série** (f)	[seri]
shape (outer form)	**forme** (f)	[fɔrm]
situation	**situation** (f)	[situasjõ]

solution	**solution** (f)	[sɔlysjõ]
standard (adj)	**standard** (adj)	[stãdar]
standard (level of quality)	**standard** (m)	[stãdar]
stop (pause)	**arrêt** (m)	[arɛ]
style	**style** (m)	[stil]
system	**système** (m)	[sistɛm]

table (chart)	**tableau** (m)	[tablo]
tempo, rate	**tempo** (m)	[tɛmpo]
term (word, expression)	**terme** (m)	[tɛrm]
thing (object, item)	**chose** (f)	[ʃoz]
truth	**vérité** (f)	[verite]
turn (please wait your ~)	**tour** (m)	[tur]
type (sort, kind)	**genre** (m)	[ʒãr]

urgent (adj)	**urgent** (adj)	[yrʒã]
urgently (adv)	**d'urgence** (adv)	[dyrʒãs]
utility (usefulness)	**utilité** (f)	[ytilite]

variant (alternative)	**version** (f)	[vɛrsjõ]
way (means, method)	**mode** (m)	[mɔd]
zone	**zone** (f)	[zon]

250. Modifiers. Adjectives. Part 1

additional (adj)	**supplémentaire** (adj)	[syplemãtɛr]
ancient (~ civilization)	**ancien** (adj)	[ãsjɛ̃]
artificial (adj)	**artificiel** (adj)	[artifisjɛl]
back, rear (adj)	**arrière** (adj)	[arjɛr]
bad (adj)	**mauvais** (adj)	[movɛ]

beautiful (~ palace)	**magnifique** (adj)	[maɲifik]
beautiful (person)	**beau** (adj)	[bo]
big (in size)	**grand** (adj)	[grã]

bitter (taste)	**amer** (adj)	[amɛr]
blind (sightless)	**aveugle** (adj)	[avœgl]
calm, quiet (adj)	**calme** (adj)	[kalm]
careless (negligent)	**négligent** (adj)	[negliʒɑ̃]
caring (~ father)	**attentionné** (adj)	[atɑ̃sjɔne]
central (adj)	**central** (adj)	[sɑ̃tral]
cheap (adj)	**bon marché** (adj)	[bɔ̃ marʃe]
cheerful (adj)	**joyeux** (adj)	[ʒwajø]
children's (adj)	**d'enfant** (adj)	[dɑ̃fɑ̃]
civil (~ law)	**civil** (adj)	[sivil]
clandestine (secret)	**clandestin** (adj)	[klɑ̃dɛstɛ̃]
clean (free from dirt)	**propre** (adj)	[prɔpr]
clear (explanation, etc.)	**clair** (adj)	[klɛr]
clever (smart)	**intelligent** (adj)	[ɛ̃teliʒɑ̃]
close (near in space)	**proche** (adj)	[prɔʃ]
closed (adj)	**fermé** (adj)	[fɛrme]
cloudless (sky)	**sans nuages** (adj)	[sɑ̃ nɥaʒ]
cold (drink, weather)	**froid** (adj)	[frwa]
compatible (adj)	**compatible** (adj)	[kɔ̃patibl]
contented (adj)	**content** (adj)	[kɔ̃tɑ̃]
continuous (adj)	**continu** (adj)	[kɔ̃tiny]
continuous (incessant)	**continu** (adj)	[kɔ̃tiny]
convenient (adj)	**convenu** (adj)	[kɔ̃vny]
cool (weather)	**frais** (adj)	[frɛ]
dangerous (adj)	**dangereux** (adj)	[dɑ̃ʒrø]
dark (room)	**sombre** (adj)	[sɔ̃br]
dead (not alive)	**mort** (adj)	[mɔr]
dense (fog, smoke)	**dense** (adj)	[dɑ̃s]
different (adj)	**différent** (adj)	[diferɑ̃]
difficult (decision)	**difficile** (adj)	[difisil]
difficult (problem, task)	**difficile** (adj)	[difisil]
dim, faint (light)	**faible** (adj)	[fɛbl]
dirty (not clean)	**sale** (adj)	[sal]
distant (faraway)	**éloigné** (adj)	[elwaɲe]
distant (in space)	**lointain** (adj)	[lwɛ̃tɛ̃]
dry (clothes, etc.)	**sec** (adj)	[sɛk]
easy (not difficult)	**facile** (adj)	[fasil]
empty (glass, room)	**vide** (adj)	[vid]
exact (amount)	**précis, exact** (adj)	[presi], [ɛgzakt]
excellent (adj)	**excellent** (adj)	[ɛkselɑ̃]
excessive (adj)	**excessif** (adj)	[ɛksesif]
expensive (adj)	**cher** (adj)	[ʃɛr]
exterior (adj)	**extérieur** (adj)	[ɛksterjœr]
fast (quick)	**rapide** (adj)	[rapid]

fatty (food)	**gras** (adj)	[gra]
fertile (land, soil)	**fertile** (adj)	[fɛrtil]
flat (~ panel display)	**plat** (adj)	[pla]
even (e.g., ~ surface)	**plat** (adj)	[pla]
foreign (adj)	**étranger** (adj)	[etrɑ̃ʒe]
fragile (china, glass)	**fragile** (adj)	[fraʒil]
free (at no cost)	**gratuit** (adj)	[gratɥi]
free (unrestricted)	**libre** (adj)	[libr]
fresh (~ water)	**douce** (adj)	[dus]
fresh (e.g., ~ bread)	**frais** (adj)	[frɛ]
frozen (food)	**surgelé** (adj)	[syrʒəle]
full (completely filled)	**plein** (adj)	[plɛ̃]
good (book, etc.)	**bon** (adj)	[bɔ̃]
good (kindhearted)	**bon** (adj)	[bɔ̃]
grateful (adj)	**reconnaissant** (adj)	[rəkɔnɛsɑ̃]
happy (adj)	**heureux** (adj)	[œrø]
hard (not soft)	**dur** (adj)	[dyr]
heavy (in weight)	**lourd** (adj)	[lur]
hostile (adj)	**hostile** (adj)	[ɔstil]
hot (adj)	**très chaud** (adj)	[trɛ ʃo]
huge (adj)	**géant** (adj)	[ʒeɑ̃]
humid (adj)	**humide** (adj)	[ymid]
hungry (adj)	**affamé** (adj)	[afame]
ill (sick, unwell)	**malade** (adj)	[malad]
immobile (adj)	**immobile** (adj)	[imɔbil]
important (adj)	**important** (adj)	[ɛ̃pɔrtɑ̃]
impossible (adj)	**impossible** (adj)	[ɛ̃pɔsibl]
incomprehensible	**indéchiffrable** (adj)	[ɛ̃deʃifrabl]
indispensable (adj)	**indispensable** (adj)	[ɛ̃dispɑ̃sabl]
inexperienced (adj)	**peu expérimenté** (adj)	[pø ɛksperimɑ̃te]
insignificant (adj)	**peu important** (adj)	[pø ɛ̃pɔrtɑ̃]
interior (adj)	**intérieur** (adj)	[ɛ̃terjœr]
joint (~ decision)	**commun** (adj)	[kɔmœ̃]
last (e.g., ~ week)	**passé** (adj)	[pɑse]
last (final)	**dernier** (adj)	[dɛrnje]
left (e.g., ~ side)	**gauche** (adj)	[goʃ]
legal (legitimate)	**légal** (adj)	[legal]
light (in weight)	**léger** (adj)	[leʒe]
light (pale color)	**clair** (adj)	[klɛr]
limited (adj)	**limité** (adj)	[limite]
liquid (fluid)	**liquide** (adj)	[likid]
long (e.g., ~ way)	**long** (adj)	[lɔ̃]
loud (voice, etc.)	**fort** (adj)	[fɔr]
low (voice)	**bas** (adj)	[ba]

251. Modifiers. Adjectives. Part 2

main (principal)	**principal** (adj)	[prɛ̃sipal]
matt (paint)	**mat** (adj)	[mat]
meticulous (job)	**méticuleux** (adj)	[metikylø]
mysterious (adj)	**mystérieux** (adj)	[misterjø]
narrow (street, etc.)	**étroit** (adj)	[etrwa]
native (of country)	**natal** (adj)	[natal]
nearby (adj)	**d'à côté, voisin**	[da kote], [vwazɛ̃]
near-sighted (adj)	**myope** (adj)	[mjɔp]
necessary (adj)	**nécessaire** (adj)	[nesesɛr]
negative (~ response)	**négatif** (adj)	[negatif]
neighboring (adj)	**voisin** (adj)	[vwazɛ̃]
nervous (adj)	**nerveux** (adj)	[nɛrvø]
new (adj)	**neuf** (adj)	[nœf]
next (e.g., ~ week)	**suivant** (adj)	[sɥivɑ̃]
nice (kind)	**gentil** (adj)	[ʒɑ̃ti]
nice (voice)	**agréable** (adj)	[agreabl]
normal (adj)	**normal** (adj)	[nɔrmal]
not big (adj)	**pas grand** (adj)	[pɑ grɑ̃]
unclear (adj)	**pas clair** (adj)	[pɑ klɛr]
not difficult (adj)	**facile** (adj)	[fasil]
obligatory (adj)	**obligatoire** (adj)	[ɔbligatwar]
old (house)	**vieux** (adj)	[vjø]
open (adj)	**ouvert** (adj)	[uvɛr]
opposite (adj)	**opposé** (adj)	[ɔpoze]
ordinary (usual)	**ordinaire** (adj)	[ɔrdinɛr]
original (unusual)	**original** (adj)	[ɔriʒinal]
past (recent)	**passé** (adj)	[pɑse]
permanent (adj)	**permanent** (adj)	[pɛrmanɑ̃]
personal (adj)	**personnel** (adj)	[pɛrsɔnɛl]
polite (adj)	**poli** (adj)	[pɔli]
poor (not rich)	**pauvre** (adj)	[povr]
possible (adj)	**possible** (adj)	[pɔsibl]
destitute (extremely poor)	**miséreux** (adj)	[mizerø]
present (current)	**présent** (adj)	[prezɑ̃]
previous (adj)	**précédent** (adj)	[presedɑ̃]
principal (main)	**principal** (adj)	[prɛ̃sipal]
private (~ jet)	**privé** (adj)	[prive]
probable (adj)	**probable** (adj)	[prɔbabl]
public (open to all)	**public** (adj)	[pyblik]
punctual (person)	**ponctuel** (adj)	[pɔ̃ktɥɛl]
quiet (tranquil)	**tranquille** (adj)	[trɑ̃kil]

rare (adj)	**rare** (adj)	[rar]
raw (uncooked)	**cru** (adj)	[kry]
right (not left)	**droit** (adj)	[drwa]
right, correct (adj)	**juste, correct** (adj)	[ʒyst], [kɔrɛkt]
ripe (fruit)	**mûr** (adj)	[myr]
risky (adj)	**risqué** (adj)	[riske]
sad (~ look)	**triste** (adj)	[trist]
sad (depressing)	**triste** (adj)	[trist]
safe (not dangerous)	**sûr** (adj)	[syr]
salty (food)	**salé** (adj)	[sale]
satisfied (customer)	**satisfait** (adj)	[satisfɛ]
second hand (adj)	**d'occasion** (adj)	[dɔkazjɔ̃]
shallow (water)	**peu profond** (adj)	[pø prɔfɔ̃]
sharp (blade, etc.)	**bien affilé** (adj)	[bjɛn afile]
short (in length)	**court** (adj)	[kur]
short, short-lived (adj)	**court** (adj)	[kur]
significant (notable)	**considérable** (adj)	[kɔ̃siderabl]
similar (adj)	**similaire, pareil** (adj)	[similɛr], [parɛj]
simple (easy)	**simple** (adj)	[sɛ̃pl]
skinny	**trop maigre** (adj)	[tro mɛgr]
thin (person)	**maigre** (adj)	[mɛgr]
small (in size)	**petit** (adj)	[pti]
smooth (surface)	**lisse** (adj)	[lis]
soft (to touch)	**mou** (adj)	[mu]
solid (~ wall)	**solide** (adj)	[sɔlid]
somber, gloomy (adj)	**sombre** (adj)	[sɔ̃br]
sour (flavor, taste)	**aigre** (adj)	[ɛgr]
spacious (house, etc.)	**spacieux** (adj)	[spasjø]
special (adj)	**spécial** (adj)	[spesjal]
straight (line, road)	**droit** (adj)	[drwa]
strong (person)	**fort** (adj)	[fɔr]
stupid (foolish)	**stupide** (adj)	[stypid]
sunny (day)	**ensoleillé** (adj)	[ɑ̃sɔleje]
superb, perfect (adj)	**parfait** (adj)	[parfɛ]
swarthy (adj)	**basané** (adj)	[bazane]
sweet (sugary)	**sucré** (adj)	[sykre]
tan (adj)	**bronzé** (adj)	[brɔ̃ze]
tasty (adj)	**bon, savoureux** (adj)	[bɔ̃], [savurø]
tender (affectionate)	**tendre** (adj)	[tɑ̃dr]
the highest (adj)	**suprême** (adj)	[syprɛm]
the most important	**le plus important**	[lə plyzɛ̃pɔrtɑ̃]
the nearest	**le plus proche**	[lə ply prɔʃ]
the same, equal (adj)	**le même, pareil** (adj)	[lə mɛm], [parɛj]

| thick (e.g., ~ fog) | **épais** (adj) | [epɛ] |
| thick (wall, slice) | **épais** (adj) | [epɛ] |

tight (~ shoes)	**serré, étroit** (adj)	[sere], [etrwa]
tired (exhausted)	**fatigué** (adj)	[fatige]
tiring (adj)	**fatiguant** (adj)	[fatigã]
transparent (adj)	**transparent** (adj)	[trãsparã]

unique (exceptional)	**unique** (adj)	[ynik]
various (adj)	**divers** (adj)	[divɛr]
warm (moderately hot)	**chaud** (adj)	[ʃo]
wet (e.g., ~ clothes)	**trempé** (adj)	[trãpe]
whole (entire, complete)	**entier** (adj)	[ãtje]
wide (e.g., ~ road)	**large** (adj)	[larʒ]
young (adj)	**jeune** (adj)	[ʒœn]

MAIN 500 VERBS

252. Verbs A-C

to accompany (vt)	**accompagner** (vt)	[akɔ̃paɲe]
to accuse (vt)	**accuser** (vt)	[akyze]
to acknowledge (admit)	**reconnaître** (vt)	[rəkɔnɛtr]
to act (take action)	**agir** (vi)	[aʒir]
to add (supplement)	**ajouter** (vt)	[aʒute]
to address (speak to)	**s'adresser** (vp)	[sadrese]
to admire (vi)	**admirer** (vt)	[admire]
to advertise (vt)	**faire de la publicité**	[fɛr də la pyblisite]
to advise (vt)	**conseiller** (vt)	[kɔ̃seje]
to affirm (insist)	**affirmer** (vt)	[afirme]
to agree (say yes)	**être d'accord**	[ɛtr dakɔr]
to allow (sb to do sth)	**permettre** (vt)	[pɛrmɛtr]
to allude (vi)	**faire allusion**	[fɛr alyzjɔ̃]
to amputate (vt)	**amputer** (vt)	[ɑ̃pyte]
to answer (vi, vt)	**répondre** (vi, vt)	[repɔ̃dr]
to apologize (vi)	**s'excuser** (vp)	[sɛkskyze]
to appear (come into view)	**apparaître** (vi)	[aparɛtr]
to applaud (vi, vt)	**applaudir** (vi)	[aplodir]
to appoint (assign)	**nommer** (vt)	[nɔme]
to approach (come closer)	**s'approcher** (vp)	[saprɔʃe]
to arrive (ab. train)	**arriver** (vi)	[arive]
to ask (~ sb to do sth)	**demander** (vt)	[dəmɑ̃de]
to aspire to …	**aspirer à …**	[aspire ɑ]
to assist (help)	**assister** (vt)	[asiste]
to attack (mil.)	**attaquer** (vt)	[atake]
to attain (objectives)	**atteindre** (vt)	[atɛ̃dr]
to revenge (vt)	**se venger** (vp)	[sɔ vɑ̃ʒo]
to avoid (danger, task)	**éviter** (vt)	[evite]
to award (give medal to)	**décorer** (vt)	[dekɔre]
to battle (vi)	**combattre** (vi)	[kɔ̃batr]
to be (~ on the table)	**se trouver** (vp)	[sə truve]
to be (vi)	**être** (vi)	[ɛtr]
to be afraid	**avoir peur**	[avwar pœr]
to be angry (with …)	**se fâcher (contre …)**	[sə faʃe kɔ̃tr]

to be at war	faire la guerre	[fɛr la gɛr]
to be based (on …)	être basé (sur …)	[ɛtr baze syr]
to be bored	s'ennuyer (vp)	[sãnɥije]
to be convinced	être convaincu de …	[ɛtr kɔ̃vɛ̃ky]
to be enough	suffire (vi)	[syfir]
to be envious	envier (vt)	[ãvje]
to be indignant	s'indigner (vp)	[sɛ̃diɲe]
to be interested in …	s'intéresser à …	[sɛ̃terese a]
to be lying down	être allongé	[ɛtr alɔ̃ʒe]
to be needed	être nécessaire	[ɛtr nesesɛr]
to be perplexed	être perplexe	[ɛtr pɛrplɛks]
to be preserved	se conserver (vp)	[sə kɔ̃sɛrve]
to be required	être indispensable	[ɛtr ɛ̃dispãsabl]
to be surprised	s'étonner (vp)	[setɔne]
to be worried	s'inquiéter (vp)	[sɛ̃kjete]
to beat (dog, person)	battre (vt)	[batr]
to become (e.g., ~ old)	devenir (vi)	[dəvnir]
to become pensive	devenir pensif	[dəvnir pãsif]
to behave (vi)	se conduire (vp)	[sə kɔ̃dɥir]
to believe (think)	croire (vi, vt)	[krwar]
to belong to …	appartenir à …	[apartənir a]
to berth (moor)	accoster (vi)	[akɔste]
to blind (other drivers)	aveugler (vt)	[avœgle]
to blow (wind)	souffler (vi)	[sufle]
to blush (vi)	rougir (vi)	[ruʒir]
to boast (vi)	se vanter (vp)	[sə vãte]
to borrow (money)	emprunter (vt)	[ãprœ̃te]
to break (branch, toy, etc.)	briser, casser (vt)	[brize], [kase]
to breathe (vi)	respirer (vi)	[rɛspire]
to bring (sth)	amener, apporter (vt)	[amne], [apɔrte]
to burn (paper, logs)	brûler (vt)	[bryle]
to buy (purchase)	acheter (vt)	[aʃte]
to call (for help)	appeler (vt)	[aple]
to call (with one's voice)	appeler (vt)	[aple]
to calm down (vt)	calmer (vt)	[kalme]
can (v aux)	pouvoir (v aux)	[puvwar]
to cancel (call off)	annuler (vt)	[anyle]
to cast off	larguer les amarres	[large lezamar]
to catch (e.g., ~ a ball)	attraper (vt)	[atrape]
to catch sight (of …)	remarquer (vt)	[rəmarke]
to cause …	être la cause de …	[ɛtr la koz də]
to change (~ one's opinion)	changer (vt)	[ʃãʒe]
to change (exchange)	changer (vt)	[ʃãʒe]
to charm (vt)	charmer (vt)	[ʃarme]

to choose (select)	**choisir** (vt)	[ʃwazir]
to chop off (with an ax)	**couper** (vt)	[kupe]
to clean (from dirt)	**nettoyer** (vt)	[nɛtwaje]
to clean (shoes, etc.)	**enlever la boue**	[ɑ̃lve la bu]
to clean (tidy)	**faire le ménage**	[fɛr le menaʒ]
to close (vt)	**fermer** (vt)	[fɛrme]
to comb one's hair	**se peigner** (vp)	[sə peɲe]
to come down (the stairs)	**descendre** (vi)	[desɑ̃dr]
to come in (enter)	**entrer** (vi)	[ɑ̃tre]
to come out (book)	**paraître** (vi)	[parɛtr]
to compare (vt)	**comparer** (vt)	[kɔ̃pare]
to compensate (vt)	**compenser** (vt)	[kɔ̃pɑ̃se]
to compete (vi)	**concurrencer** (vt)	[kɔ̃kyrɑ̃se]
to compile (~ a list)	**dresser** (vt)	[drese]
to complain (vi, vt)	**se plaindre** (vp)	[sə plɛ̃dr]
to complicate (vt)	**compliquer** (vt)	[kɔ̃plike]
to compose (music, etc.)	**composer** (vt)	[kɔ̃poze]
to compromise (reputation)	**compromettre** (vt)	[kɔ̃prɔmɛtr]
to concentrate (vi)	**se concentrer** (vp)	[sə kɔ̃sɑ̃tre]
to confess (criminal)	**avouer** (vi, vt)	[avwe]
to confuse (mix up)	**confondre** (vt)	[kɔ̃fɔ̃dr]
to congratulate (vt)	**féliciter** (vt)	[felisite]
to consult (doctor, expert)	**consulter ...**	[kɔ̃sylte]
to continue (~ to do sth)	**continuer** (vt)	[kɔ̃tinɥe]
to control (vt)	**contrôler** (vt)	[kɔ̃trole]
to convince (vt)	**convaincre** (vt)	[kɔ̃vɛ̃kr]
to cooperate (vi)	**coopérer** (vi)	[kɔɔpere]
to coordinate (vt)	**coordonner** (vt)	[kɔɔrdɔne]
to correct (an error)	**corriger** (vt)	[kɔriʒe]
to cost (vt)	**coûter** (vt)	[kute]
to count (money, etc.)	**compter** (vt)	[kɔ̃te]
to count on ...	**compter sur ...**	[kɔ̃te syr]
to crack (ceiling, wall)	**se fendre** (vp)	[sə fɑ̃dr]
to create (vt)	**créer** (vt)	[kree]
to cry (weep)	**pleurer** (vi)	[plœre]
to cut off (with a knife)	**couper** (vt)	[kupe]

253. Verbs D-G

to dare (~ to do sth)	**oser** (vt)	[oze]
to date from ...	**dater de ...**	[date də]
to deceive (vi, vt)	**tromper** (vt)	[trɔ̃pe]

to decide (~ to do sth)	**décider** (vt)	[deside]
to decorate (tree, street)	**décorer** (vt)	[dekɔre]
to dedicate (book, etc.)	**dédier** (vt)	[dedje]
to defend (a country, etc.)	**défendre** (vt)	[defɑ̃dr]
to defend oneself	**se défendre** (vp)	[sə defɑ̃dr]
to demand (request firmly)	**exiger** (vt)	[ɛgziʒe]
to denounce (vt)	**dénoncer** (vt)	[denɔ̃se]
to deny (vt)	**nier** (vt)	[nje]
to depend on …	**dépendre de …**	[depɑ̃dr də]
to deprive (vt)	**priver** (vt)	[prive]
to deserve (vt)	**mériter** (vt)	[merite]
to design (machine, etc.)	**concevoir, créer** (vt)	[kɔ̃səvwar], [kree]
to desire (want, wish)	**désirer** (vt)	[dezire]
to despise (vt)	**mépriser** (vt)	[meprize]
to destroy (documents, etc.)	**détruire** (vt)	[detrɥir]
to differ (from sth)	**être différent**	[ɛtr diferɑ̃]
to dig (tunnel, etc.)	**creuser** (vt)	[krøze]
to direct (point the way)	**diriger** (vt)	[diriʒe]
to disappear (vi)	**disparaître** (vi)	[disparɛtr]
to discover (new land, etc.)	**découvrir** (vt)	[dekuvrir]
to discuss (vt)	**discuter** (vt)	[diskyte]
to distribute (leaflets, etc.)	**diffuser** (vt)	[difyze]
to disturb (vt)	**déranger** (vt)	[derɑ̃ʒe]
to dive (vi)	**plonger** (vi)	[plɔ̃ʒe]
to divide (math)	**diviser** (vt)	[divize]
to do (vt)	**faire** (vt)	[fɛr]
to do the laundry	**faire la lessive**	[fɛr la lɛsiv]
to double (increase)	**doubler** (vt)	[duble]
to doubt (have doubts)	**douter** (vt)	[dute]
to draw a conclusion	**tirer une conclusion**	[tire yn kɔ̃klyzjɔ̃]
to dream (daydream)	**rêver** (vi)	[rɛve]
to dream (in sleep)	**rêver** (vi)	[rɛve]
to drink (vi, vt)	**boire** (vt)	[bwar]
to drive a car	**conduire une voiture**	[kɔ̃dɥir yn vwatyr]
to drive away (scare away)	**chasser** (vt)	[ʃase]
to drop (let fall)	**faire tomber**	[fɛr tɔ̃be]
to drown (ab. person)	**se noyer** (vp)	[sə nwaje]
to dry (clothes, hair)	**sécher** (vt)	[seʃe]
to eat (vi, vt)	**manger** (vi, vt)	[mɑ̃ʒe]
to eavesdrop (vi)	**écouter aux portes**	[ekute o pɔrt]
to emit (give out - odor, etc.)	**répandre** (vt)	[repɑ̃dr]
to enter (on the list)	**inscrire** (vt)	[ɛ̃skrir]

to entertain (amuse)	**amuser** (vt)	[amyze]
to equip (fit out)	**équiper** (vt)	[ekipe]
to examine (proposal)	**examiner** (vt)	[ɛgzamine]
to exchange (sth)	**s'échanger (des …)**	[seʃɑ̃ʒe de]
to exclude, to expel	**exclure, expulser** (vt)	[ɛksklyr], [ɛkspylse]
to excuse (forgive)	**excuser** (vt)	[ɛkskyze]
to exist (vi)	**exister** (vi)	[ɛgziste]
to expect (anticipate)	**s'attendre** (vp)	[satɑ̃dr]
to expect (foresee)	**prévoir** (vt)	[prevwar]
to explain (vt)	**expliquer** (vt)	[ɛksplike]
to express (vt)	**exprimer** (vt)	[ɛksprime]
to extinguish (a fire)	**éteindre** (vt)	[etɛ̃dr]
to fall in love (with …)	**tomber amoureux**	[tɔ̃be amurø]
to feed (provide food)	**nourrir** (vt)	[nurir]
to fight (against the enemy)	**lutter (contre …)**	[lyte kɔ̃tr]
to fight (vi)	**se battre** (vp)	[sə batr]
to fill (glass, bottle)	**remplir** (vt)	[rɑ̃plir]
to find (~ lost items)	**trouver** (vt)	[truve]
to finish (vt)	**finir** (vt)	[finir]
to fish (angle)	**pêcher** (vt)	[peʃe]
to fit (ab. dress, etc.)	**aller bien**	[ale bjɛ̃]
to flatter (vt)	**flatter** (vt)	[flate]
to fly (bird, plane)	**voler** (vi)	[vɔle]
to follow … (come after)	**suivre …**	[sɥivr]
to forbid (vt)	**interdire** (vt)	[ɛ̃tɛrdir]
to force (compel)	**forcer** (vt)	[fɔrse]
to forget (vi, vt)	**oublier** (vt)	[ublije]
to forgive (pardon)	**pardonner** (vt)	[pardɔne]
to form (constitute)	**former** (vt)	[fɔrme]
to get dirty (vi)	**se salir** (vp)	[sə salir]
to get infected (with …)	**attraper** (vt)	[atrape]
to get irritated	**s'irriter** (vp)	[sirite]
to get married	**se marier** (vp)	[sə marje]
to get rid of …	**se débarrasser de …**	[sə debarase də]
to get tired	**être fatigué**	[ɛtr fatigo]
to get up (arise from bed)	**se lever** (vp)	[sə ləve]
to give (vt)	**donner** (vt)	[dɔne]
to give a bath	**baigner** (vt)	[beɲe]
to give a hug, to hug (vt)	**serrer dans ses bras**	[sere dɑ̃ se bra]
to give in (yield to)	**céder** (vt)	[sede]
to go (by car, etc.)	**aller** (vi)	[ale]
to go (on foot)	**aller** (vi)	[ale]

to go for a swim	**se baigner** (vp)	[sə beɲe]
to go out (for dinner, etc.)	**sortir** (vi)	[sɔrtir]
to go to bed	**aller se coucher**	[ale sə kuʃe]
to greet (vt)	**saluer** (vt)	[salɥe]
to grow (plants)	**cultiver** (vt)	[kyltive]
to guarantee (vt)	**garantir** (vt)	[garɑ̃tir]
to guess right	**deviner** (vt)	[dəvine]

254. Verbs H-M

to hand out (distribute)	**distribuer** (vt)	[distribɥe]
to hang (curtains, etc.)	**accrocher** (vt)	[akrɔʃe]
to have (vt)	**avoir** (vt)	[avwar]
to have a try	**tenter** (vt)	[tɑ̃te]
to have breakfast	**prendre le petit déjeuner**	[prɑ̃dr ləpti deʒœne]
to have dinner	**dîner** (vi)	[dine]
to have fun	**s'amuser** (vp)	[samyze]
to have lunch	**déjeuner** (vi)	[deʒœne]
to head (group, etc.)	**être en tête (de …)**	[ɛtr ɑ̃ tɛt də]
to hear (vt)	**entendre** (vt)	[ɑ̃tɑ̃dr]
to heat (vt)	**chauffer** (vt)	[ʃofe]
to help (vt)	**aider** (vt)	[ede]
to hide (vt)	**cacher** (vt)	[kaʃe]
to hire (e.g., ~ a boat)	**louer** (vt)	[lwe]
to hire (staff)	**embaucher** (vt)	[ɑ̃boʃe]
to hope (vi, vt)	**espérer** (vi)	[ɛspere]
to hunt (for food, sport)	**chasser** (vi, vt)	[ʃase]
to hurry (sb)	**presser** (vt)	[prese]
to hurry (vi)	**être pressé**	[ɛtr prese]
to imagine (to picture)	**imaginer** (vt)	[imaʒine]
to imitate (vt)	**imiter** (vt)	[imite]
to implore (vt)	**supplier** (vt)	[syplije]
to import (vt)	**importer** (vt)	[ɛ̃pɔrte]
to increase (vi)	**augmenter** (vi)	[ogmɑ̃te]
to increase (vt)	**augmenter** (vt)	[ogmɑ̃te]
to infect (vt)	**contaminer** (vt)	[kɔ̃tamine]
to influence (vt)	**influer** (vt)	[ɛ̃flye]
to inform (~ sb about …)	**annoncer** (vt)	[anɔ̃se]
to inform (vt)	**informer** (vt)	[ɛ̃fɔrme]
to inherit (vt)	**hériter** (vt)	[erite]
to inquire (about …)	**se renseigner (sur …)**	[sə rɑ̃seɲe]
to insist (vi, vt)	**insister** (vi)	[ɛ̃siste]
to inspire (vt)	**inspirer** (vt)	[ɛ̃spire]

to instruct (teach)	**instruire** (vt)	[ɛ̃strɥir]
to insult (offend)	**insulter** (vt)	[ɛ̃sylte]
to interest (vt)	**intéresser** (vt)	[ɛ̃terese]
to intervene (vi)	**intervenir** (vi)	[ɛ̃tɛrvənir]
to introduce (present)	**présenter** (vt)	[prezɑ̃te]
to invent (machine, etc.)	**inventer** (vt)	[ɛ̃vɑ̃te]
to invite (vt)	**inviter** (vt)	[ɛ̃vite]
to iron (laundry)	**repasser** (vt)	[rəpase]
to irritate (annoy)	**irriter** (vt)	[irite]
to isolate (vt)	**isoler** (vt)	[izɔle]
to join (political party, etc.)	**se joindre** (vp)	[sə ʒwɛ̃dr]
to joke (be kidding)	**plaisanter** (vi)	[plɛzɑ̃te]
to keep (old letters, etc.)	**garder** (vt)	[garde]
to keep silent	**garder le silence**	[garde lə silɑ̃s]
to kill (vt)	**tuer** (vt)	[tɥe]
to knock (at the door)	**frapper** (vi)	[frape]
to know (sb)	**connaître** (vt)	[kɔnɛtr]
to know (sth)	**savoir** (vt)	[savwar]
to laugh (vi)	**rire** (vi)	[rir]
to launch (start up)	**lancer** (vt)	[lɑ̃se]
to leave (~ for Mexico)	**partir** (vi)	[partir]
to leave (spouse)	**quitter** (vt)	[kite]
to leave behind (forget)	**laisser** (vt)	[lese]
to liberate (city, etc.)	**libérer** (vt)	[libere]
to lie (tell untruth)	**mentir** (vi)	[mɑ̃tir]
to light (campfire, etc.)	**allumer** (vt)	[alyme]
to light up (illuminate)	**éclairer** (vt)	[eklere]
to love (e.g., ~ dancing)	**aimer** (vt)	[eme]
to like (I like ...)	**plaire à ...**	[plɛr ɑ]
to limit (vt)	**limiter** (vt)	[limite]
to listen (vi)	**écouter** (vt)	[ekute]
to live (~ in France)	**habiter** (vt)	[abite]
to live (exist)	**vivre** (vi)	[vivr]
to load (gun)	**charger** (vt)	[ʃarʒe]
to load (vehicle, etc.)	**charger** (vt)	[ʃarʒe]
to look (I'm just ~ing)	**regarder** (vi, vt)	[rəgarde]
to look for ... (search)	**chercher** (vt)	[ʃɛrʃe]
to look like (resemble)	**ressembler à ...**	[rəsɑ̃ble a]
to lose (umbrella, etc.)	**perdre** (vt)	[pɛrdr]
to love (sb)	**aimer** (vt)	[eme]
to lower (blind, head)	**abaisser** (vt)	[abese]
to make (~ dinner)	**préparer** (vt)	[prepare]
to make a mistake	**se tromper** (vp)	[sə trɔ̃pe]

to make angry	**fâcher** (vt)	[faʃe]
to make copies	**faire des copies**	[fɛr de kɔpi]
to make easier	**faciliter** (vt)	[fasilite]
to make the acquaintance	**faire connaissance**	[fɛr kɔnɛsɑ̃s]
to make use (of ...)	**se servir de ...**	[sə sɛrvir də]
to manage, to run	**diriger** (vt)	[diriʒe]
to mark (make a mark)	**marquer** (vt)	[marke]
to mean (signify)	**signifier** (vt)	[siɲifje]
to memorize (vt)	**mémoriser** (vt)	[memɔrize]
to mention (talk about)	**mentionner** (vt)	[mɑ̃sjɔne]
to miss (school, etc.)	**manquer** (vt)	[mɑ̃ke]
to mix (combine, blend)	**mélanger** (vt)	[melɑ̃ʒe]
to mock (make fun of)	**se moquer** (vp)	[sə mɔke]
to move (to shift)	**déplacer** (vt)	[deplase]
to multiply (math)	**multiplier** (vt)	[myltiplije]
must (v aux)	**devoir** (v aux)	[dəvwar]

255. Verbs N-S

to name, to call (vt)	**appeler** (vt)	[aple]
to negotiate (vi)	**négocier** (vi)	[negɔsje]
to note (write down)	**noter** (vt)	[nɔte]
to notice (see)	**apercevoir** (vt)	[apɛrsəvwar]
to obey (vi, vt)	**obéir** (vt)	[ɔbeir]
to object (vi, vt)	**objecter** (vt)	[ɔbʒɛkte]
to observe (see)	**observer** (vt)	[ɔpsɛrve]
to offend (vt)	**offenser** (vt)	[ɔfɑ̃se]
to omit (word, phrase)	**omettre** (vt)	[ɔmɛtr]
to open (vt)	**ouvrir** (vt)	[uvrir]
to order (in restaurant)	**commander** (vi, vt)	[kɔmɑ̃de]
to order (mil.)	**ordonner** (vt)	[ɔrdɔne]
to organize (concert, party)	**organiser** (vt)	[ɔrganize]
to overestimate (vt)	**surestimer** (vt)	[syrɛstime]
to own (possess)	**posséder** (vt)	[pɔsede]
to participate (vi)	**participer** (vi)	[partisipe]
to pass (go beyond)	**dépasser** (vt)	[depase]
to pay (vi, vt)	**payer** (vi, vt)	[peje]
to peep, spy on	**épier** (vt)	[epje]
to penetrate (vt)	**pénétrer** (vt)	[penetre]
to permit (vt)	**permettre** (vt)	[pɛrmɛtr]
to pick (flowers)	**cueillir** (vt)	[kœjir]
to place (put, set)	**mettre** (vt)	[mɛtr]
to plan (~ to do sth)	**planifier** (vt)	[planifje]

to play (actor)	**jouer** (vi, vt)	[ʒwe]
to play (children)	**jouer** (vi)	[ʒwe]
to point (~ the way)	**indiquer** (vt)	[ɛ̃dike]
to pour (liquid)	**verser** (vt)	[vɛrse]
to pray (vi, vt)	**prier** (vt)	[prije]
to predominate (vi)	**prédominer** (vi)	[predɔmine]
to prefer (vt)	**préférer** (vt)	[prefere]
to prepare (~ a plan)	**préparer** (vt)	[prepare]
to present (sb to sb)	**présenter** (vt)	[prezɑ̃te]
to preserve (peace, life)	**préserver** (vt)	[prezɛrve]
to progress (move forward)	**progresser** (vi)	[prɔgrese]
to promise (vt)	**promettre** (vt)	[prɔmɛtr]
to pronounce (vt)	**prononcer** (vt)	[prɔnɔ̃se]
to propose (vt)	**proposer** (vt)	[prɔpoze]
to protect (e.g., ~ nature)	**protéger** (vt)	[prɔteʒe]
to protest (vi)	**protester** (vi, vt)	[prɔtɛste]
to prove (vt)	**prouver** (vt)	[pruve]
to provoke (vt)	**provoquer** (vt)	[prɔvɔke]
to pull (~ the rope)	**tirer** (vt)	[tire]
to punish (vt)	**punir** (vt)	[pynir]
to push (~ the door)	**pousser** (vt)	[puse]
to put away (vt)	**ranger** (vt)	[rɑ̃ʒe]
to put in (insert)	**insérer** (vt)	[ɛ̃sere]
to put in order	**remettre en ordre**	[rəmɛtr anɔrdr]
to put, to place	**mettre** (vt)	[mɛtr]
to quote (cite)	**citer** (vt)	[site]
to reach (arrive at)	**atteindre** (vt)	[atɛ̃dr]
to read (vi, vt)	**lire** (vi, vt)	[lir]
to realize (a dream)	**réaliser** (vt)	[realize]
to recall (~ one's name)	**se souvenir** (vp)	[sə suvnir]
to recognize (identify sb)	**reconnaître** (vt)	[rəkɔnɛtr]
to recommend (vt)	**recommander** (vt)	[rəkɔmɑ̃de]
to recover (~ from flu)	**se rétablir** (vp)	[sə retablir]
to redo (do again)	**refaire** (vt)	[rəfɛr]
to reduce (speed, etc.)	**diminuer** (vt)	[diminɥe]
to refuse (~ sb)	**refuser** (vt)	[rəfyze]
to regret (be sorry)	**regretter** (vt)	[rəgrɛte]
to reinforce (vt)	**renforcer** (vt)	[rɑ̃fɔrse]
to remember (vt)	**se rappeler** (vp)	[sə raple]
to remind of …	**rappeler** (vt)	[raple]
to remove (~ a stain)	**enlever** (vt)	[ɑ̃lve]
to remove (~ an obstacle)	**éliminer** (vt)	[elimine]

to rent (sth from sb)	**louer** (vt)	[lwe]
to repair (mend)	**réparer** (vt)	[repare]
to repeat (say again)	**répéter** (vt)	[repete]
to report (make a report)	**faire un rapport**	[fɛr œ̃ rapɔr]
to reproach (vt)	**reprocher** (vt)	[rəprɔʃe]
to reserve, to book	**réserver** (vt)	[rezɛrve]
to restrain (hold back)	**retenir** (vt)	[rətənir]
to return (come back)	**revenir** (vi)	[rəvnir]
to risk, to take a risk	**prendre un risque**	[prɑ̃dr œ̃ risk]
to rub off (erase)	**effacer** (vt)	[efase]
to run (move fast)	**courir** (vi)	[kurir]
to satisfy (please)	**satisfaire** (vt)	[satisfɛr]
to save (rescue)	**sauver** (vt)	[sove]
to say (~ thank you)	**dire** (vt)	[dir]
to scold (vt)	**gronder** (vt)	[grɔ̃de]
to scratch (with claws)	**griffer** (vt)	[grife]
to select (to pick)	**sélectionner** (vt)	[selɛksjɔne]
to sell (goods)	**vendre** (vt)	[vɑ̃dr]
to send (a letter)	**envoyer** (vt)	[ɑ̃vwaje]
to send back (vt)	**renvoyer** (vt)	[rɑ̃vwaje]
to sense (danger)	**ressentir** (vt)	[rəsɑ̃tir]
to sentence (vt)	**condamner** (vt)	[kɔ̃dane]
to serve (in restaurant)	**servir** (vt)	[sɛrvir]
to settle (a conflict)	**régler** (vt)	[regle]
to shake (vt)	**secouer** (vt)	[səkwe]
to shave (vi)	**se raser** (vp)	[sə raze]
to shine (gleam)	**briller** (vi)	[brije]
to shiver (with cold)	**trembler** (vi)	[trɑ̃ble]
to shoot (vi)	**tirer** (vt)	[tire]
to shout (vi)	**crier** (vi)	[krije]
to show (to display)	**montrer** (vt)	[mɔ̃tre]
to shudder (vi)	**tressaillir** (vi)	[tresajir]
to sigh (vi)	**soupirer** (vi)	[supire]
to sign (document)	**signer** (vt)	[siɲe]
to signify (mean)	**signifier** (vt)	[siɲifje]
to simplify (vt)	**simplifier** (vt)	[sɛ̃plifje]
to sin (vi)	**pécher** (vi)	[peʃe]
to sit (be sitting)	**être assis**	[ɛtr asi]
to sit down (vi)	**s'asseoir** (vp)	[saswar]
to smash (~ a bug)	**écraser** (vt)	[ekraze]
to smell (scent)	**sentir** (vi, vt)	[sɑ̃tir]
to smell (sniff at)	**sentir** (vt)	[sɑ̃tir]
to smile (vi)	**sourire** (vi)	[surir]
to snap (vi, ab. rope)	**se rompre** (vp)	[sə rɔ̃pr]

to solve (problem)	résoudre (vt)	[rezudr]
to sow (seed, crop)	semer (vt)	[səme]
to spill (liquid)	renverser (vt)	[rɑ̃vɛrse]
to spill out (flour, etc.)	se renverser (vp)	[sə rɑ̃vɛrse]
to spit (vi)	cracher (vi)	[kraʃe]
to stand (toothache, cold)	supporter (vt)	[sypɔrte]
to start (begin)	commencer (vt)	[kɔmɑ̃se]
to steal (money, etc.)	voler (vt)	[vɔle]
to stop (please ~ calling me)	cesser (vt)	[sese]
to stop (for pause, etc.)	s'arrêter (vp)	[sarete]
to stop talking	se taire (vp)	[sə tɛr]
to stroke (caress)	caresser (vt)	[karese]
to study (vt)	étudier (vt)	[etydje]
to suffer (feel pain)	souffrir (vi)	[sufrir]
to support (cause, idea)	soutenir (vt)	[sutnir]
to suppose (assume)	supposer (vt)	[sypoze]
to surface (ab. submarine)	faire surface	[fɛr syrfas]
to surprise (amaze)	étonner (vt)	[etɔne]
to suspect (vt)	suspecter (vt)	[syspɛkte]
to swim (vi)	nager (vi)	[naʒe]
to turn on (computer, etc.)	allumer (vt)	[alyme]

256. Verbs T-W

to take (get hold of)	prendre (vt)	[prɑ̃dr]
to take a bath	se laver (vp)	[sə lave]
to take a rest	se reposer (vp)	[sə rəpoze]
to take aim (at …)	viser (vt)	[vize]
to take away	emporter (vt)	[ɑ̃pɔrte]
to take off (airplane)	décoller (vi)	[dekɔle]
to take off (remove)	enlever (vt)	[ɑ̃lve]
to take pictures	photographier (vi, vt)	[fɔtɔgrafje]
to talk to …	parler avec …	[parle avɛk]
to teach (give lessons)	apprendre (vt)	[aprɑ̃dr]
to tear off (vt)	arracher (vt)	[araʃe]
to tell (story, joke)	raconter (vt)	[rakɔ̃te]
to thank (vt)	remercier (vt)	[rəmɛrsje]
to think (believe)	penser (vt)	[pɑ̃se]
to think (vi, vt)	penser (vi, vt)	[pɑ̃se]
to threaten (vt)	menacer (vt)	[mənase]
to throw (stone)	jeter (vt)	[ʒete]

to tie to ...	**attacher** (vt)	[ataʃe]
to tie up (prisoner)	**ligoter** (vt)	[ligɔte]
to tire (make tired)	**fatiguer** (vt)	[fatige]
to touch (one's arm, etc.)	**toucher** (vt)	[tuʃe]
to tower (over ...)	**dominer** (vt)	[dɔmine]
to train (animals)	**dresser** (vt)	[drese]
to train (sb)	**entraîner** (vt)	[ɑ̃trene]
to train (vi)	**s'entraîner** (vp)	[sɑ̃trene]
to transform (vt)	**transformer** (vt)	[trɑ̃sfɔrme]
to translate (vt)	**traduire** (vt)	[tradɥir]
to treat (patient, illness)	**soigner** (vt)	[swaɲe]
to trust (vt)	**avoir confiance**	[avwar kɔ̃fjɑ̃s]
to try (attempt)	**essayer** (vt)	[eseje]
to turn (~ to the left)	**tourner** (vi)	[turne]
to turn away (vi)	**se détourner** (vp)	[sə deturne]
to turn off (the light)	**éteindre** (vt)	[etɛ̃dr]
to turn over (stone, etc.)	**retourner** (vt)	[rəturne]
to underestimate (vt)	**sous-estimer** (vt)	[suzɛstime]
to underline (vt)	**souligner** (vt)	[suliɲe]
to understand (vt)	**comprendre** (vt)	[kɔ̃prɑ̃dr]
to undertake (vt)	**entreprendre** (vt)	[ɑ̃trəprɑ̃dr]
to unite (vt)	**unir, réunir** (vt)	[ynir], [reynir]
to untie (vt)	**détacher** (vt)	[detaʃe]
to use (phrase, word)	**employer** (vt)	[ɑ̃plwaje]
to vaccinate (vt)	**vacciner** (vt)	[vaksine]
to vote (vi)	**voter** (vi)	[vɔte]
to wait (vt)	**attendre** (vt)	[atɑ̃dr]
to wake (sb)	**réveiller** (vt)	[reveje]
to want (wish, desire)	**vouloir** (vt)	[vulwar]
to warn (of the danger)	**avertir** (vt)	[avɛrtir]
to wash (clean)	**laver** (vt)	[lave]
to water (plants)	**arroser** (vt)	[aroze]
to wave (the hand)	**agiter** (vt)	[aʒite]
to weigh (have weight)	**peser** (vi)	[pəze]
to work (vi)	**travailler** (vi)	[travaje]
to worry (make anxious)	**inquiéter** (vt)	[ɛ̃kjete]
to worry (vi)	**s'inquiéter** (vp)	[sɛ̃kjete]
to wrap (parcel, etc.)	**envelopper** (vt)	[ɑ̃vlɔpe]
to wrestle (sport)	**lutter** (vi)	[lyte]
to write (vt)	**écrire** (vt)	[ekrir]
to write down	**prendre en note**	[prɑ̃dr ɑ̃ nɔt]

Lightning Source UK Ltd.
Milton Keynes UK
UKHW02f1941230518
323110UK00035B/486/P